# Lecture Notes in Computer Science 11849

More information about this series at http://www.springer.com/series/7412

Daoqiang Zhang · Luping Zhou ·
Biao Jie · Mingxia Liu (Eds.)

# Graph Learning in Medical Imaging

First International Workshop, GLMI 2019
Held in Conjunction with MICCAI 2019
Shenzhen, China, October 17, 2019
Proceedings

 Springer

*Editors*
Daoqiang Zhang
Nanjing University of Aeronautics
and Astronautics
Nanjing, China

Biao Jie
Anhui Normal University
Wuhu, China

Luping Zhou
University of Sydney
Sydney, NSW, Australia

Mingxia Liu ⓘ
University of North Carolina at Chapel Hill
Chapel Hill, NC, USA

ISSN 0302-9743        ISSN 1611-3349  (electronic)
Lecture Notes in Computer Science
ISBN 978-3-030-35816-7        ISBN 978-3-030-35817-4  (eBook)
https://doi.org/10.1007/978-3-030-35817-4

LNCS Sublibrary: SL6 – Image Processing, Computer Vision, Pattern Recognition, and Graphics

This Springer imprint is published by the registered company Springer Nature Switzerland AG
The registered company address is: Gewerbestrasse 11, 6330 Cham, Switzerland

# Preface

The First International Workshop on Graph Learning in Medical Imaging (GLMI 2019) was held in Shenzhen, China, on October 17, 2019, in conjunction with the 22nd International Conference on Medical Image Computing and Computer-Assisted Intervention (MICCAI 2019).

Graph object provides an effective tool to model and analyze interconnectivity. Recently, the community has witnessed a growing need and interest to represent medical imaging data as graphs. Graph-based methods have been widely applied to brain connectivity analysis, image segmentation, image registration, image fusion, image-guided therapy, image annotation, image retrieval, computer-aided diagnosis, etc. The main scope of this workshop was to help advance the scientific research within the broad field of graph learning in medical imaging. This workshop focused on major trends and challenges in this area and presented works aiming to identify new advanced techniques and their application in medical imaging. Topics of interest included, but were not limited to, graph-based methods (e.g., complex network analysis, graph mining, graph learning, graph embeddings, kernel methods for structured data, probabilistic and graphical models for structured data, spectral graph methods, machine learning in the context of graphs) with their applications to medical image analysis, brain connectivity analysis, computer-aided diagnosis, multi-modality fusion, image reconstruction, image retrieval, big medical imaging data analytics, molecular imaging, digital pathology, etc.

Along with the great advances in graph learning, a large number of papers (41 in total) were submitted and underwent a rigorous double-blinded peer-review process, with each paper being reviewed by at least 2 reviewers from the Program Committee, composed of 25 experts in the fields. Based on the reviewing scores and critiques, the 21 best papers were finally accepted (acceptance rate: 51.22%) for presentation at the workshop and chosen to be included in this Springer LNCS volume.

We are grateful to all the Program Committee members for reviewing the submitted papers and giving constructive comments and critiques and to all the authors making the workshop very fruitful and successful.

September 2019

Daoqiang Zhang
Luping Zhou
Biao Jie
Mingxia Liu

# Organization

## Workshop Organizers

| | |
|---|---|
| Daoqiang Zhang | Nanjing University of Aeronautics and Astronautics, China |
| Luping Zhou | University of Sydney, Australia |
| Biao Jie | Anhui Normal University, China |
| Mingxia Liu | University of North Carolina at Chapel Hill, USA |

## Program Committee Member

| | |
|---|---|
| Chunfeng Lian | University of North Carolina at Chapel Hill, USA |
| Dongren Yao | Institute of Automation, Chinese Academy of Sciences, China |
| Fan Wang | University of North Carolina at Chapel Hill, USA |
| Fang Chen | Nanjing University of Aeronautics and Astronautics, China |
| Jiashuang Huang | Nanjing University of Aeronautics and Astronautics, China |
| Jie Wei | University of North Carolina at Chapel Hill, USA |
| Lei Wang | University of Wollongong, Australia |
| Li Zhang | Nanjing Forestry University, China |
| Liang Sun | Nanjing University of Aeronautics and Astronautics, China |
| Liangqiong Qu | University of North Carolina at Chapel Hill, USA |
| Lishan Qiao | Liaocheng University, China |
| Luping Zhou | University of Sydney, Australia |
| Mingliang Wang | Nanjing University of Aeronautics and Astronautics, China |
| Mingxia Liu | University of North Carolina at Chapel Hill, USA |
| Peng Wan | Nanjing University of Aeronautics and Astronautics, China |
| Qi Zhu | Nanjing University of Aeronautics and Astronautics, China |
| Shuai Wang | University of North Carolina at Chapel Hill, USA |
| Shuo Huang | Nanjing University of Aeronautics and Astronautics, China |
| Wei Shao | Nanjing University of Aeronautics and Astronautics, China |
| Weixiong Jiang | University of North Carolina at Chapel Hill, USA |
| Xiaoke Hao | Hebei University of Technology, China |
| Xiaoxia Zhang | University of North Carolina at Chapel Hill, USA |
| Yongsheng Pan | University of North Carolina at Chapel Hill, USA |
| Yousefnezhad Muhammad | Nanjing University of Aeronautics and Astronautics, China |
| Zhongnian Li | Nanjing University of Aeronautics and Astronautics, China |

# Contents

# Graph Hyperalignment for Multi-subject fMRI Functional Alignment

Weida Li, Fang Chen, and Daoqiang Zhang$^{(\boxtimes)}$

College of Computer Science and Technology,
MIIT Key Laboratory of Pattern Analysis and Machine Intelligence,
Nanjing University of Aeronautics and Astronautics, Nanjing, China
vidaslee@gmail.com, {chenfang,dqzhang}@nuaa.edu.cn

**Abstract.** In fMRI analysis, the scientist seeks to aggregate multi-subject fMRI data so that inferences shared across subjects can be achieved. The challenge is to eliminate the variability of anatomical structure and functional topography of the human brain, which calls for aligning fMRI data across subjects. However, the existing methods do not exploit the geometry of the stimuli, which can be inferred by using certain domain knowledge and then serve as a priori. In this paper, such geometry is encoded in a graph matrix, and we propose an algorithm named Graph Hyperalignment for leveraging it. Specifically, a kernel-based optimization is developed to allow for non-linear feature extraction. To tackle overfitting caused by the high-spatial-and-low-temporal resolution of fMRI, the data in the new feature space are assumed to lie in a low-dimensional affine subspace, which can be implicitly integrated into the proposed optimization. Unlike other iterative existing methods, GHA reaches an optimal solution directly. Examining over four real datasets, Graph Hyperaligment achieves superior results to other methods.

**Keywords:** Brain decoding · Hyperalignment · Graph embedding

## 1 Introduction

Functional Magnetic Resonance Imaging (fMRI) plays an active role in cognitive science, as is able to capture abundant information that can help scientist to cast light on how the human brain works [1]. To reach shared cognitive findings across subjects, it is crucial to eliminate the disparities between subjects' brains. Hence, aligning multi-subject fMRI data is an integral step in fMRI analysis.

Recently, functional alignment is increasingly popular as it has achieved success in solving such variability across brains [2,3]. Specifically, functional alignment can be categorized as a concrete instance of multi-view Canonical Correlation Analysis (CCA) with some specific traits: (1) There tend to be several dozen subjects or even more. (2) The fMRI data lie in a high dimensional feature space. (3) Due to the native feature of fMRI — its high-spatial-and-low-temporal (HSLT) resolution, the collection of fMRI data of each subject suffers from small

© Springer Nature Switzerland AG 2019
D. Zhang et al. (Eds.): GLMI 2019, LNCS 11849, pp. 1–8, 2019.
https://doi.org/10.1007/978-3-030-35817-4_1

sample problem, i.e., the number of samples (volumes) is greatly smaller than the number of features (voxels). All those characteristics distinguish functional alignment from traditional multi-view CCA as they pose some particular difficulties. For example, if the time complexity of a certain model is at least a quadratic function of the number of features, then such model would be too clumsy to be used in fMRI analysis. On the other hand, given a temporally-aligned dataset, the HSLT resolution is highly likely to lead to an issue that there exists plenty of ways to align the training data perfectly by just linear functions. Therefore, insights into the geometry of the provided fMRI data are needed for avoiding overfitting. To reduce the high dimension of fMRI, some studies carried out a strategy of selecting a relatively small set of relevant voxels, e.g., based on a certain region of interest, as a preprocessing step [4]. One potential drawback of this tactic is that the joint information across voxels might be filtered.

In the existing studies of functional alignment, Hyperalignment [4] and Shared Response Model [5] are two basic models. The former serves as a decoding model, whereas the latter is an encoding one. Though they have been extensively studied and expanded into an assortment of variants [2,3,6,7], the geometry of the stimuli that represents the (dis)similarities among a certain fMRI dataset is idle. Such information could come from the categories of the given fMRI data as a priori. In this paper, we propose a model that leverage this shared geometry, which is encoded in a graph matrix. Specifically, a kernel-based optimization is developed to enable non-linear feature extraction. To tackle the issue brought by the HSLT resolution, we assume that the data in the new feature space should lie in a low-dimensional affine subspace, which can be implicitly integrated into the developed optimization. The model together with the optimization is named as Graph Hyperalignment (GHA). The contributions of this paper are as follows:

1. We propose a model to employ the geometry of the stimuli that depicts, and an efficient kernel-based optimization with low-dimension assumption to avoid overfitting posed by the HSLT resolution of fMRI.
2. Unlike other iterative methods, it reaches an optimal solution directly.

In the following, we develop the formulation of Graph Hyperalignment. Afterward, a kernel-based optimization that takes the low-dimension assumption into consideration is developed. Finally, we examine GHA over four real datasets compared with other baselines, which is followed by a conclusion.

## 2   Graph Hyperalignment

**Notation.** For consistency, the bold letters are reserved for matrices (upper) or vectors (lower), while the plain are for scalars. For any matrix $\mathbf{A}$, $\mathbf{a}_i$ denotes its $i$-th column and $A_{ij}$ is its $(i,j)$-th entry. Moreover, the subscript of $\mathbf{A}_{E \times F}$ indicates its shape.

Let $\{\mathbf{X}_i \in \mathbb{R}^{V_i \times T}\}_{i=1}^M$ be a specific temporally-aligned fMRI dataset, e.g., collecting the data while all subjects are watching one movie simultaneously, where $V_i$ is the number of features (voxels) of the $i$-th subject, $T$ refers to the number of samples (volumes), and $M$ denotes the number of subjects. To account for kernel methods, let $\Phi_i : \mathbb{R}^{V_i} \mapsto \mathbb{R}^{N_i}$ be a non-linear feature map where $N_i$ is the dimension of the new feature space. Unlike Kernel Hyperalignment [6], we allow specifying different kernels for different subjects. For the $i$-th subject, denote $\boldsymbol{\Phi}_i$ by setting $(\boldsymbol{\phi}_i)_j = \Phi_i((\mathbf{x}_i)_j)$ for $1 \leq j \leq T_i$. Further, let $\mathbf{K}_i$ be $\boldsymbol{\Phi}_i^T \boldsymbol{\Phi}_i$.

**Problem Statements.** The goal is to learn a set of aligning maps $\{f_i : \mathbb{R}^{N_i} \mapsto \mathbb{R}^K\}_{i=1}^M$ such that they aligned the transformed dataset $\{\boldsymbol{\Phi}_i \in \mathbb{R}^{N_i \times T}\}_{i=1}^M$ well. Here, $K$ refers to the number of shared features. In this paper, we focus on linear aligning maps, and thus $f_i = \mathbf{W}_i \in \mathbb{R}^{N_i \times K}$.

**The Geometry of the Stimuli.** The geometry of the stimuli can be represented by the relations among different categories of stimuli. Here, this information serves as a priori and is encoded in a graph matrix $\mathbf{G} \in \mathbb{R}^{T \times T}$ where $G_{ij}$ describes how (dis)similar the $i$-th and $j$-th stimuli are. Therefore, there is $\mathbf{G}^T = \mathbf{G}$.

To capture the temporal alignment, we adopt the so-called maximum variance multi-view CCA as an anchor [8]. Therefore, there is

$$\underset{\mathbf{W}_i, \mathbf{S}}{\operatorname{argmin}} \sum_{i=1}^M \left\| \mathbf{W}_i^T \boldsymbol{\Phi}_i - \mathbf{S} \right\|_F^2$$

$$\text{subject to } \mathbf{SS^T} = \mathbf{I} \, . \tag{1}$$

Here, $\mathbf{S} \in \mathbb{R}^{K \times T}$ is the sought-after well-aligned template and the constraint simply imposed that each shared feature should be on the same scale and any two of them should be statistically uncorrelated.

The geometry encoded in the graph matrix $\mathbf{G}$ is assumed to be reflected from the unknown well-aligned template $\mathbf{S}$. Therefore, the corresponding formulation is

$$\operatorname{argmin}_{\mathbf{S}} \frac{1}{2} \sum_{i=1}^T \sum_{j=1}^T G_{ij} \left\| \mathbf{s}_i - \mathbf{s}_j \right\|_F^2 = \operatorname{tr}\left(\mathbf{SLS}^T\right)$$

$$\text{subject to } \mathbf{SS^T} = \mathbf{I} \, . \tag{2}$$

where $\mathbf{L} = \mathbf{D} - \mathbf{G}$ and $\mathbf{D}$ is a diagonal matrix with $D_{ii} = \sum_{j=1}^T G_{ij}$. Here, $\mathbf{L}$ is the Laplacian matrix of the graph matrix $\mathbf{G}$ [9]. The objective function above seeks to separate the $i$-th and $j$-th well-aligned samples if $G_{ij} < 0$ and makes them as close as possible when $G_{ij} > 0$.

Combining the problems (1) and (2) with a balancing hyperparameter $\alpha \in [0, 1)$, the proposed model is expressed as

$$\operatorname{argmin}_{\mathbf{W}_i, \mathbf{S}} (1 - \alpha) \sum_{i=1}^M \left\| \mathbf{W}_i^T \boldsymbol{\Phi}_i - \mathbf{S} \right\|_F^2 + \alpha \operatorname{tr}\left(\mathbf{SLS}^T\right)$$

$$\text{subject to } \mathbf{SS^T} = \mathbf{I}$$

$$(\mathbf{w}_i)_j \in \mathrm{R}(\boldsymbol{\Phi}_i) \text{ for } 1 \leq i \leq M \text{ and } 1 \leq j \leq K \tag{3}$$

where $\mathrm{R}(\boldsymbol{\Phi}_i)$ denotes the subspace spanned by the columns of $\boldsymbol{\Phi}_i$. The latter constraint is out of the following consideration: Suppose an optimal solution

$\{\mathbf{W}_i^*\}_{i=1}^M$ is know and there is $\{\mathbf{Z}_i \in \mathbb{R}^{N_i \times K}\}_{i=1}^M$ where each column of $\mathbf{Z}_i$ belongs to the null space of $\mathbf{\Phi}_i$, then $\{\mathbf{W}_i^* + \mathbf{Z}_i\}_{i=1}^M$ is anther optimal solution as the trivial part $\{\mathbf{Z}_i\}_{i=1}^M$ does not help produce a lower objective value while optimizing. With linear kernels, such superfluous parts must exist due the HSLT resolution of fMRI. In a nutshell, the latter constrain simply excludes the minor parts.

## 3   Optimization

In the problem (3), while $\mathbf{S}$ is fixed, for each $i$, the optimal solution is $\mathbf{W}_i^* = (\mathbf{\Phi}_i^\dagger)^T \mathbf{S}^T$ where $\mathbf{\Phi}_i^\dagger$ is the pseudo-inverse of $\mathbf{\Phi}_i$. Substituting $\{\mathbf{W}_i^*\}_{i=1}^M$, there is

$$\sum_{i=1}^M \left\| (\mathbf{W}_i^*)^T \mathbf{\Phi}_i - \mathbf{S} \right\|_F^2 = M \|\mathbf{S}\|_F^2 + \sum_{i=1}^M \left( \langle \mathbf{S}\mathbf{\Phi}_i^\dagger \mathbf{\Phi}_i, \mathbf{S}\mathbf{\Phi}_i^\dagger \mathbf{\Phi}_i \rangle - 2\langle \mathbf{S}\mathbf{\Phi}_i^\dagger \mathbf{\Phi}_i, \mathbf{S} \rangle \right)$$

$$= M \|\mathbf{S}\|_F^2 - \mathrm{tr}\left( \mathbf{S} \left( \sum_{i=1}^M \mathbf{\Phi}_i^\dagger \mathbf{\Phi}_i \right) \mathbf{S}^T \right) . \tag{4}$$

Hence, the problem (3) is equivalent to

$$\underset{\mathbf{S}}{\mathrm{argmin}}\ \mathrm{tr}\left( \mathbf{S} \left( \alpha \mathbf{L} + (\alpha - 1)\mathbf{M} \right) \mathbf{S}^T \right)$$

$$\text{subject to } \mathbf{S}\mathbf{S}^T = \mathbf{I} . \tag{5}$$

where $\mathbf{M} = \sum_{i=1}^M \mathbf{\Phi}_i^\dagger \mathbf{\Phi}_i$. By spectral decomposition, $\alpha \mathbf{L} + (\alpha - 1)\mathbf{M} = \mathbf{E}\mathbf{\Sigma}\mathbf{E}$ where the eigenvalues along the diagonal of $\mathbf{\Sigma}$ is in ascending order. Then the first $K$ columns of $\mathbf{E}$ is an optimal solution for the problem (5), which is denoted by $\hat{\mathbf{E}}$. Therefore, in the problem (3), for each $i$, an optimal aligning map is $\mathbf{W}_i^* = (\mathbf{\Phi}_i^\dagger)^T (\mathbf{S}^*)^T = (\mathbf{\Phi}_i^\dagger)^T \hat{\mathbf{E}}^T$.

Here are some tricks to facilitate the optimization. By spectral decomposition, $\mathbf{K}_i = \mathbf{V}_i \mathbf{D}_i \mathbf{V}_i^T$ where the zero eigenvalues are excluded. With $\mathbf{U}_i = \mathbf{\Phi}_i \mathbf{V}_i \mathbf{D}_i^{-\frac{1}{2}}$, a Singular Value Decomposition of $\mathbf{\Phi}_i$ is

$$\mathbf{\Phi}_i = \mathbf{U}_i \mathbf{D}_i^{\frac{1}{2}} \mathbf{V}_i^T . \tag{6}$$

Since $\mathbf{\Phi}_i^\dagger = \mathbf{V}_i \mathbf{D}_i^{-\frac{1}{2}} \mathbf{U}_i^T$, there are $\mathbf{\Phi}_i^\dagger \mathbf{\Phi}_i = \mathbf{V}_i \mathbf{V}_i^T$ and $\mathbf{W}_i^* = \mathbf{\Phi}_i \mathbf{V}_i \mathbf{D}_i^{-1} \mathbf{V}_i^T \hat{\mathbf{E}}$.

**The Overfitting Issue.** With linear kernels, suppose $\mathbf{X}_i$ is full-column rank for each $i$, which is almost the case due to the HSLT resolution of fMRI. Then, $(\mathbf{W}_i^*)^T \mathbf{X}_i = \mathbf{S}^* \mathbf{X}_i^\dagger \mathbf{X}_i = \mathbf{S}^* \mathbf{I} = \mathbf{S}^*$, which means that the generated optimal solution $\{\mathbf{W}_i^*\}_{i=1}^M$ aligns the training data perfectly. In other words, the optimal solution of the problem (3) indicates overfitting.

The culprit here is the potential full-column rank of each $\mathbf{X}_i$. To solve this issue, we assume that the data of the $i$-th subject should lie in a low-dimensional affine subspace in the new feature space. If the dimension of the affine subspace

---

**Algorithm 1.** Graph Hyperalignment (GHA)

---

**Input:** Aligning data $\{\mathbf{X}_i \in \mathbb{R}^{V_i \times T}\}_{i=1}^{M}$, the number of the shared features $K$, the energy $\{p_i\%\}_{i=1}^{M}$ to be preserved, a priori $\mathbf{L}$, the hyperparameter $\alpha$ and kernel functions for each subject.

1: For each $i$, standardize $\mathbf{X}_i$ such that it has zero mean along the second dimension and the variance of each feature (voxel) is 1.

2: Generate $\{\mathbf{K}_i\}_{i=1}^{M}$ by the specified kernel functions and then centralize them by $\mathbf{K}_i \leftarrow \mathbf{K}_i + T^{-2}\mathbf{J}\mathbf{K}_i\mathbf{J} - T^{-1}\mathbf{J}\mathbf{K}_i - T^{-1}\mathbf{K}_i\mathbf{J}$ where $\mathbf{J} \in \mathbb{R}^{T \times T}$.

3: **for** $i \leftarrow 1$ **to** $M$ **do**

4:     $\mathbf{K}_i = \mathbf{V}_i \mathbf{D}_i \mathbf{V}_i^T$ by spectral decomposition where the eigenvalues in $\mathbf{D}_i$ is in descending order.

5:     Find $L_i$ so that the first $L_i$ singular values in $\mathbf{D}_i^{\frac{1}{2}}$ contains roughly $p_i\%$ energy.

6:     Let $\hat{\mathbf{V}}_i$ be the first $L_i$ columns of $\mathbf{V}_i$.

7:     Let $\hat{\mathbf{D}}_i$ be the top left $L_i \times L_i$ submatrix of $\mathbf{D}_i$.

8: **end for**

9: $\mathbf{M} \leftarrow \sum_{i=1}^{M} \hat{\mathbf{V}}_i \hat{\mathbf{V}}_i^T$ and $\mathbf{P} \leftarrow \alpha\mathbf{L} + (\alpha - 1)\mathbf{M}$.

10: By spectral decomposition, $\mathbf{P} = \mathbf{E}\mathbf{\Sigma}\mathbf{E}^T$ where the eigenvalues are in ascending order. Let $\hat{\mathbf{E}}$ be the first $K$ columns of $\mathbf{E}$.

11: For $1 \leq i \leq M$, $\mathbf{W}_i^* \leftarrow \mathbf{\Phi}_i \hat{\mathbf{V}}_i \hat{\mathbf{D}}_i^{-1} \hat{\mathbf{V}}_i^T \hat{\mathbf{E}}$.

---

is $L_i(L_i \leq T)$, we find the one that best fits the training data by solving the following problem:

$$\underset{\mathbf{B}_i \in \mathbb{R}^{N_i \times L_i}, \mathbf{m}_i}{\operatorname{argmin}} \sum_{j=1}^{T} \left\| \mathbf{B}_i \mathbf{B}_i^T ((\boldsymbol{\phi}_i)_j - \mathbf{m}_i) - ((\boldsymbol{\phi}_i)_j - \mathbf{m}_i) \right\|_F^2 \tag{7}$$

$$\text{subject to } \mathbf{B}_i^T \mathbf{B}_i = \mathbf{I}.$$

An optimal solution is that $\mathbf{m}_i^* = T^{-1} \sum_{j=1}^{T} (\boldsymbol{\phi}_i)_j$ and $\mathbf{B}_i^*$ be the first $L_i$ columns of $\mathbf{U}_i$ in equation (6) where $(\boldsymbol{\phi}_i)_j \leftarrow (\boldsymbol{\phi}_i)_j - \mathbf{m}_i^*$.

For the $i$-th subject, suppose $\mathbf{Z}_i \in \mathbb{R}^{N_i \times E_i}$ is another data in the new feature space. To apply $\mathbf{m}_i$, we can centralize the Gram matrix $\mathbf{Z}_i^T \mathbf{\Phi}_i$ by

$$\mathbf{Z}_i^T \mathbf{\Phi}_i + T^{-2}\mathbf{J}_{E_i \times T}\mathbf{\Phi}_i^T \mathbf{\Phi}_i \mathbf{J}_{T \times T} - T^{-1}\mathbf{J}_{E_i \times T}\mathbf{\Phi}_i^T \mathbf{\Phi}_i - T^{-1}\mathbf{Z}_i^T \mathbf{\Phi}_i \mathbf{J}_{T \times T} \tag{8}$$

where $\mathbf{J}$ denotes all-one matrix. From now on, suppose all Gram matrices have been centralized. Considering the equation (6), let $S_i$ be the number of (non-zero) singular values in $\mathbf{D}_i^{\frac{1}{2}}$. Assume the singular values are in descending order and the first $L_i$ of them contain approximately $p_i \in (0, 100]$ percent of energy, i.e., $\sum_{j=1}^{L_i} (D_i^{\frac{1}{2}})_{jj} / \sum_{j=1}^{S_i} (D_i^{\frac{1}{2}})_{jj} \approx p\%$. Therefore, the low-dimension $L_i$ is controlled by $p_i\%$. Let $\hat{\mathbf{U}}_i$ and $\hat{\mathbf{V}}_i$ be the first $L_i$ columns of $\mathbf{U}_i$ and $\mathbf{V}_i$, respectively. Then, $\mathbf{B}_i^* = \hat{\mathbf{U}}_i$ can be implemented implicitly in the proposed optimization since $\mathbf{Z}_i^T \hat{\mathbf{U}}_i \hat{\mathbf{U}}_i^T \hat{\mathbf{U}}_i \hat{\mathbf{U}}_i^T \mathbf{\Phi}_i \hat{\mathbf{V}}_i = \mathbf{Z}_i^T \hat{\mathbf{U}}_i \hat{\mathbf{U}}_i^T \mathbf{\Phi}_i \hat{\mathbf{V}}_i = \mathbf{Z}_i^T \mathbf{\Phi}_i \hat{\mathbf{V}}_i$. The optimization procedure of GHA is shown in Algorithm 1.

**Table 1.** The larger the better. Each performance is reported by averaging accuracies over all folds with standard deviation. The bold indicates the best performance on each dataset.

| Dataset(#class) | ν-SVM | KHA [6] | SVDHA [10] | SRM [5] | RSRM [3] | RHA [7] | GHA |
|---|---|---|---|---|---|---|---|
| DS105WB(8) [11] | 11.67 ± 1.80 | 39.22 ± 4.50 | 30.48 ± 3.52 | 39.69 ± 3.95 | 40.01 ± 3.84 | 52.50 ± 4.28 | **61.22 ± 5.44** |
| DS105ROI(8) [11] | 13.06 ± 2.93 | 48.22 ± 3.34 | 41.33 ± 4.19 | 48.14 ± 3.17 | 48.51 ± 3.80 | 57.63 ± 5.55 | **62.54 ± 4.66** |
| DS011(2) [12] | 51.80 ± 3.73 | 85.79 ± 3.82 | 74.42 ± 4.40 | 85.47 ± 3.53 | 85.58 ± 3.89 | 91.80 ± 2.65 | **92.41 ± 2.57** |
| DS232(4) [13] | 25.89 ± 2.46 | 69.38 ± 3.16 | 56.77 ± 4.52 | 69.18 ± 3.27 | 69.25 ± 3.20 | 77.64 ± 2.75 | **82.58 ± 1.42** |
| DS001(4) [14] | 34.32 ± 2.08 | 57.10 ± 1.97 | 51.99 ± 1.87 | 56.83 ± 1.54 | 57.20 ± 1.30 | 57.87 ± 0.61 | **61.49 ± 1.95** |

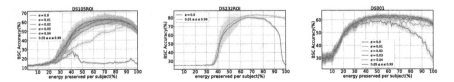

**Fig. 1.** BSC accuracy is reported with standard deviation.

## 4    Experiments

**Datasets.** Four datasets shared by openfmri.org or Chen *et al.* [5] are involved. Raw datasets are preprocessed by using FSL (https://fsl.fmrib.ox. ac.uk/), following a standard process: slice timing, anatomical alignment, normalization, smoothing. The default parameters in FSL were taken when the dataset does not provide. Here are the descriptions of them:

**DS011.** Fourteen subjects learned to predict weather outcomes (rain or sun) for two different cities. After learning, they predicted weather [12]. There are 271 samples per subject with 19174 features.

**DS105.** The data were collected while six subjects were viewing gray-scale images of faces, houses, cats, bottles, scissors, shoes, chairs, and nonsense images [11]. Here, DS105WB contains the whole-brain fMRI data (19174 features) while the data in DS105ROI are based on a region of interest (2294 features). There are 994 samples from each subject.

**DS001.** Sixteen subjects were told to inflate a control balloon or a reward balloon on a screen. For a control balloon, subjects had only one choice. For another case, they could choose to pump or cash out. The balloon may explode or expand after pumping [14]. There are 485 samples per subject with 19174 features.

**DS232.** Ten subjects were instructed to respond to images of faces, scenes, objects and phrase-scrambled versions of the scene images [13]. There are 1691 samples per subject with 9947 features.

**Measure for the Performance of Alignment.** Since each dataset employed includes labels, the performance is evaluated by between-subject classification (BSC) accuracy [4], i.e., testing how well a trained classifier can generalize to new subjects. Following previous studies, ν-SVM is used for classification.

**Experiment Scheme.** The data of each subject is equally divided into two parts with each category being equally split. One part is for alignment, whereas the other is for training or testing a classifier. Switching the roles of the two parts and leave-$k$-subject-out strategy are adopted for cross-validation. For instance, with 16 subjects, leave-4-subject-out leads to $16 \div 4 \times 2 = 8$ folds for cross-validation.

Experiment on each fold has two phrases: (1) One part of subjects' data is fed to a functional alignment method to yield the aligning maps $\{f_i : \mathbb{R}^{V_i} \mapsto \mathbb{R}^K\}_{i=1}^M$. Then, the left data of each subject are mapped into the shared space by its generated aligning map. (2) The mapped data of the $M - k$ subjects are used to train a classifier, while those of the other $k$ subjects are for testing the classifier.

**Baselines.** Five state-of-the-art functional alignment methods were implements by ourselves in Python: Regularized Hyperalignment (RHA) [7], Kernel Hyperalignment (KHA) [6], SVD-Hyperalignment (SVDHA) [10], Shared Response Model (SRM) [5] and Robust SRM (RSRM) [3].

**Settings.** For each dataset, the parameter $\nu$ in $\nu$-SVM with linear kernel is fixed for all methods. For other methods, we choose the best hyperparameter according to the original papers. For GHA: (1) A linear kernel is fixed here. (2) Since each dataset contains label, a priori is specified by setting $G_{ij} = 1$ if the $i$-th and $j$-th samples are in the same category and $G_{ij} = -1$ otherwise. Following the description order of datasets, $\nu$ is set as $0.3, 0.8, 0.5$ and $0.8$. Further, $K$, energy $p_i\%(1 \leq i \leq M)$ and $\alpha$ are always fixed as 10, 80% and 0.5, respectively.

**Examination Over Temporally-Aligned Datasets.** Examining over four real datasets, the results are shown in Table 1. GHA achieves the best performance over each dataset compared with other baselines.

**Studies Over Hyperparameters.** The influence of $\alpha$ and $\{p_i\%\}_{i=1}^M$ are provided in Fig. 1. For each $\alpha$, the best result is not coupled with full energy, which infers the necessity of low-dimension assumption in the new feature space. Plus, it also attests to the importance of leveraging the geometry of the stimuli.

## 5   Conclusion

Functional alignment is an indispensable step in fMRI analysis to reach shared traits across subjects. So far, the geometry of the stimuli that serves as a priori is unemployed. In this paper, this geometry is encoded in a graph matrix and a model is proposed to take advantage of it. Specifically, a kernel-based optimization is developed to account for non-linear feature extraction. Further, a low-dimension assumption is imposed on each new feature space to avoid overfitting caused by the HSLT resolution of fMRI. The empirical studies over four real datasets confirm that GHA beats other existing methods. In the future, we are planning to study how to construct a more informative graph matrix.

**Acknowledgement.** This work was supported by the National Natural Science Foundation of China (Nos. 61876082, 61861130366, 61703301) and the Royal Society-Academy of Medical Sciences Newton Advanced Fellowship (No. NAF\R1\180371).

# References

1. Haxby, J.V., Connolly, A.C., Guntupalli, J.S.: Decoding neural representational spaces using multivariate pattern analysis. Ann. Rev. Neurosci. **37**, 435–456 (2014)
2. Turek, J.S., Willke, T.L., Chen, P.H., Ramadge, P.J.: A semi-supervised method for multi-subject FMRI functional alignment. In: 2017 IEEE International Conference on Acoustics, Speech and Signal Processing (ICASSP), pp. 1098–1102 IEEE (2017)
3. Turek, J.S., Ellis, C.T., Skalaban, L.J., Turk-Browne, N.B., Willke, T.L.: Capturing shared and individual information in FMRI data. In: 2018 IEEE International Conference on Acoustics, Speech and Signal Processing (ICASSP), pp. 826–830 IEEE (2018)
4. Haxby, J.V., et al.: A common, high-dimensional model of the representational space in human ventral temporal cortex. Neuron **72**(2), 404–416 (2011)
5. Chen, P.H.C., Chen, J., Yeshurun, Y., Hasson, U., Haxby, J., Ramadge, P.J.: A reduced-dimension FMRI shared response model. In: Advances in Neural Information Processing Systems (NIPS), pp. 460–468 (2015)
6. Lorbert, A., Ramadge, P.J.: Kernel hyperalignment. In: Advances in Neural Information Processing Systems (NIPS), pp. 1790–1798 (2012)
7. Xu, H., Lorbert, A., Ramadge, P.J., Guntupalli, J.S., Haxby, J.V.: Regularized hyperalignment of multi-set fmri data. In: 2012 IEEE Statistical Signal Processing Workshop (SSP), pp. 229–232. IEEE (2012)
8. Kettenring, J.R.: Canonical analysis of several sets of variables. Biometrika **58**(3), 433–451 (1971)
9. Chung, F.R., Graham, F.C.: Spectral Graph Theory, vol. 92. American Mathematical Society, Providence (1997)
10. Chen, P.H., Guntupalli, J.S., Haxby, J.V., Ramadge, P.J.: Joint SVD-hyperalignment for multi-subject FMRI data alignment. In: 2014 IEEE International Workshop on Machine Learning for Signal Processing (MLSP), pp. 1–6 IEEE (2014)
11. Haxby, J.V., Gobbini, M.I., Furey, M.L., Ishai, A., Schouten, J.L., Pietrini, P.: Distributed and overlapping representations of faces and objects in ventral temporal cortex. Science **293**(5539), 2425–2430 (2001)
12. Foerde, K., Knowlton, B.J., Poldrack, R.A.: Modulation of competing memory systems by distraction. Proc. Nat. Acad. Sci. **103**(31), 11778–11783 (2006)
13. Carlin, J.D., Kriegeskorte, N.: Adjudicating between face-coding models with individual-face FMRI responses. PLoS Comput. Biol. **13**(7), e1005604 (2017)
14. Schonberg, T., Fox, C.R., Mumford, J.A., Congdon, E., Trepel, C., Poldrack, R.A.: Decreasing ventromedial prefrontal cortex activity during sequential risk-taking: an fmri investigation of the balloon analog risk task. Front. Neurosci. **6**, 80 (2012)

# Interactive 3D Segmentation Editing and Refinement via Gated Graph Neural Networks

Xiaosong Wang$^{(\boxtimes)}$, Ling Zhang, Holger Roth, Daguang Xu, and Ziyue Xu

Nvidia Corporation, Bethesda, MD, USA
xiaosongw@nvidia.com

**Abstract.** The extraction of organ and lesion regions is an important yet challenging problem in medical image analysis. The accuracy of the segmentation is essential to the quantitative evaluation in many clinical applications. Nevertheless, automated segmentation approaches often suffer from a variety of errors, e.g., over-segmentation, under-detection, and dull edges, which often requires manual corrections on the algorithm-generated results. Therefore, an efficient segmentation editing and refinement tool is desired due to the need of (1) minimizing the repeated effort of human annotators on similar errors (e.g., under-segmentation cross several slices in 3D volumes); (2) an "intelligent" algorithm that can preserve the correct part of the segmentation while it can also align the erroneous part with the true boundary based on users' limited input. This paper presents a novel solution that utilizes the gated graph neural networks to refine the 3D image volume segmentation from certain automated methods in an interactive mode. The pre-computed segmentation is converted to polygons in a slice-by-slice manner, and then we construct the graph by defining polygon vertices cross slices as nodes in a directed graph. The nodes are modeled with gated recurrent units to first propagate the features among neighboring nodes. Afterward, our framework outputs the movement prediction of each polygon vertex based on the converged states of nodes. We quantitatively demonstrate the refinement performance of our framework on the artificially degraded segmentation data. Up to 10% improvement in IOUs are achieved for the segmentation with a variety of error degrees and percentages.

**Keywords:** Interactive · Segmentation refinement · Gated graph neural network

## 1 Introduction

Even in the deep learning era, image segmentation remains a challenging problem in many medical imaging applications. High quality annotated data are usually required for data-hungry deep learning paradigms, while manual labeling is indeed a laborsome effort for human annotators, especially in labeling

© Springer Nature Switzerland AG 2019
D. Zhang et al. (Eds.): GLMI 2019, LNCS 11849, pp. 9–17, 2019.
https://doi.org/10.1007/978-3-030-35817-4_2

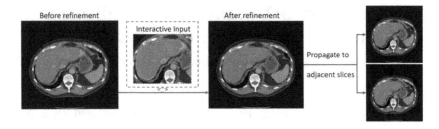

**Fig. 1.** Overview of segmentation refinement with or without interactive inputs.

segmentation masks. It has been a common practice to initialize the annotation with a segmentation results from an automated approach that was trained either on a small amount of data (in an active learning scenario) or on data from other domain (for transfer learning). Automated segmentation approaches often suffer from a range of different errors, e.g., over-segmentation, under-detection, and dull edges. Therefore, an efficient segmentation refinement and editing tool is desired so as to minimize the effort of human annotators on repeated errors, e.g., similar under-segmentation in several adjacent slices.

There have been many interactive segmentation editing methods with various interactions [7,8]. We believe polygon editing is one of the efficient way for users to editing contours and it is straight-forward to model the polygon vertices with graphs, especially for 3D polygons. Efforts are made to generalize neural networks to graph data. In [2], convoluational neural networks (CNN) are employed in the spectral domain to operate the convolution on the graph. Another trend is to recurrently apply neural networks to every node of the graph [3], e.g., gated graphic neural networks (GGNN). Acuna et al. [1] first applied GGNN to upsample the polygon generated using LSTMs based sequential output model. In this work, we employed the GGNN model to propagate the annotator's editing (on one polygon vertex) to nearby nodes in the spatial neighborhood and adjacent slices as well (shown in Fig. 1).

Another challenge we face here is to move all vertices closer to the true object boundary and meanwhile preserve the ones that were already on the boundary. It is indeed an essential requirement for automatically refining the segmentation contours since we assume the majority of the points in the initial segmentation contour are close to the object true boundary, although we later demonstrate the prominent performance of our proposed method on some extreme cases with significant under- or over-segmentation. We employ three different strategies to fulfill this requirement based on a vanilla GGNN: (1) having a separate output branch to classify if the moved vertex is on the boundary or not, in addition to the movement prediction branch; (2) applying the refinement sequentially to encourage the vertices far from the boundary to converge towards the true contour in small steps; (3) designing a controlled training strategy by feeding mixed training samples with different distances of movements and including a relatively large portion of no movement samples.

We evaluate our proposed framework on both artificially degraded segmentation results (computed from the groundtruth) and real results from a classic 3D U-Net approach [5] (as an initialization). On the artificial data, our approach is able to improve the segmentation up to 10% in IOU (according to different error rates). By adopting the sequential output, we can achieve a further $\sim 1\%$ improvements upon the refinement results. Finally, we illustrate some sample image results with editing and refinement.

## 2 Method

Before the user can edit the segmentation mask, we transform the 3D segmentation masks to the corresponding polygons in a slice-by-slice manner. In this work, we consider two ways of editing the polygon interactively, either the user moving one of the vertex in the polygon to a point on the true boundary or clicking a button to get a refined segmentation in an automatic fashion. Vertices on the polygons in each slice will only be adjusted inside the current slice for both situations. In the following sections, we discuss the basics of GGNN first and then introduce more details regarding our addition on the GGNN model and its application for interactive segmentation editing and refinement.

### 2.1 Graph Gated Neural Networks

Our gated graphic neural network architecture is defined based on a directed graph structure $\mathcal{G} = (\mathcal{V}, \mathcal{E})$. Each vertex $v_i \in \mathcal{V}$ represents a point in polygons from previous generated segmentation results. Edges $e = (v, v') \in \mathcal{E} = \mathcal{V} \times \mathcal{V}$ connects vertices, which indicates adjacent relations between two neighboring polygon vertices. A sample graph structure modeling based on a 3D polygon is shown in Fig. 2. In this work, $L = 3$ different types of edges are considered spatially, e.g., immediate adjacent neighbors (green edges in Fig. 2) and relatively far neighbors (blue edges in Fig. 2). In addition, two closest vertices from the polygons on the adjacent slices are also connected for each polygon vertex (orange edges in Fig. 2). $IN(v) = \{v|(v', v) \in \mathcal{E}\}$ returns the set of predecessor vertices $v'$ with edges $v'-> v$, while $OUT(v) = \{v|(v, v') \in \mathcal{E}\}$ is the set of successor vertices $v'$ with edges $v-> v'$. The set of all nodes in $v$'s 3D neighborhood is defined as $N(v) = IN(v) \bigcup OUT(v))$. The state of each vertex is represented using a state vector $\mathbf{h}_v \in \mathcal{R}^D$ for each vertex $v$. $D$ states the dimension of such embedding.

Unlike a convolutional neural networks, GGNN modeling consists of two stages to map graphs to outputs, namely the propagation model and the output model. A propagation model promotes the communication between vertices so that the state $\mathbf{h}_v$ can evolve according to its own features and its neighbors' as well and finalize the representations for each vertex in several time steps. Then, an output model maps from the resulting state of each vertex to an desired output $o_v$ for each $v \in \mathcal{V}$, i.e. the movement of each vertex and the logits indicate if it is on the boundary in this case. The system is built using recurrent neural

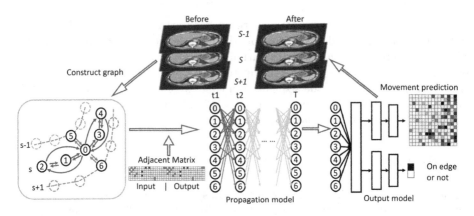

**Fig. 2.** Overview of segmentation refinement with or without interactive inputs. (Color figure online)

networks and is differentiable from end-to-end, so all parameters are learned jointly using gradient-based optimization.

**Propagation Model:** The propagation process adopts gated recurrent units (GRU) [2] for modeling the communication between vertices and the recurrence of such communications for a fixed number of steps $T$. The neighboring relationships between vertices is defined in the 3D adjacent matrix $\mathbf{A} \in R^{|\mathcal{V}| \times 2L|\mathcal{V}|}$ (a sample shown in Fig. 2).

$$\mathbf{a}_v^t = \mathbf{A}_v : [\mathbf{h}_1^{t-1}, ..., \mathbf{h}_{|N|}^{t-1}] + b \tag{1}$$

It determines how the state $\mathbf{h}_v^{(t)}$ of each vertex will be updated based on all states $\mathbf{h}_{v'}^{t-1}, v' \in N(v)$ (a sample shown in Fig. 2).

$$\mathbf{h}_v^{(1)} = [\mathbf{x}_v, \mathbf{0}], \mathbf{h}_v^t = GRU(\mathbf{h}_v^{t-1}, \mathbf{a}_v^t) \tag{2}$$

The state $\mathbf{h}_v^1$ is initialized with the image feature computed for vertex $v$. Here, we adopted a skip-layer architecture [1,4] to extract and concatenate CNN features from a number of convolutional layers, namely output of conv1, res1, res2, and res4 blocks from an ResNet-50 CNN.

In a fixed time steps, the state of each vertex will be updated with a weighted average of all features from its neighbors and even neighbors' neighbors. These weights are learned from multiple factors during the training, including the weights on edges (which decide how much it will be updated from each neighbor), the similarity of features compared to its neighbors' (computed in reset and update gate in GRU, which decide if it will be updated or reset), and the condition if itself is on the boundary(gradient flow from the output model, which decide if it should remain in the current state).

**Output Model:** The output model has a two-branch architecture as shown in Fig. 2. In a similar fashion as stated in [1], the movement of each vertex (centered in a $M \times M$ grid) will be outputted via a neural network branch based on both the state $\mathbf{h}_v^T$ and the features $\mathbf{x}_v^T$ of vertex $v$. All vertices share the network and it essentially become a classification problem (which spot in its $M \times M$ neighborhood grid should the vertex move to).

$$o_v = f(Tanh(g(\mathbf{h}_v^T, \mathbf{x}_v^T))) \tag{3}$$

$f, g$ are neural networks, i.e., multilayer perceptrons (MLP) in this case. On the other paralleled branch, both the state $\mathbf{h}_v^T$ and the features $\mathbf{x}_v^T$ of vertex $v$ will be inputted into a classifier to see if the current state represents a vertex on the boundary. Another set of MLPs (similar to the ones on the movement branch) are used to output a binary classification results. The groundtruth points on the boundary are computed along with the polygons (using the $findcontours()$ in the OpenCV library), which indeed is a dense version of the corresponding polygon. This classification branch will encourage the propagation model (through gradient flow) not only to embed a state for vertex location adjustment but also enforce the state to learn the feature of a vertex on true boundary. In such setting, those vertices that are already on boundary will remain in their initial state (i.e., image features representing boundaries).

**Sequential Output:** Because the movement of each vertex is limited to a grid (with a size of $15 \times 15$) centered at the target vertex location, some of the vertices may require further corrections if they are far from the true contour (i.e., more than 7 grid blocks away). We applied our algorithm for several times to update the results sequentially so as to move all vertices closer to the object boundary and meanwhile preserve the ones that were already on the boundary.

**Training Strategies:** A straight-forward idea is to use the results from a certain segmentation algorithm as the initialization to train our proposed framework towards the segmentation groundtruth. However, it will be hard to generalize the model to other situations since the trained model will then intend to restore certain segmentation errors that is unique to this particular algorithm, e.g always under-segmentation or always over-segmentation. Therefore, we leverage artificially degraded data (computed from the groundtruth segmentation mask) as the training data. The benefits of adopting artificially degraded data are two-fold. Firstly, we can simulate all different segmentation errors in different extents. In practice, we move the vertices on the groundtruth polygons away from their original locations with different directions and distances. In addition, we also keep certain percentage of the groundtruth vertices untouched so as to learn how these correct vertices look like and how to remain them in their origin.

## 3   Results and Discussion

To demonstrate the performance of our proposed framework, we adopted the CT liver data in the medical segmentation Dechathlon challenge [6] in the experiments, which totally contains 131 volumes from different patients. We randomly split the dataset to have 91 volumes for the training, 10 as the validation set and

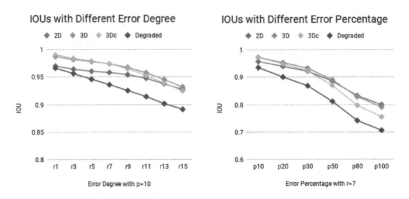

**Fig. 3.** Evaluation of polygon refinement in IOUs using 2D, 3D, and 3Dc method. **Left**: IOUs of refined Polygons on degraged polygons with Error Degree from 1 to 15 and Error Percentage $p = 10\%$. **Right**: IOUs of refined Polygons on degraged polygons with $p$ from 10% to 100% and $r = 7$.

30 as the testing set. Only the slices having groundtruth masks will be utilized, i.e., 14020 slices for training/Validation and 4237 slices for testing. The input image size of our model is $224 \times 224$. Image data and associated masks are first cropped (20 pixels padding outside the masks) and re-sampled to the model input size. The concatenated image features are extracted and computed from a ImageNet pretrained ResNet-50 with the size of $112 \times 112 \times 256$. The final model was trained in 10 epochs using Adam optimizer with an initial learning rate of

**Table 1.** Evaluation of the proposed method on the artificially degraded polygons with a variety of Error Degree (r) and Error Percentage (p).

| model (r = 7, p = 10) | | 2D | 3D | 3Dc | Error |
|---|---|---|---|---|---|
| Error Percentage (p) = 10% | | | | | |
| r = 1 | IOU | $0.970 \pm 0.038$ | $0.988 \pm 0.012$ | $\mathbf{0.991 \pm 0.018}$ | $0.966 \pm 0.028$ |
| | DICE | $0.984 \pm 0.020$ | $0.993 \pm 0.006$ | $\mathbf{0.995 \pm 0.009}$ | $0.982 \pm 0.016$ |
| r = 7 | IOU | $0.958 \pm 0.037$ | $0.974 \pm 0.018$ | $\mathbf{0.974 \pm 0.022}$ | $0.936 \pm 0.039$ |
| | DICE | $0.978 \pm 0.019$ | $0.987 \pm 0.009$ | $\mathbf{0.987 \pm 0.012}$ | $0.966 \pm 0.023$ |
| r = 15 | IOU | $0.927 \pm 0.048$ | $\mathbf{0.931 \pm 0.048}$ | $0.925 \pm 0.049$ | $0.891 \pm 0.058$ |
| | DICE | $0.961 \pm 0.026$ | $\mathbf{0.964 \pm 0.028}$ | $0.960 \pm 0.028$ | $0.941 \pm 0.037$ |
| Error Degree (r) = 7 | | | | | |
| p = 10 | IOU | $0.958 \pm 0.036$ | $0.973 \pm 0.018$ | $\mathbf{0.973 \pm 0.022}$ | $0.935 \pm 0.039$ |
| | DICE | $0.978 \pm 0.019$ | $0.986 \pm 0.009$ | $\mathbf{0.986 \pm 0.011}$ | $0.966 \pm 0.023$ |
| p = 50 | IOU | $0.885 \pm 0.043$ | $\mathbf{0.890 \pm 0.045}$ | $0.869 \pm 0.045$ | $0.811 \pm 0.061$ |
| | DICE | $0.938 \pm 0.026$ | $\mathbf{0.941 \pm 0.027}$ | $0.929 \pm 0.028$ | $0.894 \pm 0.042$ |
| p = 100 | IOU | $\mathbf{0.799 \pm 0.067}$ | $0.791 \pm 0.076$ | $0.755 \pm 0.064$ | $0.706 \pm 0.074$ |
| | DICE | $\mathbf{0.887 \pm 0.045}$ | $0.881 \pm 0.051$ | $0.859 \pm 0.045$ | $0.825 \pm 0.057$ |

**Table 2.** Evaluation of the sequential refinement of polygons (varied in $s$).

| model (r = 7, p = 50) | | r = 7, p = 10 | r = 15, p = 10 | r = 7, p = 100 |
|---|---|---|---|---|
| Error | IOU | $0.931 \pm 0.046$ | $0.864 \pm 0.073$ | $0.636 \pm 0.087$ |
| | DICE | $0.963 \pm 0.027$ | $0.925 \pm 0.046$ | $0.774 \pm 0.071$ |
| s = 0 | IOU | $0.964 \pm 0.021$ | $0.880 \pm 0.068$ | $0.739 \pm 0.106$ |
| | DICE | $0.981 \pm 0.011$ | $0.935 \pm 0.042$ | $0.845 \pm 0.076$ |
| s = 1 | IOU | $\mathbf{0.965 \pm 0.020}$ | $0.889 \pm 0.069$ | $0.744 \pm 0.105$ |
| | DICE | $\mathbf{0.982 \pm 0.010}$ | $0.939 \pm 0.043$ | $0.848 \pm 0.075$ |
| s = 3 | IOU | $0.964 \pm 0.021$ | $0.894 \pm 0.066$ | $0.746 \pm 0.103$ |
| | DICE | $0.981 \pm 0.011$ | $0.942 \pm 0.041$ | $0.850 \pm 0.073$ |
| s = 5 | IOU | $0.964 \pm 0.023$ | $\mathbf{0.895 \pm 0.066}$ | $\mathbf{0.746 \pm 0.104}$ |
| | DICE | $0.981 \pm 0.012$ | $\mathbf{0.943 \pm 0.041}$ | $\mathbf{0.850 \pm 0.075}$ |

0.001. Due to the limits of GPU memory, we only consider polygons from three continuous slices at a time during training.

**Quantitative Analysis:** Two standard evaluation matrix, i.e., intersect over union (IOU) and the Dice coefficient (DICE) are used to measure the accuracy of segmentation results compared to the groundtruth. The resulting polygons from our proposed method are mapped back to the segmentation mask before the evaluation.

To evaluate the tolerance of our proposed method, we artificially degrade the polygons generated from the groundtruth with different Error Degrees (r) and different Error Percentages (p). Error degrees controls how far each polygon vertex will be deviated from its original location while error percentage limits how many of the vertices in each polygon will be intentionally degraded.

We compare three variants of our proposed approach in editing various errors, i.e., on single polygons (2D), on 3D polygons (cross slices) with the movement prediction only (3D) and 3D version with additional classification branch (3Dc). The Error column shows the statistics of degraded polygons. No interactive input is included in this experiment. As illustrated in Fig. 3 and Table 1, 3Dc achieved the best performance in data with minor error degrees and small error percentages. 3D dominates the refinement performance when both error degrees and percentages increases. The classification branch will enforce the convergence of vertices (near the boundary) towards the true boundary while it may not help the movement prediction when all vertices are largely deviated from the groundtruth. We also notice that 2D will perform better when all the vertices (p = 100) are degraded. In this case, 3D neighboring vertices will not help (pass the correct features). We also experiments with applying the refinement for several times so that vertices with large displacement will have the chance to return the origin gradually in small steps. Extreme cases are demonstrated here with $r = 15$ or $p = 100\%$. As shown in Table 2, the trained model(3D with $r = 7$

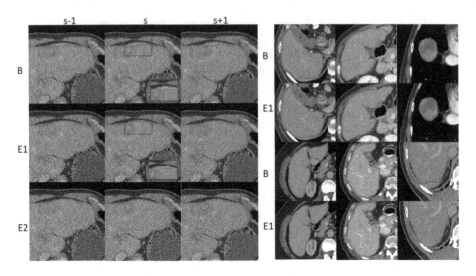

**Fig. 4. Left**: Refinement results with 2 edits on 3 adjacent slices . **Right**: More results with various errors. User-edited vertices in green, B: before, E: edit. (Color figure online)

and $p = 50\%$) reached the highest accuracy (up to another 1.5% improvement) in $s = 1$ for relative "easy" case and in $s = 5$ for the two extreme cases.

**Qualitative Result:** Sample qualitative results are illustrated in Fig. 4 based on the real segmentation results from the 3D U-Net model. The U-Net model is trained using the same data split. Results with continuous under-segmentation are shown on 3 adjacent slices in the left of Fig. 4. Two User's edits (E1 and E2) on single vertex are successfully propagated to all 3D neighboring vertices. Another 6 groups of sample results are shown with the segmentation before and after the editing (with moved polygon vertex marked in green). Different cases are presented, e.g., over/under segmentation. In all cases, the results demonstrate that the proposed method is not only able to propagate the users' editing to neighboring nodes but also to preserve the rest of polygon vertices' location.

## 4    Conclusion

Here, we demonstrate an efficient and accurate graph-based approach to reduce the annotation efforts by propagating the user's editing to its 3D neighbors while preserving the correct part of contours. The proposed method is more flexible in terms of modeling 3D image slice data in comparison to conventional CNN based method and has the potential to be extended to an fully automated segmentation approach.

# References

1. Acuna, D., Ling, H., Kar, A., Fidler, S.: Efficient interactive annotation of segmentation datasets with polygon-RNN++. In: Proceedings of the IEEE Conference on CVPR, pp. 859–868 (2018)
2. Cho, K., Van Merriënboer, B., Bahdanau, D., Bengio, Y.: On the properties of neural machine translation: Encoder-decoder approaches (2014). arXiv:1409.1259
3. Li, Y., Tarlow, D., Brockschmidt, M., Zemel, R.: Gated graph sequence neural networks (2015). arXiv preprint arXiv:1511.05493
4. Long, J., Shelhamer, E., Darrell, T.: Fully convolutional networks for semantic segmentation. In: Proceedings of the IEEE Conference on CVPR, pp. 3431–3440 (2015)
5. Ronneberger, O., Fischer, P., Brox, T.: U-Net: convolutional networks for biomedical image segmentation. In: Navab, N., Hornegger, J., Wells, W.M., Frangi, A.F. (eds.) MICCAI 2015. LNCS, vol. 9351, pp. 234–241. Springer, Cham (2015). https://doi.org/10.1007/978-3-319-24574-4_28
6. Simpson, A.L., et al.: A large annotated medical image dataset for the development and evaluation of segmentation algorithms (2019). arXiv preprint arXiv:1902.09063
7. Wang, G., et al.: Interactive medical image segmentation using deep learning with image-specific fine tuning. IEEE Trans. Med. Imag. **37**(7), 1562–1573 (2018)
8. Zhao, F., Xie, X.: An overview of interactive medical image segmentation. Ann. BMVA **2013**(7), 1–22 (2013)

# Adaptive Thresholding of Functional Connectivity Networks for fMRI-Based Brain Disease Analysis

Zhengdong Wang[1], Biao Jie[1(✉)], Weixin Bian[1], Daoqiang Zhang[2], Dinggang Shen[3], and Mingxia Liu[3(✉)]

[1] School of Computer Science and Information,
Anhui Normal University, Anhui 241003, China
jbiao@nuaa.edu.cn
[2] Department of Computer Science and Engineering,
Nanjing University of Aeronautics and Astronautics, Nanjing 210016, China
[3] Department of Radiology and BRIC, University of North Carolina at Chapel Hill,
Chapel Hill, NC 27599, USA
mxliu@med.unc.edu

**Abstract.** Functional connectivity (FC) networks based on functional magnetic resonance imaging (fMRI) data have been widely applied to automated identification of brain diseases, such as attention deficit hyperactivity disorder (ADHD) and Alzheimer's disease (AD). To generate compact representations of FC networks for disease analysis, various thresholding strategies have been developed for analyzing brain FC networks. However, existing studies typically employ predefined values or percentages of connections to threshold the whole FC networks, thus ignoring the *diversity of temporal correlations (particularly strong correlations)* among different brain regions. In addition, in practice, it is usually very challenging to decide the optimal threshold or connection percentage in FC network analysis. To address these problems, in this paper, we propose a weight distribution based thresholding (WDT) method for FC network analysis with resting-state function MRI data. Specifically, for FC between a pair of brain regions, we calculate its optimal threshold value by using the weight (*i.e.*, temporal correlation) distributions of the FC across two subject groups (*i.e.*, patient and normal groups). The proposed WDT method can adaptively yields FC-specific thresholds, thus preserving the diversity information of FCs among different brain regions. Experiment results on both ADNI and ADHD-200 datasets with rs-fMRI data demonstrate the effectiveness of our proposed WDT method.

## 1 Introduction

The human brain is a complex system that depends on functional interaction among distributed brain regions. This system can be characterized as a connectivity network, where each node represents a brain region and each edge quantifies the connectivity between a pair of brain regions. Network analysis provides

D. Zhang et al. (Eds.): GLMI 2019, LNCS 11849, pp. 18–26, 2019.
https://doi.org/10.1007/978-3-030-35817-4_3

an important tool to explore the core organization of the human brain, as well as the association between brain functional deficits and structural disruption caused by brain diseases [1]. Previous studies have investigated network properties associated with various brain diseases, such as attention deficit hyperactivity disorder (ADHD), Alzheimer's disease (AD) and its prodromal stage (*i.e.*, mild cognitive impairment, MCI). In the past decades, advanced imaging techniques, such as functional magnetic resonance imaging (fMRI), provide efficient ways to map functional connectivity (FC) of the brain [2], to help better understand the pathology of brain disorders. Using fMRI data, many studies focus on employing FC networks to quantify the temporal correlation between intrinsic blood oxygen level-dependent (BOLD) signal fluctuations of brain regions for brain disease analysis [3].

Among various studies, graph learning has shown its superiority in the analysis of brain FC networks, which not only provides a quantitative measurement of network properties (characterizing the segregated and integrated nature of brain activity), but also offers a general framework for comparison of heterogeneous graphs/networks [4]. In existing graph learning methods, FC networks are generally fully-connected weighted graphs, where each node (e.g., brain region) is connected to all the other nodes in the graph and weight values (*e.g.*temporal correlations) of edges are continuous within the range $[-1, 1]$. Given $P$ nodes, there will be $(P - 1)P/2$ edges in a fully-connected graph. To characterize the topological properties of FC networks and facilitate computer-aided analysis, the thresholding methods are usually used to threshold a FC network for constructing a binary network, where the connection (*i.e.*, edge) between brain regions is either present or not.

Network thresholding methods offer at least three advantages. First, since the connectivity in an FC network represents the temporal correlation between brain regions, some weak and unimportant connections could be obscure the network topology, when using together with strong and important connections. Previous studies have found that brain regions have sparse anatomical connections (*i.e.*, a brain region may be only connected with specific brain regions) [5]. Therefore, it is important to remove those weak or unimportant connections by using thresholding methods [6]. Second, it is simpler to extract meaningful measures from thresholded networks for network analysis [1], because most of the existing network measures are defined on thresholded networks and a large number of connections makes it difficult to extract meaningful network representation [7]. Also, thresholding FC networks can reduce the computational burden of computer-aided network analysis methods [8].

Currently, most of the existing threshold methods can be divided into two categories: (1) single-threshold based methods, and (2) sparsity-based methods. Methods in the first category usually threshold the whole brain network using a predefined value. That is, for any pair of brain regions, there exists an edge between them if and only if the corresponding edge weight (*e.g.*, temporal correlation) is larger than the predefined threshold. In contrast, methods belonging to the second category typically preserve a predefined percentage (*e.g.*, top 30%) of connections with the strongest temporal correlation. However, these two types of methods ignore the *diversity of temporal correlations (particularly strong correlations)* among different brain regions, thus could not reflect the real difference of FC networks of different subject groups. Figure 1 illustrates two brain FC networks for a normal control (NC) and a patient, respectively. Each network contains three brain regions, denoted as A, B, and C, respectively. For each subject, the weights (*i.e.*, temporal correlations) of FCs between different pairs of brain regions are different, *e.g.*, for the normal, weight of connection is 0.9 for FC between region A and B, and is 0.7 for FC between region B and C. And weights of three FCs in the patient's network have been changed by a brain disease. As shown in Fig. 1, both thresholded networks achieved by the single-threshold based method (see Fig. 1 (a)) and the sparsity-based method (see Fig. 1 (b)) can not characterize the real difference of functional connectivity between brain networks of the NC and the patient.

Intuitively, we could employ FC-specific thresholds to preserve the diversity information of FC among different brain regions. As shown in Fig. 1 (c), we employ a specific threshold for each FC, yielding two thresholded networks that can characterize the real difference between FC networks of two subjects. However, it is challenging to determine the optimal threshold for each FC in brain networks. In practice, we often explore the network properties over a broad range of available thresholds to determine the optimal one [9], which significantly increases the computation burden.

To address these problems, in this paper, we propose a weight distribution based thresholding (WDT) method for brain disease analysis by using fMRI data. Specifically, for FC between each pair of brain regions, we adaptively construct a threshold by using weight distributions of the FC across two subject groups (*i.e.*, patient and normal control), where each distribution is estimated by using weights of the FC from subjects in same group. Our WDT method can adaptively yield FC-specific thresholds to preserve the diversity information of FCs between different brain regions, thus better reflect the difference of FC networks between different subject groups. The proposed method is evaluated on two fMRI datasets for brain disease diagnosis, with experimental results demonstrating promising results compared with existing threshold methods.

## 2 Method

### 2.1 Subjects and Image Preprocessing

In this study, we use two datasets with resting state fMRI (rs-fMRI) data. The first dataset is download from the ADNI database, containing 43 later MCI (lMCI, 26 male (M) and 17 female (F), aged 72.1 ± 8.2 years), 56 early MCI (eMCI) (21M/35F, aged 71.2 ± 6.8 years), and 50 NCs (21M/29F, aged 75.0 ± 6.9 years). Data acquisition is performed as follows: the image resolution is 2.29 – 3.31 mm for inplane, and slice thickness is 3.31 mm, TE = 30 ms and TR = 2.2–3.1 s. Another dataset is ADHD-200 from New York University site, including 118 ADHD (25M/93F, aged 11.2 ± 2.7 years) and 98 NCs (51M/47F,

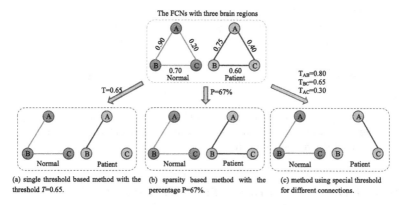

**Fig. 1.** Examples of functional connectivity (FC) networks (top) for a normal control (NC) and a patient, and the corresponding thresholded networks (bottom). (a) Thresholded networks using a single-threshold based method with threshold $T = 0.65$. (b) Thresholded networks using a sparsity-based method with the percentage of $P = 67\%$. (c) Thresholded networks using with specific thresholds for different connections. Note that there are different temporal correlations (*i.e.*, weights) for different connections in the FC network of the NC (or patient) subject, and the connection weights in the patient's network have been changed. From (a) and (b), we can see that the thresholded networks using a single-threshold or a percentage of connections can not characterize the diversity of functional connectivity in networks of the NC and the patient. We may need threshold FCNs with specific values for different connections, as shown in (c).

aged 12.2 ± 2.1 years). The acquisition of data in ADHD-200 is performed as follows: the matrix size is 49 × 58, axial slices is 47, slice thickness is 4 mm, FOV = 240 mm, TR = 2 s, TE = 15 ms, flip angle = 90, and the voxel size is 3 × 3 × 4 mm³.

Following [10], we preprocess images from the ADNI dataset using the standard pipeline, including (1) removing the first 10 rs-fMRI volumes, (2) slice timing and head motion correction, (3) dividing the brain space of fMRI scans into 90 regions-of-interest (ROIs) using the Automated Anatomical Labeling (AAL) template [11], (4) band-pass filtering within a frequency interval of [0.025Hz, 0.100Hz], (5) extracting BOLD signals from the gray matter tissue, and (6) computing the mean time series of ROIs to construct FC networks using the Pearson correlation coefficients (PCCs) as the measures of FC between ROIs. For ADHD-200, we directly used the time series from the Athena preprocessed data, with details shown on the Athena website[1]. Briefly, the data pre-processing steps include: (1) removing the first 4 image volumes, (2) slice timing and head motion correction, (3) extracting the fMRI time series from gray matter regions, (4) temporal band-pass filtering [0.009Hz, 0.08Hz], (5) partitioning the brain space into 90 ROIs using AAL template, and (6) extracting mean time series of ROIs, and (7) constructing FC networks based on PCC.

---

[1] http://www.nitrc.org/plugins/mwiki/index.php/neurobureau:AthenaPipeline.

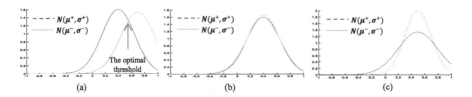

**Fig. 2.** Illustration of normal distributions of FC for the patient and NC groups, including three cases, *i.e.*, (a) two distributions with different means, (b) the same or similar distributions, and (c) two distributions with the same or similar mean.

## 2.2   Weight Distribution Based Thresholding Method

To better characterize the diversity of temporal correlations between different pairs of brain regions, we develop a weight distribution based thresholding (WDT) method to adaptively determine the optimal threshold for each FC in brain networks. Given $N$ training subjects along with their response vectors $Y = [y_1, y_2, \cdots, y_N]$, we denote $\mathcal{F} = [F_1, F_2, \cdots, F_N]$ as their FC networks, where $F_i$ is the FC network (*i.e.*, adjacency matrix) of the $i^{th}$ subject and $y_i$ is the corresponding class label (*i.e.*, patient or NC). We partition all training subjects into two groups (*i.e.*, patient and NC groups) according to their class label, denoted as $\mathcal{F}^+ = [F_1^+, F_2^+, \cdots, F_{N_1}^+]$ and $\mathcal{F}^- = [F_1^-, F_2^-, \cdots, F_{N_2}^-]$, respectively.

For FC of a pair of brain regions $i$ and $j$, we compute its optimal threshold $T_{ij}$ according to weight distributions of the FC across two subject groups. Here, we suppose that the weights of the FC in subjects from the same group follows the normal distribution, denoted as $\mathcal{N}^{+1}(\mu^{+1}, \sigma^{+1})$ and $\mathcal{N}^{-1}(\mu^{-1}, \sigma^{-1})$ for patient and NC groups, respectively. The parameters of two normal distributions can be estimated using the subjects in the corresponding group (*i.e.*, $\mathcal{F}^+$ or $\mathcal{F}^-$). As shown in Fig. 2, there are three cases for these two normal distributions. (1) Two distributions are significantly different with different means, as shown in Fig. 2 (a), implying that FC has been significantly changed in the patient group compared with that in the NC group. Therefore, the optimal threshold is the intersection point of two distributions, located in the range of $[\mu_1, \mu_2]$. (2) These two distributions are the same or very similar, as shown in Fig. 2 (b), suggesting that there is no significant difference for FC between patient and NC groups. For simplicity, we remove their connection (*i.e.*, setting the corresponding threshold $T_{ij} = 1$). (3) These two distributions are different, but their means (*i.e.*, $\mu^{+1}$ and $\mu^{-1}$) are the same (or similar), as shown in Fig. 2 (c), indicating that the corresponding FC is unstable for subjects in the same group. This implies that it is difficult to find the stable patterns of FC between the patient and NC groups. After removing the corresponding connection, we can compute the threshold $T_{ij}$ as follows:

$$T_{ij} = \begin{cases} p, & if \;\; KL(\mathcal{N}^{+1}, \mathcal{N}^{-1}) > \delta \;\; and \;\; |\mu^{+1} - \mu^{-1}| > \theta, \\ 1, & otherwise. \end{cases} \tag{1}$$

---

**Algorithm 1:** Proposed Weight distribution based thresholding (WDT) method

---

**Input:** A set of FC Networks $\mathcal{F}$, a response vector $Y$, and two parameters $\delta$ and $\theta$

**Output:** A threshold matrix $T$

1  Divide all training subjects into patient group (denoted as $\mathcal{F}^+$) and NC group (denoted as $\mathcal{F}^-$) according to their class labels.

2  **foreach** *FC between pair of brain regions i and j* **do**

3  $\quad$ Estimate the distributions of $\mathcal{N}^{+1}(\mu^{+1}, \sigma^{+1})$ and $\mathcal{N}^{-1}(\mu^{-1}, \sigma^{-1})$ using subjects in $\mathcal{F}^+$ and $\mathcal{F}^-$, respectively;

4  $\quad$ Compute $KL(\mathcal{N}^{+1}, \mathcal{N}^{-1})$ using Eq. 2;

5  $\quad$ **if** $KL(\mathcal{N}^{+1}, \mathcal{N}^{-1}) > \delta$ *and* $|\mu^{+1} - \mu^{-1}| > \theta$ **then**

6  $\quad\quad$ Calculate the intersection points of two normal distributions;

7  $\quad\quad$ Select the intersection point located in the range of $[\mu_1, \mu_2]$ as $p$

8  $\quad\quad$ Set $T_{ij} = p$

9  $\quad$ **else**

10  $\quad\quad$ Set $T_{ij} = 1$

11  return $T$

---

where $\delta$ and $\theta$ are two predefined positive values. Also, $p$ is the intersection point of two distributions, locating in the range of $[\mu_1, \mu_2]$. The term $KL(\mathcal{N}^{+1}, \mathcal{N}^{-1})$ denotes the Kullback-Leibler divergence that computes the similarity between two distributions, and can be defined as:

$$KL(\mathcal{N}^{+1}, \mathcal{N}^{-1}) = log(\frac{\sigma^{+1}}{\sigma^{-1}}) + \frac{(\sigma^{-1})^2 + (\mu_1 - \mu_2)^2}{2(\sigma^{+1})^2} - \frac{1}{2}. \tag{2}$$

Therefore, the proposed WDT method can adaptively determine an optimal threshold for each FC in FC network. Thus, we can obtain a threshold matrix $T$ for the whole FC network, which reflects the diversity of FCs between different pairs of brain regions. Algorithm 1 summaries the detailed process of the proposed WDT method for adaptive thresholding of brain FC networks.

## 3  Experiments

**Experimental Setup:** To evaluate the effectiveness of our WDT method, we test the classification performance of thresholded FC networks in brain disease diagnosis. Specifically, we first extract two kinds of network measures [7] (*i.e.*, local clustering coefficients and community structure) from thresholded FCNs as features of each subject. The clustering coefficient features reflect the prevalence of clustered connectivity around individual brain region. And the community structure features characterize the appearance of densely connected groups of brain regions, with sparser connections between groups.

We first compare our WDT method with two existing methods, *i.e.*, single-threshold based method (called **ST**) and percentage-based threshold method

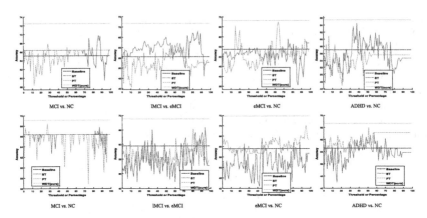

**Fig. 3.** The accuracy of all four methods in four classification tasks *w.r.t.* different thresholds or percentages of connections when using (top row) clustering coefficient features and (bottom row) community structure features.

(called **PT**). In the ST and PT methods, we extract the local clustering coefficient features and community structure features for classification, respectively. For the fair comparison, we compute the best performance of ST with the threshold ranging from 0.01 to 0.99 (step size: 0.01), and compute the best performance of PT with the percentage from 1% to 99% (step size: 1%). We also compare WDT with the **baseline** method without network thresholding. That is, we directly extract the weighted network measures [7] (*i.e.*, weighted clustering coefficients and weighted modularity) from the FC networks constructed using PCCs as features for classification. In four methods (*i.e.*, WDT, ST, PT and baseline), we perform feature selection using the standard $t$-test algorithm (with $p$-value less than 0.05) to select informative features, followed by a linear support vector machine (SVM) with a default parameter (*i.e.*, $C = 1$) for classification.

To evaluate the performance of different methods, we conduct four classification tasks, *i.e.*, (1) MCI vs. NC, (2) eMCI vs. lMCI, (3) eMCI vs. NC, and (4) ADHD vs. NC classification, by using a 10-fold cross-validation. We evaluate the performance via four metrics, including accuracy (*i.e.*, the percentage of subjects that are correctly classified), sensitivity (*i.e.*, the percentage of patients that are correctly classified), specificity (*i.e.*, the percentage of NC that are correctly classified), and the area under the receiver operating characteristic (ROC) curve (AUC).

**Results and Analysis:** Tables 1 and 2 present the results achieved by four methods in four classification tasks using two types of network measures, respectively. As can be seen from Tables 1 and 2, the proposed WDT method usually outperforms the competing methods in four tasks. For instance, the proposed WDT method, respectively, achieves the accuracy of 72.4%, 71.7%, 68.1% and 65.4% for four classification tasks (*i.e.*, MCI vs. NC, eMCI vs. lMCI, eMCI vs. NC and ADHD vs. NC classifications) when using clustering coefficient features, while the best accuracies obtained by the competing methods are 69.7%, 67.9%, 67.3% and 64.5%, respectively. Besides, the proposed WDT method, respectively, achieves the accuracy of 69.1%, 68.8%, 74.6% and 66.6% for four classification tasks when using community structure features, while the best accuracies obtained by the competing methods are of 68.4%, 68.0%, 70.1% and 64.9%, respectively. These results suggest the efficacy of our WDT method.

**Table 1.** Performance of all four methods in four classification tasks when using clustering coefficient features. ACC: ACCuracy; SEN: SENsitivity; SPE: SPEcificity.

| Method | MCI vs. NC | | | | lMCI vs. eMCI | | | | eMCI vs. NC | | | | ADHD vs. NC | | | |
|---|---|---|---|---|---|---|---|---|---|---|---|---|---|---|---|---|
| | ACC | SEN | SPE | AUC | ACC | SEN | SPE | AUC | ACC | SEN | SPE | AUC | ACC | SEN | SPE | AUC |
| Baseline | 65.1 | 100.0 | 0.0 | 51.0 | 55.6 | 46.5 | 53.6 | 55.0 | 53.6 | 23.3 | 76.8 | 52.0 | 57.0 | 56.1 | 57.6 | 53.2 |
| ST | 69.7 | 85.9 | 38.0 | 60.9 | 67.9 | 80.4 | 54.0 | 71.3 | 58.9 | 46.5 | 67.9 | 58.1 | 64.5 | 55.1 | 72.0 | 66.6 |
| PT | 67.8 | 82.8 | 38.0 | 61.1 | 62.2 | 60.7 | 64.0 | 63.0 | 67.3 | 69.8 | 64.3 | 63.3 | 60.8 | 51.0 | 68.6 | 63.1 |
| WDT (Ours) | 72.4 | 83.8 | 50.0 | 62.0 | 71.7 | 78.6 | 64.0 | 66.9 | 68.1 | 51.2 | 80.4 | 61.4 | 65.4 | 59.2 | 70.3 | 60.6 |

**Table 2.** Performance of all four methods in four classification tasks when using community structure features. ACC: ACCuracy; SEN: SENsitivity; SPE: SPEcificity.

| Method | MCI vs. NC | | | | lMCI vs. eMCI | | | | eMCI vs. NC | | | | ADHD vs. NC | | | |
|---|---|---|---|---|---|---|---|---|---|---|---|---|---|---|---|---|
| | ACC | SEN | SPE | AUC | ACC | SEN | SPE | AUC | ACC | SEN | SPE | AUC | ACC | SEN | SPE | AUC |
| Baseline | 66.4 | 100.0 | 0.0 | 50.0 | 59.5 | 57.1 | 62.0 | 60.0 | 58.9 | 20.9 | 87.5 | 46.8 | 56.4 | 50.0 | 61.9 | 55.2 |
| ST | 67.7 | 98.0 | 8.0 | 61.2 | 66.0 | 71.4 | 60.0 | 62.8 | 63.9 | 60.5 | 66.1 | 64.7 | 62.7 | 61.2 | 63.6 | 60.7 |
| PT | 68.4 | 99.0 | 8.0 | 54.1 | 68.0 | 66.1 | 70.0 | 67.8 | 70.1 | 55.8 | 80.4 | 66.9 | 64.9 | 39.8 | 85.6 | 63.2 |
| WDT (Ours) | 69.1 | 99.0 | 10.0 | 52.6 | 68.8 | 73.2 | 64.0 | 64.7 | 74.6 | 48.8 | 92.9 | 70.4 | 66.6 | 52.0 | 78.8 | 60.5 |

Furthermore, Figure 3 plots classification accuracies of two competing methods (*i.e.*, ST and PT) with different thresholds or percentages of connections. For comparison, in Fig. 3, we also present the results achieved by our WDT method and the baseline method. As can be seen from Fig. 3, the proposed WDT method outperforms the competing methods with most of thresholds or percentages, suggesting the effectiveness of the proposed method. In addition, from Fig. 3, we can see that the accuracy of two competing methods (*i.e.*, ST and PT) are largely affected by different thresholds or percentages of connections in four classification tasks, which indicates the selection of threshold or percentage is very important for characterizing network properties and subsequent classification. These results also demonstrate the advantage of WDT in adaptively determining the optimal threshold for FC network analysis.

## 4 Conclusion

In this paper, we proposed a weight distribution based thresholding (WDT) method for the analysis of brain functional connectivity networks. Different from existing methods that threshold the whole networks by using a predefined value or percentage of connections, our WDT method can adaptively determine an optimal threshold for FC between each pair of brain regions, thus preserving the diversity of temporal correlations between different brain regions. Experiment results on both ADNI and ADHD-200 datasets demonstrate that the proposed method can significantly improve the performance of disease classification compared with existing thresholding methods.

**Acknowledgment.** This study was supported by NSFC (Nos. 61573023, 61976006, 61703301, and 61902003), Anhui-NSFC (Nos. 1708085MF145 and 1808085MF171), and AHNU-FOYHE (No. gxyqZD2017010).

# References

1. Bullmore, E., Sporns, O.: Complex brain networks: graph theoretical analysis of structural and functional systems. Nat. Rev. Neurosci. **10**(3), 186–198 (2009)
2. Dumoulin, S.O., Fracasso, A., Zwaag, W.V.D., Siero, J.C.W., Petridou, N.: Ultrahigh field MRI: advancing systems neuroscience towards mesoscopic human brain function. NeuroImage **168**, 345–357 (2018)
3. Brier, M.R., et al.: Functional connectivity and graph theory in preclinical Alzheimer's disease. Neurobiol. Aging **35**(4), 757–768 (2014)
4. Tijms, B.M., et al.: Alzheimer's disease: connecting findings from graph theoretical studies of brain networks. Neurobiol. Aging **34**(8), 2023–2036 (2013)
5. Sporns, O.: The human connectome: a complex network. Ann. New York Acad. Sci. **1224**(1), 109–125 (2011)
6. Simpson, S.L., Bowman, D.B., Laurienti, P.J.: Analyzing complex functional brain networks: fusing statistics and network science to understand the brain. Stat. Surv. **7**, 1–36 (2013)
7. Rubinov, M., Sporns, O.: Complex network measures of brain connectivity: uses and interpretations. NeuroImage **52**(3), 1059–1069 (2010)
8. Garrison, K.A., Scheinost, D., Finn, E.S., Shen, X., Constable, R.T.: The (in)stability of functional brain network measures across thresholds. NeuroImage **118**(15), 651–661 (2015)
9. Supekar, K., Menon, V., Rubin, D., Musen, M., Greicius, M.D.: Network analysis of intrinsic functional brain connectivity in Alzheimer's disease. PLoS Comput. Biol. **4**(6), e1000100:1–e1000100:11 (2008)
10. Jie, B., Liu, M., Zhang, D., Shen, D.: Sub-network kernels for measuring similarity of brain connectivity networks in disease diagnosis. IEEE Trans. Image Process. **27**(5), 2340–2353 (2018)
11. Tzourio-Mazoyer, N., et al.: Automated anatomical labeling of activations in SPM using a macroscopic anatomical parcellation of the MNI MRI single-subject brain. NeuroImage **15**(1), 273–289 (2002)

# Graph-Kernel-Based Multi-task Structured Feature Selection on Multi-level Functional Connectivity Networks for Brain Disease Classification

Zhengdong Wang[1], Biao Jie[1(✉)], Mi Wang[1], Chunxiang Feng[1], Wen Zhou[1], Dinggang Shen[2], and Mingxia Liu[2(✉)]

[1] School of Computer Science and Information, Anhui Normal University,
Anhui 241003, China
jbiao@nuaa.edu.cn
[2] Department of Radiology and BRIC, University of North Carolina at Chapel Hill,
Chapel Hill, NC 27599, USA
mxliu@med.unc.edu

**Abstract.** Function connectivity networks (FCNs) based on resting-state functional magnetic resonance imaging (rs-fMRI) have been used for analysis of brain diseases, such as Alzheimer's disease (AD) and Attention Deficit Hyperactivity Disorder (ADHD). However, existing studies usually extract meaningful measures (*e.g.*, local clustering coefficients) from FCNs as a feature vector for brain disease classification, and perform vector-based feature selection methods (*e.g.*, *t*-test) to improve the performance of learning model, thus ignoring important structural information of FCNs. To address this problem, we propose a graph-kernel-based structured feature selection (gk-MTSFS) method for brain disease classification using rs-fMRI data. Different with existing method that focus on vector-based feature selection, our proposed gk-MTSFS method adopts the graph kernel (*i.e.*, kernel constructed on graphs) to preserve the structural information of FCNs, and uses the multi-task learning to explore the complementary information of multi-level thresholded FCNs (*i.e.*, thresholded FCNs with different thresholds). Specifically, in the proposed gk-MTSFS model, we first develop a novel graph-kernel based Laplacian regularizer to preserve the structural information of FCNs. Then, we employ an $L_{2,1}$-norm based group sparsity regularizer to joint select a small amount of discriminative features from multi-level FCNs for brain disease classification. Experimental results on both ADNI and ADHD-200 datasets with rs-fMRI data demonstrate the effectiveness of our proposed gk-MTSFS method in rs-fMRI-based brain disease diagnosis.

## 1 Introduction

Advanced neuroimaging technologies, such as magnetic resonance imaging (MRI), provide non-invasive ways to explore the function and structure of the human brain, thus providing important insights into the basic cognitive processes

© Springer Nature Switzerland AG 2019
D. Zhang et al. (Eds.): GLMI 2019, LNCS 11849, pp. 27–35, 2019.
https://doi.org/10.1007/978-3-030-35817-4_4

of the brain [1], and also provide the important way to achieve performances applicable in diagnosis of brain diseases [2], including Alzheimer's disease (AD) and its prodromal stage (*i.e.*, mild cognitive impairment, MCI), and Attention Deficit Hyperactivity Disorder (ADHD). Functional connectivity networks (FCNs) based on resting-state functional MRI (rs-fMRI) data, which characterize the interactions of distributed brain regions, have been widely applied to the analysis of various brain diseases. Some abnormal functional connectivities in FCNs have been found in AD/MCI/ADHD patiens. Recently, FCNs are also applied to computer-aided diagnosis of brain diseases by using machine learning methods, and achieved the promising results [3].

In typical FCN-based classification methods, studies first extract meaningful measures (e.g., local clustering coefficients [4], connectivity strengths [5], and Regional homogeneity [3]) from constructed FCN as a feature vector, and then perform vector-based feature selection methods (*e.g.*, *t*-test [3,4], F-scores [5] and Lasso [6]) to select the most discriminative features for improving the performance of learning model. These studies have demonstrated that feature selection can not only improve the performances of brain disease classification, but also help identify neuroimage-based biomarkers to better understand the pathology of brain disorders. However, since these measures only characterize the local topological properties of FCN, thus some important global structural information conveyed by FCN are ignored in these studies.

In additional, to characterize the topological properties of FCNs and reduce the computational complex of FCN analysis, the thresholding methods are usually used to threshold the FCNs. Since different thresholds will generate different thresholded FCNs with different levels of topological structure (*i.e.*, the thresholded FCNs with larger threshold will preserve fewer edges, and thus are sparser in edges). Recent studies have shown that, compared with methods using single threshold, the methods with multiple thresholds can take advantage of the complementary information conveyed by multiple thresholded FCNs and thus improve the classification performance of learning model [7]. However, these studies often integrate the complementary information of multiple thresholded FCNs by assembling multiple classifiers (*e.g.*, multi-kernel support vector machine). Few work explores complementary information of multiple thresholded FCNs in feature selection step, which could reduce classification performance of learning model.

To address these problems, we propose a graph-kernel-based multi-task structured feature selection (called gk-MTSFS) method for brain disease classification using rs-fMRI data. Different from previous feature selection methods that focus on vector-based feature selection, the proposed gk-MTSFS method first uses graph kernels (*i.e.*, kernels defined on graphs/networks) to measure the topological similarity of FCNs, thus naturally preserving the structural information of FCNs. Then, we use the multi-task learning to explore the complementary information of multi-level FCNs (*i.e.*, thresholded FCNs with different thresholds), thus help to induce more discriminative features for further improving classification performance. Here, we use multiple thresholds to simultaneously threshold the FCNs constructed from rs-fMRI data, and denote the features learning on each thresholded FCN as a single task. Specifically, our gk-MTSFS model contains two regularization items: (1) a graph-kernel-based Laplacian regularizer that can preserve the local-to-global structural information of FCN data, and (2) a $L_{2,1}$-norm based group sparsity regularizer to capture the intrinsic relatedness among multiple learning tasks, joint select a small number of common features from multiple tasks for subsequent classification. We validate our proposed gk-MTSFS method on two public datasets with baseline rs-fMRI data, *i.e.*, ADNI dataset[1] and ADHD-200 dataset[2]. The experimental results demonstrate the efficacy of our proposed gk-MTSFS method.

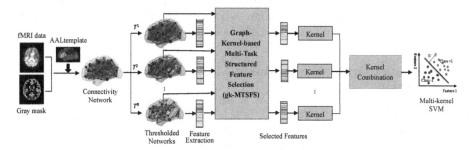

**Fig. 1.** Illustration of our proposed gk-MTSFS learning framework.

## 2    Method

Figure 1 illustrates the proposed gk-MTSFS based learning framework, which including three main steps: image pre-processing and FCN construction, feature extraction and feature selection, and classification.

### 2.1    Subjects and Image Preprocessing

In this study, we use two datasets with resting state fMRI (rs-fMRI) data. The first dataset is download from the ADNI database, containing 43 later MCI (lMCI), 56 early MCI (eMCI), and 50 HCs. Data acquisition is performed as follows: the image resolution is 2.29–3.31 mm for inplane, and slice thickness is 3.31 mm, TE = 30 ms and TR = 2.2–3.1 s. Another dataset is ADHD-200 from New York University site, including 118 ADHD (25M/93F, aged 11.2 ± 2.7 years) and 98 NCs (51M/47F, aged 12.2 ± 2.1 years). The acquisition of data in ADHD-200 is performed as follows: the matrix size is 49 × 58, axial slices is 47, slice thickness is 4 mm, FOV = 240 mm, TR = 2 s, TE = 15 ms, flip angle = 90, and the voxel size is $3 \times 3 \times 4\,mm^3$.

Following [8], we preprocess images from the ADNI dataset using the standard pipeline, including (1) removing the first 10 rs-fMRI volumes, (2) slice

---

[1] http://adni.loni.usc.edu.

[2] http://fcon_1000.projects.nitrc.org/indi/adhd200/.

timing and head motion correction, (3) dividing the brain space of fMRI scans into 90 regions-of-interest (ROIs) using the Automated Anatomical Labeling (AAL) template, (4) band-pass filtering within a frequency interval of [0.025 Hz, 0.100 Hz], (5) extracting BOLD signals from the gray matter tissue, and (6) computing the mean time series of ROIs to construct FC networks using the Pearson correlation coefficients (PCCs) as the measures of FC between ROIs. For ADHD-200, we directly used the time series from the Athena preprocessed data, with details shown on the Athena website[3]. Briefly, the data pre-processing steps include: (1) removing the first 4 image volumes, (2) slice timing and head motion correction, (3) extracting the fMRI time series from gray matter regions, (4) temporal band-pass filtering [0.009 Hz, 0.08 Hz], (5) partitioning the brain space into 90 ROIs using AAL template, and (6) extracting mean time series of ROIs, and (7) constructing FC networks based on PCC.

## 2.2   Proposed Graph-Kernel-Based Multi-task Structured Feature Selection

Given a thresholded network set $\mathcal{E}^r = \{\widetilde{E}_1^r, \widetilde{E}_2^r, \cdots, \widetilde{E}_N^r\}$, where $\widetilde{E}_i^r$ denotes the thresholded network of the $i$-th subject using the $r$-th threshold, $N$ is the number of subjects, $R$ is the number of thresholds. Let $X^r = [x_1^r, x_2^r, \cdots, x_N^r] \in R^{N \times d}$ denotes a set of feature vectors extracted from the $r$-th thresholded FCN of all subjects (with each vector corresponding to a specific subject). For example, $x_i^r$ denotes the region-specific clustering coefficient features extracted from the $r$-th thresholded FCN of $i$-th subject, and $d$ is the feature dimension. Let $Y = [y_1, y_2, \cdots, y_N] \in R^N$ denote the response vector, where $y_i$ represents the class label of the $i$-th subject. To preserve the distribution information of FCN data, we first introduce a graph-kernel-based Laplacian regularization term, $i.e.$,

$$\min_{w^1, w^2, \dots, w^R} \sum_{r=1}^{R} \sum_{i,j}^{N} \|w^{rT} x_i^r - w^{rT} x_j^r\|_2^2 = 2 \sum_{r=1}^{R} (X^r w^r)^T M^r (X^r w^r) \qquad (1)$$

where $M^r = C^r - S^r$ is a Laplacian matrix, $S^r = S_{i,j}^r$ is a similarity matrix that measures the similarity between subjects, $C^r$ is a diagonal matrix whose diagonal elements is defined as $C_{ii}^r = \sum_{j=1}^{N} S_{(i,j)}^r$.

To preserve the structural information of FCNs, we use the graph kernel to measure the similarity of a pair of networks, $i.e.$,

$$S_{i,j}^r = k(\widetilde{E}_i^r, \widetilde{E}_j^r) \qquad (2)$$

where $k(\widetilde{E}_i^r, \widetilde{E}_j^r)$ is a graph kernel, which calculates the similarity between network $\widetilde{E}_i^r$ and $\widetilde{E}_j^r$. In our experiments, we use a subtree-based graph kernel defined in [9] to measures the similarity of a pair of FCNs.

From Eqs. 1–2, we can see that if two subjects have similar network structures, they will be encouraged to be as close as possible after mapping. Obviously,

---

[3] http://www.nitrc.org/plugins/mwiki/index.php/neurobureau:AthenaPipeline.

Eq. 2 can be expected to well preserve the structural information of networks, by using graph kernel approach in the mapping process.

Based on the formulation in Eq. 2, the objective function of our proposed graph-kernel based structured feature selection (gk-MTSFS) model is defined as following:

$$\min_{w} \frac{1}{2} \sum_{r=1}^{R} \|Y - X^r w^r\|_2^2 + \beta \sum_{r=1}^{R} (X^r w^r)^T M^r (X^r w^r) + \lambda \|W\|_{2,1} \qquad (3)$$

where $W = [w^1, w^2, \ldots, w^R]$, $M^r$ is a Laplacian matrix defined by Eq. 2, $\beta$ and $\lambda$ are two positive constants that balance the contributions of three items. In practice, we use inner cross validation on the training data to determine their optimal values.

According to definition in Eq. 3, the objective function of our proposed gk-MTSFS method contains three items. The first item is a quadratic loss function that measures the difference between estimated and true values for training subjects. The second item is a graph-kernel-based Laplacian regularizer that preserves the distribution information of FCN data and structural information of each FCN. Here, we use the graph kernel to compute the similarity of FCNs, which can capture the local and global structural information of networks, thus helping to learn more discriminative features. The last item is a group sparsity regularizer with $L_{2,1}$-norm that capture the complementary information among multiple learning tasks, and joint select a small number of common features from multiple tasks for subsequent classification. The features corresponding to non-zero factors in $W$ will be selected for classification. The objective function in Eq. 3 can be effectively solved via using accelerated proximal gradient algorithm.

## 2.3  gk-MTSFS Based Learning Framework

**Network Thresholding.** Since weights of edges correspond to the Pearson correlation coefficient among ROIs, the constructed FCN of each subject is a full-connected weighted network. To characterize the topology of networks, we parallelly threshold FCNs of all subjects using a set of thresholds $T = [T^1, T^2, \ldots, T^R]$, where $R$ is the number of thresholds. Specifically, given a threshold $T^r$, for $i$-th FCN (*i.e.*, adjacency matrix $E_i$), we threshold it via the following formulation:

$$\widetilde{E}_i^r(p, q) = \begin{cases} 0, & \text{if } E_i(p, q) < T^r \\ 1, & \text{otherwise} \end{cases} \qquad (4)$$

where $E_i(p, q)$ is the element of matrix $E_i$, corresponding to the weight (*i.e.*, Pearson correlation coefficient) of edge between ROIs $p$ and $q$. In this way, for any pair of ROIs $p$, $q$, there has an edge between $p$ and $q$ when $E_i(p, q) > T^r$. Thus, we can obtain $R$ thresholded FCNs $\widetilde{E}_r, \{r = 1, \cdots, R\}$ for subsequent feature extraction and selection.

**Feature Extraction and Feature Selection.** Following works in [7], we also extract the local clustering coefficient of each ROI in the each thresholded FCN as the feature, and then concatenate all features of all ROIs as a feature vector for representing each subject. Based on extracted feature vector and thresholded FCNs, as shown in Fig. 1, we further perform our proposed gk-MTSFS method to select the most discriminative features for improving the classification performance.

**Classification.** Following works in [10], we use the multi-kernel SVM technique for classification, Specifically, we first compute a linear kernel on features selected by the proposed gk-MTSFS method across training subjects. We can get $R$ kernels with $R$ thresholds. Then, we use the following method to integrate these kernels:

$$k(E_i, E_j) = \sum_{r=1}^{R} \alpha^r k^r(x_i^r, x_j^r), \tag{5}$$

where $k^r(x_i^r, x_j^r)$ is the kernel over features from the $r-$th thresholded FCN across two subjects $\mathbf{x}^i$ and $\mathbf{x}^j$ (we use the linear kernel in our experiment), $\alpha_r$ denotes the combining weight on features from the $r-$th thresholded FCN, with the constraint of $\sum_{r=1}^{R} \alpha_r = 1$. We use a coarse-grid search strategy via cross-validation on the training subjects to find the optimal $\alpha_r$. Once obtaining the optimal $\alpha_r$, we can integrate multiple kernels into a mixed kernel, and perform the standard SVM for classification.

## 3   Experiments

### 3.1   Experimental Setup

We extensively perform experiments to evaluate the performance of our proposed gk-MTSFS method. Specifically, we perform three tasks: (1) lMCI vs. eMCI, (2) eMCI vs. HC and (3) ADHD vs. HC classifications. A 10-fold cross validation strategy is used in the experiments. Specifically, for each task, all subjects are first equivalently partitioned into 10 subsets. In each fold cross validation, one subset is alternatively used as the testing data, and the remaining subsets are combined as the training set. In addition, the process of data partition is independently repeated 10 times to avoid any bias. We evaluate the performance of the proposed gk-MTSFS method via four evaluation metrics, including accuracy, sensitivity, specificity, and the area under the receiver operating characteristic (ROC) curve (AUC).

We compare our proposed gk-MTSFS feature selection method with several Multi-task methods, including a multi-task feature selection method based on group Lasso (called as gLasso), A method of performing Lasso feature selection on each task and classifying it with a multi-kernel SVM (called as Lasso) and the method that have no feature selection performed on each task and directly perform classification using multi-kernel SVM method (denoted as MMT). In all competing methods (*i.e.*, gLasso, Lasso, MMT), the optimal parameter values are still determined via using inner cross validation on training data. In addition, we also compare with the baseline method without performing thresholding step, and directly extracting weighted clustering coefficients from the original FCNs constructed from rs-fMRI data as features, performing $t$−test method for feature selection, and using a linear SVM for classification.

## 3.2   Classification Performance

Table 1 summaries the results of all methods in three classification tasks. Figure 2 plots the corresponding ROC curves of these methods in three tasks. As can be seen from Table 1 and Fig. 2, compared with all competing methods, our proposed gk-MTSFS method can achieve better classification performance. For example, our proposed method achieves the accuracy of 76.5%, 76.9% and 68.0% for lMCI vs. eMCI, eMCI vs. HC and ADHD vs. HC classifications, respectively, while the best accuracy values achieved by the competing methods are 70.6%, 69.3% and 64.0%. Moreover, our proposed gk-MTSFS method obtains the AUC values of 0.81, 0.79 and 0.70 in three tasks, respectively. These results demonstrate that our proposed method can achieve good performance in AD/MCI classification and ADHD classification, indicating the proposed gk-MTSFS can capture the structural information of FCNs, and further improve the performance of brain disease classification.

From Table 1 and Fig. 2, we can also see that methods (*i.e.*, Lasso, gLasso, gk-MTSFS) with feature selection can achieve better performance than the method without performing feature selection (*i.e.*., MMT), indicating the important contribution of feature selection for improving performance in brain disease classification. In addition, from Table 1, we can see that, compared with baseline method, the multi-threshold methods (*i.e.*, MMT, Lasso and gLasso) can obtain better classification results, suggesting that thresholded networks with multiple thresholds can contain complementary information, thus help to further improve the performance of disease classification.

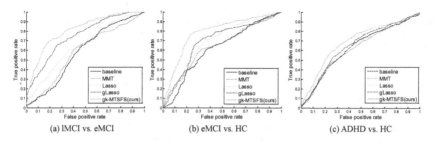

(a) lMCI vs. eMCI          (b) eMCI vs. HC          (c) ADHD vs. HC

**Fig. 2.** The ROC curves achieved by all five methods in three classification tasks: (a) lMCI vs. eMCI, (b) eMCI vs. HC and (c) ADHD vs. HC.

**Table 1.** Classification performance of five methods in three classification tasks. ACC: ACCuracy; SEN: SENsitivity; SPE: SPEcificity.

| Method | lMCI vs. eMCI | | | | eMCI vs. HC | | | | ADHD vs. HC | | | |
|---|---|---|---|---|---|---|---|---|---|---|---|---|
| | ACC (%) | SEN (%) | SPE (%) | AUC | ACC (%) | SEN (%) | SPE (%) | AUC | ACC (%) | SEN (%) | SPE (%) | AUC |
| baseline | 56.8 | 47.0 | 63.6 | 0.58 | 62.0 | 61.6 | 62.2 | 0.62 | 61.4 | 47.6 | 73.1 | 0.63 |
| MMT | 60.2 | 59.8 | 60.2 | 0.58 | 66.6 | 66.8 | 65.8 | 0.69 | 63.4 | 53.9 | 71.3 | 0.64 |
| Lasso | 62.7 | 57.9 | 65.4 | 0.65 | 63.9 | 60.5 | 67.8 | 0.64 | 62.3 | 48.3 | 74.2 | 0.63 |
| gLasso | 70.6 | 64.9 | 74.1 | 0.75 | 69.3 | 69.5 | 69.2 | 0.79 | 64.0 | 54.5 | 71.9 | 0.65 |
| gk-MTSFS (Ours) | **76.5** | **67.2** | **82.7** | **0.81** | **76.9** | **76.3** | **77.2** | **0.79** | **68.0** | **58.1** | 75.8 | **0.70** |

### 3.3 Effect of Regularization Parameters

There are two regularization parameters, *i.e.*, $\beta$ and $\lambda$ in the proposed gk-MTSFS method. To assess the effect of these two parameters on classification accuracy of our proposed method, we also perform three tasks with varying the value of $\beta$ from 2 to 20 with step of 2, varying the value of $\lambda$ from 2 to 30 with step of 2. Figure 3 graphically shows the obtained results. From Fig. 3 we can see that our proposed gk-MTSFS method *w.r.t.* different combinations of $\beta > 0$ and $\lambda > 0$ consistently outperform the LASSO method (*i.e.*, $\beta = 0$ and $\lambda > 0$), indicating importance of introducing the graph-kernel-based Laplacian regularization item.

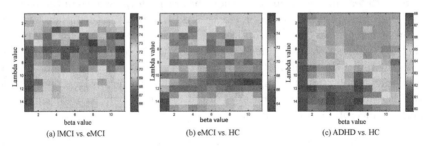

(a) lMCI vs. eMCI          (b) eMCI vs. HC          (c) ADHD vs. HC

**Fig. 3.** The accuracy of the proposed gk-MTSFS method *w.r.t.* the combinations of $\lambda$ and $\beta$ values in three classification tasks of (a) lMCI vs. eMCI, (b) eMCI vs. HC and (c) ADHD vs. HC.

## 4   Conclusion

In this paper, we propose a novel graph-kernel-based multi-task feature selection method for brain disease classification with fMRI data. Different with existing method that focus on vector-based feature selection, our proposed gk-MTSFS method adopts the graph kernel to preserve the structural information of FCNs, and uses the multi-task learning technique to explore the complementary information of multi-level thresholded FCNs. We further develop a gk-MTSFS based learning framework for automatic brain disease diagnosis. Experimental results on two real datasets with rs-fMRI data demonstrate that our proposed gk-MTSFS method can achieve the better classification performance in comparison with state-of-the-art methods.

**Acknowledgment.** This study was supported by NSFC (Nos. 61573023, 61976006, 61703301, and 61902003), Anhui-NSFC (Nos. 1708085MF145 and 1808085MF171), and AHNU-FOYHE (No. xyqZD2017010).

# References

1. Greicius, M.D., Krasnow, B., Reiss, A.L., Menon, V.: Functional connectivity in the resting brain: a network analysis of the default mode hypothesis. Proc. Natl. Acad. Sci. **100**(1), 253–258 (2003)
2. Lian, C., Liu, M., Zhang, J., Shen, D.: Hierarchical fully convolutional network for joint atrophy localization and Alzheimer's disease diagnosis using structural MRI. IEEE Trans. Pattern Anal. Mach. Intell. **35**, 1798–1828 (2019)
3. Wang, X., Jiao, Y., Tang, T., Wang, H., Lu, Z.: Altered regional homogeneity patterns in adults with attention-deficit hyperactivity disorder. Eur. J. Radiol. **82**(9), 1552–1557 (2013)
4. Wee, C.Y., et al.: Identification of MCI individuals using structural and functional connectivity networks. NeuroImage **59**(3), 2045–2056 (2012)
5. Liu, F., et al.: Multivariate classification of social anxiety disorder using whole brain functional connectivity. Brain Struct. Funct. **220**(1), 101–115 (2015)
6. Jie, B., Zhang, D., Gao, W., Wang, Q., Wee, C.Y., Shen, D.: Integration of network topological and connectivity properties for neuroimaging classification. IEEE Trans. Biomed. Eng. **61**(2), 576–589 (2014)
7. Jie, B., Zhang, D., Wee, C.Y., Shen, D.: Topological graph kernel on multiple thresholded functional connectivity networks for mild cognitive impairment classification. Hum. Brain Mapp. **35**(7), 2876–2897 (2014)
8. Jie, B., Liu, M., Zhang, D., Shen, D.: Sub-network kernels for measuring similarity of brain connectivity networks in disease diagnosis. IEEE Trans. Image Process. **27**(5), 2340–2353 (2018)
9. Shervashidze, N., Schweitzer, P., Van Leeuwen, E.J., Mehlhorn, K., Borgwardt, K.M.: Weisfeiler-Lehman graph kernels. J. Mach. Learn. Res. **12**, 2539–2561 (2011)
10. Zhang, D., Wang, Y., Zhou, L., Yuan, H., Shen, D.: Multimodal classification of Alzheimer's disease and mild cognitive impairment. NeuroImage **55**(3), 856–867 (2011)

# Linking Convolutional Neural Networks with Graph Convolutional Networks: Application in Pulmonary Artery-Vein Separation

Zhiwei Zhai[1(✉)], Marius Staring[1], Xuhui Zhou[3], Qiuxia Xie[3], Xiaojuan Xiao[3], M. Els Bakker[1], Lucia J. Kroft[1], Boudewijn P. F. Lelieveldt[1], Gudula J. A. M. Boon[2], Frederikus A. Klok[2], and Berend C. Stoel[1]

[1] Department of Radiology, Leiden University Medical Center,
Leiden, The Netherlands
Z.Zhai@lumc.nl
[2] Department of Thrombosis and Hemostasis, Leiden University Medical Center,
Leiden, The Netherlands
[3] Department of Radiology, Sun Yat-sen University, Shenzhen, China

**Abstract.** Graph Convolutional Networks (GCNs) are a novel and powerful method for dealing with non-Euclidean data, while Convolutional Neural Networks (CNNs) can learn features from Euclidean data such as images. In this work, we propose a novel method to combine CNNs with GCNs (CNN-GCN), that can consider both Euclidean and non-Euclidean features and can be trained end-to-end. We applied this method to separate the pulmonary vascular trees into arteries and veins (A/V). Chest CT scans were pre-processed by vessel segmentation and skeletonization, from which a graph was constructed: voxels on the skeletons resulting in a vertex set and their connections in an adjacency matrix. 3D patches centered around each vertex were extracted from the CT scans, oriented perpendicularly to the vessel. The proposed CNN-GCN classifier was trained and applied on the constructed vessel graphs, where each node is then labeled as artery or vein. The proposed method was trained and validated on data from one hospital (11 patient, 22 lungs), and tested on independent data from a different hospital (10 patients, 10 lungs). A baseline CNN method and human observer performance were used for comparison. The CNN-GCN method obtained a median accuracy of 0.773 (0.738) in the validation (test) set, compared to a median accuracy of 0.817 by the observers, and 0.727 (0.693) by the CNN. In conclusion, the proposed CNN-GCN method combines local image information with graph connectivity information, improving pulmonary A/V separation over a baseline CNN method, approaching the performance of human observers.

## 1 Introduction

Graph Convolutional Networks (GCN) are a variant of Convolutional Neural Networks (CNN) applied on graphs [1,2]. Recently, there are many research

© Springer Nature Switzerland AG 2019
D. Zhang et al. (Eds.): GLMI 2019, LNCS 11849, pp. 36–43, 2019.
https://doi.org/10.1007/978-3-030-35817-4_5

fields processing graphs (non-Euclidean data), such as social networks, citation networks, applied chemistry, computer vision, anatomical structures etc. GCNs and their variants have obtained state-of-the-art performance in these fields [1,3].

In the medical imaging domain, GCNs achieved promising results as well. Parisot et al. [4] proposed a semi-supervised method for disease prediction using GCNs, where individuals were represented as nodes; the features consisted of both image and non-image information; a sparse graph was constructed among all individuals and partially labeled. The GCN was trained on the labeled nodes and inferred classes of unlabeled nodes, based on node features and their connections. Shin et al. [5] proposed a deep vessel segmentation by combining CNNs and GCNs, where a CNN was trained for generating features and vessel probabilities; a GCN was trained to predict the presence of a vessel, based on the features and connectivity, and an inference module to generate the final segmentation. The method achieved competitive results in both retinal vessel and coronary artery data sets. However, this classifier cannot be trained end-to-end, which may yield sub-optimal results. In this work, we propose therefore a network linking CNNs with GCNs, which can be trained end-to-end.

Separation of pulmonary arteries/veins (A/V) is a challenging problem, because of the complexity of their anatomical structures and the similarity in intensity and morphology. In recent years, only a few methods have been developed for separating A/V, including traditional methods [6,7] and deep learning based methods [8]. Both local and global information were considered by the traditional methods [6,7], including the property of parallel configuration and close proximity of arteries and bronchus, anatomical information on the A/V roots, and connectivity information. Nardelli et al. [8] proposed a CNN method for classifying vessel particles to A/V based on local patches and subsequently applied a graph-cut optimization to refine the classifications, which combined connectivity information and predictions by the CNN classifier.

In this work, we propose a novel network linking CNNs and GCNs (CNN-GCN), which considers both local image and graph connectivity features and the classifier can be trained end-to-end. To enable large graphs with huge amounts of nodes containing features from 3D patches to fit in GPU memory, we propose a batch-based strategy on graphs for CNN-GCN training and validation, instead of using entire graphs. The CNN-GCN method was applied to separate pulmonary A/V. These images were pre-processed by vessel graph construction and 3D patch extraction, and subsequently the classes of each node in the vessel graph was predicted by the CNN-GCN classifier, and A/V volume was re-built based on the classification of the nodes.

## 2   Methods

In this section, we provide the theoretical background of GCNs, and motivation for linking CNNs with GCNs. We demonstrate its usage by an application in separating pulmonary arteries-veins.

## 2.1   Graph Convolution Networks

We follow the works of Kipf et al. [1] and Wu et al. [2] to introduce the theoretical background of GCNs. A graph is defined as $\mathcal{G} = (\mathcal{V}, A)$, where $\mathcal{V} = \{v_i, i = 1, \ldots, N\}$ is the vertex set consisting of $N$ nodes, and $A = (a_{ij})_{N \times N}$ is the adjacency matrix of the graph: $a_{ij} = 1$ if nodes $v_i$ and $v_j$ are connected, otherwise $a_{ij} = 0$. For consistency, each node is always connected to itself, i.e. $a_{ii} = 1$. Each node $v_i$ has an $F$-dimensional feature vector $x_i \in \mathbb{R}^F$, and the feature matrix for all nodes is $X = [x_1, \ldots, x_N]^T$ i.e. $X \in \mathbb{R}^{N \times F}$. Each node $v_i$ belongs to a class $c$ out of $C$, which can be encoded as a one-hot vector $y_i \in \{0, 1\}^C$.

In a graph convolution layer, the operations can be divided into three stages: feature representation, feature transform and nonlinear activation. Commonly, the input layer $H^{(0)}$ is the input feature matrix: $H^{(0)} = X$. Within a GCN, the input for the $k^{th}$ layer is the output from the $(k-1)^{th}$ layer: $H^{(k-1)}$ with size $N \times F^{(k-1)}$, and as output $H^{(k)}$ of size $N \times F^{(k)}$. The processing within this layer is expressed as:

$$H^{(k)} = \sigma \left( W H^{(k-1)} \Theta^{(k)} \right), \tag{1}$$

where $W$ is an $N \times N$ weight matrix among nodes $\mathcal{V}$; $\Theta^{(k)}$ is a layer-specific trainable parameter matrix of size $F^{(k-1)} \times F^{(k)}$; $\sigma(\cdot)$ is an activation function, like ReLU. The operation $\hat{H}^{(k)} = W H^{(k-1)}$ is considered to be a 'feature representation', which averages the feature vectors of neighbors around nodes. Based on the spectral graph convolution, Kipf et al. [1] estimated the weight matrix using Chebyshev polynomials: $W = D^{-\frac{1}{2}} A D^{-\frac{1}{2}}$, with $D$ the diagonal degree matrix of $A$ and $w_{ij} = \frac{a_{ij}}{\sqrt{d_i \cdot d_j}}$, i.e. not trainable. Instead of using a fixed hand-crafted weight matrix, Monti et al. [3] proposed a method to calculate $W$ using parametric kernels $w_{ij} = k(x_i, x_j | \theta)$, where $\theta$ represents the trainable parameters and $k(\cdot)$ is a Gaussian kernel. In this study we use the trainable method. The operation: $\tilde{H}^{(k)} = \hat{H}^{(k)} \Theta^{(k)}$ corresponds to a 'feature transform', where the feature vector can be transformed from $F^{(k-1)}$ dimensions to $F^{(k)}$ dimensions. If needed, a trainable bias $\epsilon$ of size $1 \times F^{(k)}$ can be involved as well after transformation. Finally, a 'nonlinear activation' operation is applied: $H^{(k)} = \sigma \left( \tilde{H}^{(k)} \right)$.

## 2.2   Linking CNN with GCN

A GCN can combine both local and connectivity information, which may be useful to analyze vascular trees. To combine CNNs with GCNs we let the feature matrix $X$ be learned by a CNN: $x_i = \Phi(p_i | \Theta)$, where $\Phi(\cdot)$ is a general CNN with an arbitrary sequence of layers, and $p_i$ a local image patch with size $S$. Then, the CNN and GCN can be linked as follows:

$$H = \sigma \left( W_\theta X \Theta \right), \text{ where } X = \Phi \left( P | \Theta \right), \tag{2}$$

---

**Algorithm 1.** Model linking CNN with GCN

---

1: **procedure** CNNGCNMODEL($B$, $NB$)
2:     Inputs of the model
3:     Batch: $B$ with size $b \times S$
4:     Neighborhood Batch: $NB$ with size $b \times n \times S$
5:     $\tilde{X} = \Phi(B|\Theta)$                    ▷ $\Phi(\cdot)$ is a shared function with sequential layers
6:     $\tilde{NX} = \Phi(NB|\Theta)$
7:     $H = GcnLayer(\tilde{X}, \tilde{NX})$
8:     $Y = softmax(H)$                    ▷ other activation may also be used here
9:     **return** $Y$

---

**Algorithm 2.** Graph convolutional layer with batch strategy on graphs

---

1: **procedure** GCNLAYER($X$, $NX$)
2:     **Inputs:** $X$, $NX$                    ▷ $X$ with size $b \times F$; $NX$ with size $b \times n \times F$
3:     $W = k(X, NX|\theta)$                        ▷ $k(\cdot)$ is a trainable function.
4:     $\tilde{W} = expend\_dims(W, axis = 1)$    ▷ $W$ with size $b \times n$; $\tilde{W}$ with size $b \times 1 \times n$
5:     $\hat{X} = K.reshape(K.batchdot(\tilde{W}, NX), (b, F))$              ▷ $\hat{X}$ with shape $b \times F$
6:     $\hat{H} = (X + \tilde{X})/(1 + sum(W))$        ▷ feature representation and normalization.
7:     $\tilde{H} = \hat{H}\Theta$                                ▷ feature transform
8:     $H = Relu(\tilde{H})$                        ▷ other activations may be used here
9:     **return** $H$

---

with $P = [p_1, ..., p_N]^T$ the set of all patches. In other words, $X$ are the learned feature maps from the CNN, which is then followed by a step of a normal GCN akin to Eq. (1). The CNN-GCN classifier is linked as a function chain, which can be straightforwardly optimized by gradient decent using back-propagation. The patch $p_i$ of each node is processed with a shared CNN function $\Phi(\cdot)$. Pseudo-code of the proposed method is given in Algorithm 1.

Straightforward training of the CNN-GCN requires loading the entire graph in GPU memory. As features are learned, local patches of all nodes need to be available as well, i.e. the entire matrix $P$ which has size around $45000 \times S$. Since this is not feasible with current GPUs, we propose a sampling strategy on graphs instead of using entire graphs, similarly to batch processing for training CNNs. Given a graph $\mathcal{G}$, we randomly select $b$ nodes with their patches as an input batch $B$, with size $b \times S$. Since we use a graph structure, we also need the image patches of these neighbors. This is denoted by $NB$ which has size $b \times n \times S$, where $n$ is the number of neighbors. Both the batch $B$ and the neighborhood batch $NB$ are processed with a shared CNN function $\Phi(\cdot)$, which may consist of multiple layers, such as convolution layers, max-pooling layers, activation layers etc. In every iteration a new selection of $B$ and $NB$ is made. Pseudo-code of a GCN layer with batch strategy on graphs is presented in Algorithm 2.

## 2.3   Application to Pulmonary Artery-Vein Separation

Lung vessel trees were extracted from the chest CT scans by a vessel segmentation method [9] and then skeletonized by a skeletonization method [10] (using

MevisLab 2.7.1). All voxels on the vessel skeleton were added as a set of nodes $\mathcal{V}$, and the adjacency matrix $A$ was constructed based on their connections. In this study, only one-degree (direct) neighbors were considered. A graph $\mathcal{G}$ was constructed for left and right lung separately. For each voxel on the vessel skeleton, a local patch $p_i$ perpendicular to the vessel orientation and of size $S = [32, 32, 5]$ was extracted from the CT images. A patch $p_i$ is labeled either artery or vein, i.e. $y_i \in \{0, 1\}^2$, based on the label of the center voxel. The CNN architecture $\Phi(\cdot|\Theta)$ for processing patches is adopted from [8]. Following the proposed batch strategy, input batch $B$ and its neighbors $NB$ were processed with the shared function $\Phi(\cdot|\Theta)$ to the feature vectors $X$ and $NX$, respectively. The feature vectors $X$ and $NX$ were inserted into a GCN layer, represented and transformed to a new dimension. After an activation layer, the output is predicted with 2 dimensions. The architecture for pulmonary artery-vein separation by linking CNN and GCN is demonstrated in Fig. 1. Based on the predictions of center voxels, the A/V volume is re-built, where each voxel on the cross-sectional area is labeled with the prediction of corresponding center-voxel.

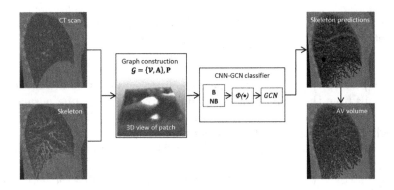

**Fig. 1.** An overview of proposed method for pulmonary arteries-veins separation.

## 3   Experiments

The CNN-GCN method was implemented in 'TensorFlow.Keras', version 1.12.2, where the GCN layer was implemented inheriting from the 'Keras.layers.Layer' class. Categorical cross-entropy was used as loss function and the Stochastic Gradient Descent method was used as optimizer. Training was performed on a local GPU cluster (Nvidia Titan Xp 12 GB). The source code is publicly available via https://github.com/chushan89/Linking-CNN-GCN.git.

We collected contrast enhanced CT scans of 11 cases, scanned with a Toshiba Aquilion ONE, from Sun Yat-sen University Hospital (SunYs data set) and contrast enhanced CT scans of 10 cases, scanned with a Toshiba Aquilion 64, from Leiden University Medical Center (LUMC data set). All CT scans were resampled by a cubic B-spline filter to obtain isotropic voxels, with a size of $0.625 \, \text{mm}^3$.

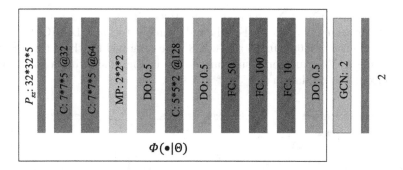

**Fig. 2.** Architecture of CNN-GCN model for pulmonary arteries-veins separation, by linking CNN and GCN layer. C: convolution layer; MP: max-pooling layer; DO: dropout layer; FC: fully-connected layer (or dense layer); $\Phi(\cdot|\Theta)$: a CNN function with multiple layers; GCN: graph convolutional layer.

Lung vessels were segmented and provided for each case [9]. For the SunYs data set, two radiologists of Sun Yat-sen University Hospital labeled the segmented lung vessels into arteries or veins, as initial annotations. The initial labels were checked and corrected by three experts at the LUMC. The corrected annotations were used as ground truth, where initial annotation was used to assess observer performance. In total 22 lungs from 11 patients (consisting of 1,041,463 patches) with fully annotated pulmonary arteries-veins were obtained, referred to as the SunYs dataset. From this data set, 16 lungs (722,013 patches) were used for training and 6 lungs (319,450 patches) for validation. For the LUMC data set, either right or left lung vessels of each case were labeled by two experts independently, in total 10 lungs (504,527 patches) with fully A/V annotations were prepared as an independent test set, from a different patient population, CT protocol and scanner, that was not seen during training.

The CNN3D architecture proposed by Nardelli et al. [8] was used for comparison. The weights of the function $\Phi(\cdot)$ in the CNN-GCN method were initialized randomly using the Glorot uniform initializer, as demonstrated in Fig. 2. Alternatively, we transferred the learned weights from the CNN3D for initialization of the CNN-GCN method, which we refer to as 'CNN-GCNt'. All three methods were trained and validated with the same data, and their hyper-parameter settings were kept the same: learning rate $= 1e-3$, batch size $= 128$, epoch $= 100$. As a benchmark, the initial annotations of observers were validated against the ground truth. Accuracy was used as a key measure for comparing all methods and observer performance.

## 4   Results

The trained classification models were used to predict labels of pulmonary A/V, and results were evaluated against the ground truth. The results are available in Fig. 3. With the validation set from the SunYs data set, the automatic methods obtained median accuracies of 0.727, 0.764 and 0.778 for the CNN3D,

CNN-GCN, and CNN-GCNt method, respectively. This compares to a median inter-observer accuracy of 0.817. For the independent test set (LUMC data set), median accuracies of 0.693, 0.723 and 0.738 were obtained for these three methods. Example A/V separation results are shown in Fig. 4, showing a good and a bad case from the validation set.

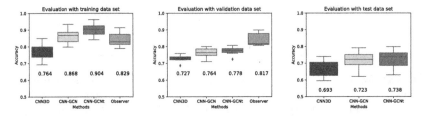

**Fig. 3.** Accuracy of the automatic methods and observers in training, validation and test sets, respectively.

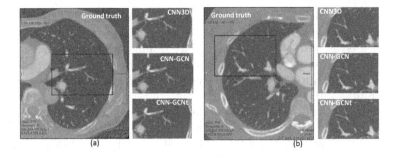

**Fig. 4.** A 2D visualization of a good and bad result in (a) and (b), respectively, where the accuracies of CNN3D, CNN-GCN and CNN-GCNt in the good one were 0.759, 0.800 and 0.807, respectively; the accuracies in the bad one were 0.687, 0.710 and 0.724, respectively.

## 5    Discussion and Conclusion

We proposed a novel deep-learning-based method by linking CNNs with GCNs, which can be trained end-to-end. The CNN-GCN method can consider both local image and connectivity information. A local batch strategy on graphs was proposed, in order to make graphs with huge amounts of nodes trainable within GPU memory. In the application of pulmonary artery-vein separation, the CNN-GCN method could provide a primary separation, which performs better than the CNN method and obtains slightly worse results compared to observers. There are some limitations of this study. In the test data set, we didn't independently verify the observers' annotations, therefore observer performance wasn't provided during testing. In the future, annotation correction will be added in the test set. Probably over-fitting occurred during training, which may be overcome by adding regularizers or more training samples. Even with GCN, some connectivity errors still remained. Including high-order information (such as branch information) or high-degree neighbors may be helpful in solving these remaining errors. Despite these limitations, we obtained encouraging results from the independent test set, especially considering the fact that these are from a different patient population, CT-protocol and CT-scanner. In conclusion, the proposed CNN-GCN method, with end-to-end training, successfully combines information from images and graphs.

**Acknowledgements.** This research was supported by the China Scholarship Council (No. 201406120046) and supported in part by a research grant from the Investigator-Initiated Studies Program of Merck Sharp & Dohme Limited and Bayer AG. The opinions expressed in this paper are those of the authors and do not necessarily represent those of Merck Sharp & Dohme Limited or Bayer AG.

# References

1. Kipf, T.N., Welling, M.: Semi-supervised classification with graph convolutional networks. arXiv preprint arXiv:1609.02907 (2016)
2. Wu, F., Zhang, T., et al.: Simplifying Graph Convolutional Networks. arXiv preprint arXiv:1902.07153 (2019)
3. Monti, F., Boscaini, D., et al.: Geometric deep learning on graphs and manifolds using mixture model CNNs. In: Proceedings of the IEEE Conference on Computer Vision and Pattern Recognition, pp. 5115–5124 (2017)
4. Parisot, S., Ktena, S.I., et al.: Disease prediction using graph convolutional networks: application to Autism Spectrum Disorder and Alzheimer's disease. Med. Image Anal. **48**, 117–130 (2018)
5. Shin, S.Y., Lee, S., et al.: Deep vessel segmentation by learning graphical connectivity. arXiv preprint arXiv:1806.02279 (2018)
6. Charbonnier, J.P., Brink, M., et al.: Automatic pulmonary artery-vein separation and classification in computed tomography using tree partitioning and peripheral vessel matching. IEEE Trans. Med. Imaging **35**(3), 882–892 (2015)
7. Payer, C., Pienn, M., et al.: Automated integer programming based separation of arteries and veins from thoracic CT images. Med. Image Anal. **34**, 109–122 (2016)
8. Nardelli, P., Jimenez-Carretero, D., et al.: Pulmonary artery-vein classification in CT images using deep learning. IEEE Trans. Med. Imaging **37**(11), 2428–2440 (2018)
9. Zhai, Z., Staring, M., et al.: Automatic quantitative analysis of pulmonary vascular morphology in CT images [published online ahead of print June 18, 2019; Medical Physics (2019). https://doi.org/10.1002/mp.13659]
10. Selle, D., Preim, B., et al.: Analysis of vasculature for liver surgical planning. IEEE Trans. Med. Imaging **21**(11), 1344–1357 (2002)

# Comparative Analysis of Magnetic Resonance Fingerprinting Dictionaries via Dimensionality Reduction

Oleh Dzyubachyk[1]([:envelope:])(iD), Kirsten Koolstra[2](iD), Nicola Pezzotti[3,4](iD),
Boudewijn P. F. Lelieveldt[1,5](iD), Andrew Webb[2], and Peter Börnert[2,6]

[1] Division of Image Processing, Department of Radiology,
Leiden University Medical Center, Leiden, The Netherlands
`o.dzyubachyk@lumc.nl`
[2] C.J. Gorter Center for High Field MRI, Department of Radiology,
Leiden University Medical Center, Leiden, The Netherlands
[3] Computer Graphics and Visualization Group, Delft University of Technology,
Delft, The Netherlands
[4] Philips Research Eindhoven, Eindhoven, The Netherlands
[5] Intelligent Systems Department, Delft University of Technology,
Delft, The Netherlands
[6] Philips Research Hamburg, Hamburg, Germany

**Abstract.** Quality assessment of different Magnetic Resonance Fingerprinting (MRF) sequences and their corresponding dictionaries remains an unsolved problem. In this work we present a method in which we approach analysis of MRF dictionaries by performing dimensionality reduction and representing them as low-dimensional point sets (embeddings). Dimensionality reduction was performed using a modification of the t-Distributed Stochastic Neighbor Embedding (t-SNE) algorithm. First, we demonstrated stability of calculated embeddings that allows neglecting the stochastic nature of t-SNE. Next, we proposed and analyzed two algorithms for comparing the embeddings. Finally, we performed two simulations in which we reduced the MRF sequence/dictionary in length or size and analyzed the influence of this reduction on the resulting embedding. We believe that this research can pave the way to development of a software tool for analysis, including better understanding, optimization and comparison, of different MRF sequences.

**Keywords:** Dimensionality reduction · t-SNE · Magnetic Resonance Fingerprinting (MRF) · Point cloud registration

## 1 Introduction

In Magnetic Resonance Fingerprinting (MRF) [1,2] multiple tissue parameters $(T_1, T_2, M_0)$ are encoded during a single scan, by using a variable flip angle pattern in the data acquisition process, creating a unique signal evolution for each

© Springer Nature Switzerland AG 2019
D. Zhang et al. (Eds.): GLMI 2019, LNCS 11849, pp. 44–52, 2019.
https://doi.org/10.1007/978-3-030-35817-4_6

$(T_1, T_2)$ combination. Signal evolutions can be simulated for different $(T_1, T_2)$ pairs and stored in a so-called dictionary. If combined with efficient sampling schemes, such as the spiral, these dictionaries allow one to recover tissue parameters from heavily undersampled data. This technique is schematically shown in Fig. 1. Comparison of different MRF sequences or their respective dictionaries regarding the encoding capability is challenging and represents a largely unaddressed problem [3].

Dimensionality reduction is a powerful tool for analysis of high-dimensional data [4]. However, such methods (Principal component analysis, Isomap, t-SNE) operate on a per-data set basis and hence cannot be directly applied for comparison of two different high-dimensional data sets. For example, embeddings produced by t-Distributed Stochastic Neighbor Embedding (t-SNE) [5], currently one of the most popular and advanced dimensionality reduction techniques, are guided by pairwise distances between its points. Thus, these embeddings exhibit freedom with respect to translation and rotation. Moreover, their scaling factors can also differ. Finally, as t-SNE is a stochastic technique, it does not guarantee repeatability if the same data set is embedded multiple times.

The goal of this work is to develop and validate a method that enables comparative analysis of different MRF dictionaries [1], which we approach as a dimensionality reduction problem. Representing calculated embeddings as low-dimensional (2D or 3D) point clouds, we apply the Iterative Closest Point (ICP) algorithm [6,7] for aligning them (Sect. 2). We validate our method on a commonly used MRF sequence and its corresponding dictionary [2].

In Sect. 3.1 we demonstrate the stability of the embedding by performing repetitive dimensionality reduction with t-SNE on the same data set. In Sect. 3.2 we investigate two different approaches for comparing the embeddings: (i) By separately embedding the data sets followed by registration; and (ii) By embedding the data sets together and consequently co-registering them. In Sect. 3.2 and in Sect. 3.3 we analyze the influence of the MRF dictionary size, both in terms of the length of each dictionary element and the number of elements and sampling sparsity, on the embedding. We believe that this research can facilitate development of a tool that would provide a better insight into MRF encoding principles, their optimization and potential improvement of parameter quantification in MRF.

## 2   Methods

### 2.1   MRF Dictionary

One MRF dictionary was calculated for the flip angle pattern shown in Fig. 1A, described in [2], using the extended phase graph formalism [8]. The repetition time (TR) was set to a constant value of 15 ms. $T_1$ values ranged from 20 to 5000 ms in steps of 30 ms. $T_2$ values ranged from 10 to 500 ms in steps of 10 ms. All the dictionary elements were normalized to a unit norm. This resulted in a dictionary with 7 925 elements, each represented by 1000 time points of the MRF signal curve. $T_1$ values shorter than $T_2$ were ignored in the dictionary calculation. This dictionary, denoted $D_{ref}$ and further referred to as the "reference dictionary", was used as a validation set in all our experiments.

## 2.2  Dimensionality Reduction via Hierarchical SNE

Dimensionality reduction was performed in the time dimension, with each feature vector containing 1000 points. The main principle of the t-SNE is that it projects higher-dimensional data onto a lower-dimensional manifold while preserving similarity (pairwise distances) between data points. As a particular implementation we used Hierarchical Stochastic Neighbor Embedding, which was preferred over other variants of t-SNE as it is proven to be much more capable of reconstructing the underlying low-dimensional manifolds [9].

## 2.3  Registration of the Embeddings

ICP performs global alignment of two point clouds. As, in general, t-SNE embeddings might also have different scale, we used a modification of the ICP with built-in scale estimation [7]. Since in our particular case all the correspondences between the point pairs are known, we have skipped the point matching step, which did not affect the results but significantly simplified and sped-up the algorithm. In fact, in such a setting the ICP reduces to mere calculation of three transformation parameters (rotation, translation and scaling) from the known pairs of the corresponding points.

# 3  Experiments and Results

In this section, we present results of several experiments targeting different properties of the produced low-dimensional embeddings. Although we performed all the experiments by embedding the dictionaries to both 2D and 3D, here we report our results for the 2D case only. Results for the 3D case are quite similar to their 2D counterparts, since most of the produced embeddings of our validation data can be well approximated by a 2D manifold (plane). Co-registered embeddings were compared to each other by analyzing the distribution of the Euclidean distance between the corresponding points in the two data sets.

## 3.1  Embedding Stability

The stochastic nature of t-SNE can, in general, cause embeddings obtained after repetitive runs on the same data to be different. To estimate this difference, we embedded the reference dictionary $D_{ref}$ ten times and compared the results. For simplicity, without loss of generality, all the embeddings denoted as $E_{ref}(n = \overline{2,9})$ were registered to $E_{ref}(n = 1)$, where the numbers in the parenthesis denote the repetition number. Results of this experiment, presented in Fig. 2, clearly indicate that produced embeddings are very similar to each other with the average error being nearly two orders of magnitude smaller than the distance between the neighboring points in the embedding.

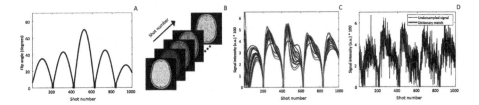

**Fig. 1.** Schematic overview of MRF. (A) In the MRF acquisition a variable flip angle train is used to create a unique signal evolution for each tissue. (B) After each flip angle an image is acquired, usually sampled using an efficient scheme such as the spiral. Images are typically heavily undersampled and show serious artifacts. (C) Signal evolutions are simulated for many $(T_1, T_2)$ pairs and stored in a dictionary; different colors denote different dictionary entries. (D) Noisy signal curves from undersampled images are matched to the dictionary to find $T_1$ and $T_2$ values for each voxel.

## 3.2  Dictionary Length

In this section we analyze the influence of the dictionary length on the resulting embedding. Having shorter dictionaries is favorable as it requires a shorter MRI data acquisition time. On the other hand, shortening the dictionaries might result in loss of encoding capability. To test this, we progressively decreased the length of the reference dictionary by 100 elements at a time. This resulted in nine sub-dictionaries $D_{i=\overline{1,9}}$, with trace length ranging from 100 to 900. Each sub-dictionary was embedded using t-SNE, (i) separately, resulting in $E_i$, as well as (ii) together with the reference dictionary $D_{ref}$, resulting in two embeddings $E_i^*$ and $E_{ref;i}^*$. The latter case requires special attention as t-SNE is only able to embed data sets that have constant length in the feature dimension. To resolve this issue, each of the sub-dictionaries was zero-padded to the original trace length (1000 elements), which mimics adding extra zero-degree flip angles to the MRF train, and, consequently, concatenated with the reference dictionary along the feature dimension.

We performed two different experiments. In the first one, the embeddings $E_i$ of the separately embedded sub-dictionaries $D_i$ were registered to the embedding $E_{ref}(1)$ of the reference dictionary $D_{ref}$. This provides additional insight on the stability of the embedding and the registration processes. The embeddings were registered in two different ways: (i) directly and (ii) progressively, by co-registering the embeddings of the "neighboring" sub-dictionaries and composing the obtained transforms for aligning the embedding of each sub-dictionary to that of the reference one.

Results of this experiment, illustrated in Figs. 3, 4, conform to our expectations: embeddings of the shorter dictionaries show clear progression as their length increases and start resembling more and more the embedding of the full dictionary $D_{ref}$. The latter was confirmed both quantitatively (Fig. 3) and qualitatively (Fig. 4). From these results we can draw two important conclusions: (i) Both registration approaches produce very similar results; and (ii) Starting

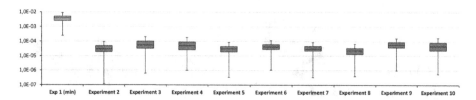

**Fig. 2.** Stability of 2D embedding on the validation data set. Label "Experiment 1 (min)" denotes the distribution of the distances between each point in $E_{ref}(1)$ and its closest neighbor. Labels "Experiment 2" to "Experiment 9" denote distributions of the distances between the corresponding points in $E_{ref}(1)$ and $E_{ref}(n = \overline{2,9})$. Whiskers indicate the maximum and the minimum of the corresponding distribution. The plots indicate excellent repeatability of the embedding with negligible stochastic effects.

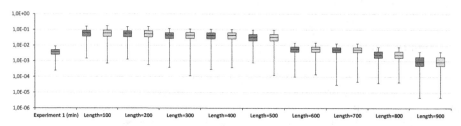

**Fig. 3.** Comparison between the reference dictionary $D_{ref}$ and its shorter counterparts $D_{i=\overline{1,9}}$. Label "Experiment 1 (min)" (orange box) denotes distribution of the distances between each point in the reference embedding $E_{ref}(1)$ and its closest neighbor. Distribution of distances between the points of the reference embedding and each of its shorter counterparts $E_i$ for the case of direct (green boxes) and progressive registration (yellow boxes) is shown. Whiskers indicate the maximum and the minimum of the corresponding distribution. The plots exhibit decreasing trend as embeddings of shorter dictionaries start resembling more and more the embedding of the full dictionary. (Color figure online)

from $D_6$, the plots exhibit a clear distance drop indicating that these sub-dictionaries are very similar to $D_{ref}$.

In the second experiment, we compared embedding the sub-dictionaries separately and together with the reference dictionary. The former is faster and does not require modifying the data by zero-padding. On the other hand, this approach raises a question if (and how) two embeddings obtained in this way can be compared to each other. Consequently, we co-registered the following embedding pairs: $E_i^*$ and $E_{ref;i}^*$ (without scaling); $E_{ref}(1)$ and $E_{ref;i}^*$; $E_i$ and $E_i^*$, and compared the results to these of the experiment described above.

Results of this experiment are shown in Figs. 5, 6. In particular, quantitative results presented in Fig. 5 (green boxes) confirm that embedding the reference dictionary $D_{ref}$ together with shorter sub-dictionaries produces results that are very similar to $E_{ref}$ obtained by embedding it separately. This observation can also be confirmed qualitatively by comparing the results illustrated in Fig. 6 to

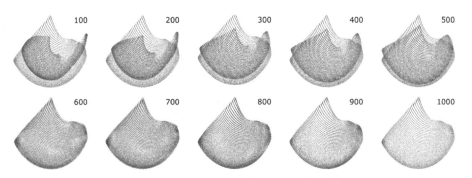

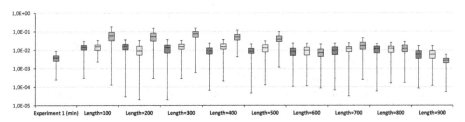

**Fig. 4.** Comparative visualization of embeddings of dictionaries for different sequence length. Each point of the scatter plot represents an embedded lower-dimensional dictionary element. Proximity of the embedding points is directly related to similarity of the corresponding dictionary elements. The dictionaries were embedded separately and co-registered using the direct registration scheme. The reference embedding $E_{ref}(1)$ is plotted in red and the corresponding embeddings $E_{i=\overline{1,9}}$ of the shorter sub-dictionaries $D_i$ are shown in green. Labels above the embeddings indicate the length of the MRF flip angle train in the corresponding sub-dictionary. Embeddings of shorter dictionaries exhibit clear progression towards the embedding of the full dictionary. (Color figure online)

**Fig. 5.** Comparison between the reference dictionary $D_{ref}$ and its shorter counterparts $(D_{i=\overline{1,9}})$, embedded together. The reference dictionary $D_{ref}$ and each of the shorter sub-dictionaries $D_i$ were embedded together and co-registered. Distribution of distances between the points of $E_{ref}(1)$ and $E^*_{ref;i}$ (green boxes); $E_i$ and $E^*_i$ (yellow boxes); and $E^*_i$ and $E^*_{ref;i}$ (blue boxes) is shown. Label "Experiment 1 (min)" (orange box) denotes distribution of the distances between each point in the reference embedding $E_{ref}(1)$ and its closest neighbor. Whiskers indicate the maximum and the minimum of the corresponding distribution. The plots of all three groups exhibit decreasing distance trend as embeddings of shorter dictionaries start resembling more and more the embedding of the full dictionary, although this trend is less strict than the one depicted in Fig. 3. (Color figure online)

those in Fig. 4: both figures show similar progression of the embeddings with respect to dictionary length, although some clear differences can be observed for short sub-dictionaries. Similarly, the results plotted in Fig. 5 (blue boxes) are similar to these in Fig. 3, although, also in this case, the decreasing distance trend is violated for $i \in \{7, 8\}$.

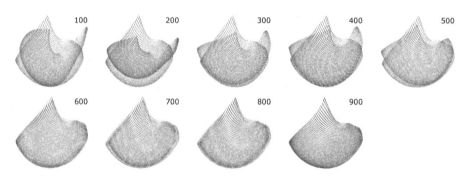

**Fig. 6.** Comparative visualization of embeddings of dictionaries of different length. The reference dictionary $D_{ref}$ and each of the shorter sub-dictionaries $D_{i=\overline{1,9}}$ were embedded together and co-registered. Embeddings $E^*_{ref;i}$ are plotted in red and the corresponding embeddings of the shorter sub-dictionaries $E^*_i$ are shown in green. Labels above the embeddings indicate the length of the corresponding sub-dictionary. Embeddings of shorter dictionaries exhibit progression towards the embedding of the full dictionary, although less clear than that shown in Fig. 4. (Color figure online)

### 3.3 Dependence of Produced Embeddings on Dictionary Size

To get more insight into the embedding process, we have designed another experiment in which we truncated the number of elements or applied sparser sampling along the $T_2$ axis. For this we have created another dictionary in a similar manner to the one described in Sect. 2.1, using the same step size along the $T_2$ axis. However, this dictionary contained 250 elements along the $T_2$ axis instead of 50, resulting in a dictionary with 31 292 elements. This dictionary, despite including also rather high $T_2$ values (up to 2500 ms) is still realistic as cerebral spinal fluid has a very long $T_2$ value. We generated three sub-dictionaries by truncating this dictionary to 100, 150, and 200 elements along the $T_2$ axis. In addition, another sub-dictionary was created by performing sparse sampling along this axis, during which every third entry was kept. All the dictionaries were embedded separately and co-registered with that of the original dictionary. Ideally, points in the embedded reduced dictionaries are expected to overlap with the corresponding points from the embedded original dictionary.

Results of this experiment are shown in Fig. 7. Although co-registered embeddings of the reduced dictionaries exhibit the correct trend, they do not coincide with the corresponding parts of the embedding of the full dictionary. From this observation we can conclude that size of the embedded data set in terms of number of elements has a significant influence on the final result. At this moment it is not clear if this effect is a direct consequence of using our particular implementation, or it is a property of the entire t-SNE family.

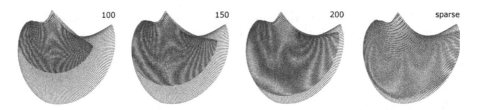

**Fig. 7.** Comparative visualization of embeddings of dictionaries of different size. The embedding with the longest fully-sampled $T_2$ axis is plotted in red and the corresponding co-registered embeddings of smaller/sparser dictionaries are shown in green. Numbers above the embeddings indicate the length of the $T_2$ axis of the corresponding dictionary. These scatter plots illustrate that embeddings of the reduced dictionaries resemble the corresponding parts of the full dictionary. At the same time it can be noticed that data sets of different size in terms of number of elements are embedded differently. (Color figure online)

## 4  Discussion and Conclusions

Several important conclusions can be drawn from the experiments. First, the described dimensionality reduction approach is stable, meaning that different runs produce very similar embeddings, which allows us to neglect the stochastic nature of t-SNE. Second, we have shown that different high-dimensional data sets can be compared to each other by embedding them together as well as separately, in both cases followed by point cloud registration. These two approaches differ in the sense that in the former case the embeddings are influenced by each other, whereas for the latter case they are calculated using solely the points of the corresponding data set. Both cases produce similar embeddings, although results of the separate embedding seem to be more consistent. Hence, they are preferred for also being faster. Finally, we have also investigated dependence of the produced embeddings on the dictionary size (in terms of the number of elements along one of the axes), from which we concluded that larger dictionaries are embedded in a slightly different way from smaller ones.

Our method was designed to be as generic as possible, in the sense that it can be applied to a wide range of MR sequences, not limited to MRF data. In particular, we have tested the embedding stability on several different MRF dictionaries (results not shown) and concluded high repeatability of the embedding process, in line with results presented in Sect. 3.1.

In the future we are planning to use the presented approach for developing a tool for comparison of different MRF sequences. A preliminary example of how this methodology can be applied for analyzing different flip angle sequence lengths was given in Sect. 3.2, where we have shown, both quantitatively (Fig. 3) and qualitatively (Fig. 4), that, starting from the length of 600 time points, the truncated sub-dictionaries are very similar to the full dictionary (1000 time points). This might imply that the MRF sequence length can be reduced without compromising the encoding capability. To confirm this, further experiments are needed that take into account the noise-like structure in the signal coming from highly undersampled acquisitions typically performed in MRF. Finally, we would also like to investigate the robustness of our approach by replacing t-SNE with other, possibly linear, dimensionality reduction approaches.

# References

1. Ma, D., et al.: Magnetic resonance fingerprinting. Nature **495**, 187 (2013)
2. Jiang, Y., Ma, D., Seiberlich, N., Gulani, V., Griswold, M.A.: MR fingerprinting using fast imaging with steady state precession (FISP) with spiral readout. Magn. Reson. Med. **74**(6), 1621–1631 (2015)
3. Cohen, O., Rosen, M.S.: Algorithm comparison for schedule optimization in MR fingerprinting. Magn. Reson. Imag. **41**, 15–21 (2017)
4. Van der Maaten, L., Postma, E., Van den Herik, J.: Dimensionality reduction: a comparative review. J. Mach. Learn. Res. **10**, 66–71 (2009)
5. Van der Maaten, L., Hinton, G.: Visualizing data using t-SNE. J. Mach. Learn. Res. **9**, 2579–2605 (2008)
6. Chen, Y., Medioni, G.: Object modelling by registration of multiple range images. Image Vision Comput. **10**(3), 145–155 (1992)
7. Zinßer, T., Schmidt, J., Niemann, H.: Point set registration with integrated scale estimation. In: Proceedings of International Conference on Pattern Recognition and Information Processing, pp. 116–119, January 2005
8. Scheffler, K.: A pictorial description of steady-states in rapid magnetic resonance imaging. Concept. Magn. Reson. **11**(5), 291–304 (1999)
9. Pezzotti, N., Höllt, T., Lelieveldt, B.P.F., Eisemann, E., Vilanova, A.: Hierarchical stochastic neighbor embedding. Comput. Graph. Forum **35**, 21–30 (2016)

# Learning Deformable Point Set Registration with Regularized Dynamic Graph CNNs for Large Lung Motion in COPD Patients

Lasse Hansen[✉], Doris Dittmer, and Mattias P. Heinrich

Institute of Medical Informatics, University of Lübeck, Lübeck, Germany
{hansen,dittmer,heinrich}@imi.uni-luebeck.de

**Abstract.** Deformable registration continues to be one of the key challenges in medical image analysis. While iconic registration methods have started to benefit from the recent advances in medical deep learning, the same does not yet apply for the registration of point sets, e.g. registration based on surfaces, keypoints or landmarks. This is mainly due to the restriction of the convolution operator in modern CNNs to densely gridded input. However, with the newly developed methods from the field of geometric deep learning suitable tools are now emerging, which enable powerful analysis of medical data on irregular domains. In this work, we present a new method that enables the learning of regularized feature descriptors with dynamic graph CNNs. By incorporating the learned geometric features as prior probabilities into the well-established coherent point drift (CPD) algorithm, formulated as differentiable network layer, we establish an end-to-end framework for robust registration of two point sets. Our approach is evaluated on the challenging task of aligning keypoints extracted from lung CT scans in inhale and exhale states with large deformations and without any additional intensity information. Our results indicate that the inherent geometric structure of the extracted keypoints is sufficient to establish descriptive point features, which yield a significantly improved performance and robustness of our registration framework.

**Keywords:** Geometric deep learning · Deformable point set registration

## 1 Introduction and Related Work

Registration, i.e. determining a spatial transformation that aligns two images or point sets, is a fundamental task in medical image and shape analysis and a prerequisite for numerous clinical applications. It is widely used for image-guided intervention, motion compensation in radiation therapy, atlas-based segmentation or monitoring of disease progression. Non-rigid registration is ill-posed and thus a non-convex optimization problem with a very high number of degrees

© Springer Nature Switzerland AG 2019
D. Zhang et al. (Eds.): GLMI 2019, LNCS 11849, pp. 53–61, 2019.
https://doi.org/10.1007/978-3-030-35817-4_7

of freedom. In addition, the medical domain poses particular challenges on the registration task, e.g. non-linear intensity differences in multi-modal images or high inter-patient variations in anatomical shape and appearance.

**Iconic registration:** Voxel-based intensity-driven medical image registration has been an active area of research, which can e.g. be solved using discrete [7] optimization of a similarity metric and a regularization constraint on the smoothness of the deformation field. Data driven deep learning methods based on convolutional neural networks (CNNs), have only recently been used in the field of medical image registration. In [14] an iconic and unsupervised learning approach is introduced that learns features to drive a registration and replaces the iterative optimization with a feed-forward CNN. While achieving impressive runtimes of under a second on a GPU the accuracy for CT lung motion estimation is inferior to conventional methods. Weak supervision in the form of landmarks or multi-label segmentations was used in the CNN framework of [9], where the similarity measure is based on the alignment of the registered labels.

**Geometric registration:** To capture large deformations, e.g. present in intra-patient inhale-exhale examinations of COPD patients [5] or vessel-guided brain shift compensation [1], geometric registration models - based on keypoints or surfaces - offer a promising solution. Point-based registration has not yet profited from the advantages of deep feature learning due to the restriction of conventional CNNs to densely gridded input. Many current geometric methods (e.g. [1] and [12]) are based on the well-established coherent point drift (CPD) algorithm [10]. In addition to 3D coordinates, they incorporate further image or segmentation-derived features, such as point orientations or scalar fractional anisotropy (FA) values [12].

**Deep geometric learning:** While these hand-crafted features clearly improved on the results of the CPD, recent methods from the field of geometric deep learning [4] would enable a data-driven feature extraction directly from point sets. The PointNet framework [11] was one of the first approaches to apply deep learning methods to unordered point sets. A limitation of the approach is that is does not consider local neighborhood information, which was addressed in [15] by dynamically building a k-nearest-neighbour graph on the point set and thus also enabling feature propagation along edges in that graph. Combining convolutional feature learning with a differentiable and robustly regularized fitting process has first been proposed for multi-camera scene reconstruction in [3] (DSAC), but has so far been limited to rigid alignment.

**Large deformation lung registration:** Both iconic and geometric approaches have often been found to yield relative large residual errors for large motion lung registration (forced inhale-to-exhale): e.g. 4.68 mm for the discrete optimization algorithm in [7] applied to the DIR-lab COPD data [5] and 3.61 mm (on the inhale-exhale pairs of the EMPIRE10 challenge) for [6], which used both keypoint- and intensity-based information. Learning the alignment of such difficult data appears to be so far impossible with intensity-driven CNN approaches that already struggle with more shallow breathing in 4D-CT [14]. Thus being able to directly match vessel- and airway trees based on geometric features alone can provide a valuable pre-alignment for further intensity-based registration (cf. [8]) or be directly used in clinical applications to perform atlas-based labelling of anatomical segments and branchpoints for physiological studies [13].

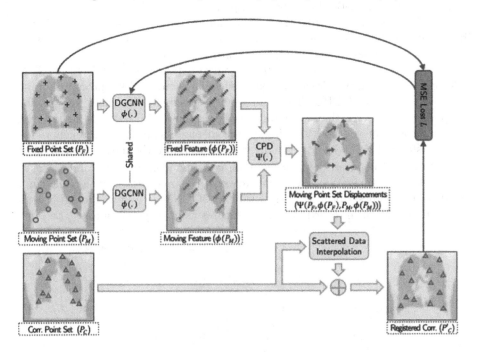

**Fig. 1.** Illustration of our proposed method for supervised non-rigid point set registration. While we investigate the problem of 3D registration, here, point sets are depicted in two dimensions for simplicity. Also, point sets are underlaid with coronal lung CT slices as visualization aides. No image information is used in our registration pipeline.

### 1.1  Contributions

Our work contributes two important steps towards data-driven point set registration that enables the incorporation of deep feature learning into a regularized CPD fitting algorithm. First, we utilize dynamic graph CNNs [15] in an auxiliary metric learning task to establish robust correspondences between a moving and a fixed point set. These learned features are shown to yield an improved modeling of prior probabilities in the CPD algorithm. Since all operations of the CPD algorithm are differentiable, we secondly show that it is possible to further optimize the parameters of the feature extraction network directly on the registration task. To evaluate our method we register keypoints extracted from inhale and exhale states in lung CT-scans from the challenging DIR-Lab COPD dataset [5] showing the general feasibility of a deep learning point set registration framework in an end-to-end manner and with only geometric information.

## 2    Methods

In this section, we introduce our proposed method for deformable point set registration with deeply learned features. Figure 1 summarizes the methods general idea. Input to our method are the fixed point set $P_F$ and the moving point set $P_M$. While we make no assumptions on the number of points or correspondences in the input point sets, we assume a further set of keypoint correspondences with $P_F$ for the supervised learning task, which is denoted as $P_C$. We compute geometric features from $P_F$ and $P_M$ with a shared dynamic graph CNN (DGCNN [15]) $\phi$. The spatial positions together with the extracted descriptors are input to the feature based CPD algorithm that produces displacement vectors for all points in $P_M$. We then employ thin-plate splines (TPS) [2] as a scattered data interpolation method to compute the displacements for $P_C$, which yields the transformed point set $P_C'$. Finally, we can compute the mean squared error (MSE) of the Euclidean distance between correspondences in $P_F$ and $P_C'$ as a loss $L$ for the optimization of the feature extraction network $\phi$. In the following, we describe the descriptor learning with the DGCNN as well as the extensions to the CPD algorithm to exploit point features as prior probabilities.

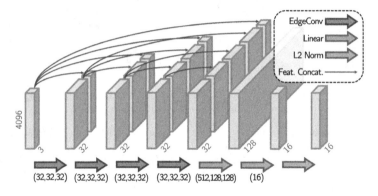

**Fig. 2.** Proposed network architecture for geometric feature extraction from the fixed and moving point set. Input is a three-dimensional point set and the network computes a 16-dimensional geometric descriptor for each of the 4096 points. The number of layer neurons for each operation is specified in the corresponding brackets.

### 2.1    Descriptor Learning on Point Sets with Dynamic Graph CNNs

Our proposed network architecture for geometric feature extraction is illustrated in Fig. 2. A key component is the edge convolution introduced in [15], that dynamically builds a k-Nearest-Neighbor (kNN) graph from the points in the input feature space and then aggregates information from neighbouring points to output a final feature map. We employ several edge convolutions with DenseNet style feature concatenation to efficiently capture both local and global geometry. The final feature descriptor is obtained by fully connected layers that reduce the point information to a given dimensionality. We restrict the output descriptor space by $L_2$ normalization to enable constant parametrization of subsequent operations in the registration pipeline which stabilizes network training. To establish robust initial correspondences between the moving and fixed point set the model is pretrained in an auxiliary metric learning task using a triplet loss.

## 2.2 Feature-Based Coherent Point Drift

The CPD algorithm formulates the alignment of two point sets as a probability density estimation problem. The points in the moving point set $P_M$ are described as centroids of gaussian mixture models (GMMs) and are fitted to the points in the fixed point set $P_F$ by maximizing the likelihood. To find the displacements for $P_M$ the Expectation Maximization (EM) algorithm is used, where in the E-step point correspondence probabilities $\mathbf{C}$ are computed and in the M-step the displacement vectors are updated. We incorporate the learned geometric feature descriptors $\phi(P_F)$ and $\phi(P_M)$ as additional prior probabilities with

$$\mathbf{C}(P_F, \phi(P_F), P_M, \phi(P_M)) = \mathbf{C_{pos}}(P_F, P_M) + \alpha \cdot \mathbf{C_{feat}}(\phi(P_F), \phi(P_M)), \quad (1)$$

where $\mathbf{C_{pos}}$ denotes the spatial point correspondence described in [10], $\alpha$ is a trade-off and scaling parameter and

$$\mathbf{C_{feat_{mn}}}(\phi(P_F)_n, \phi(P_M)_m) = \exp(-\frac{1}{2 \cdot \rho^2} \|\phi(P_F)_n - \phi(P_M)_m\|^2) \quad (2)$$

with $n = 1 \ldots N$ and $m = 1 \ldots M$. $N$ and $M$ denote the number of points in $P_F$ and $P_M$, respectively. In addition to the parameter $\rho$ in (2), that controls the width of the Gaussian, the CPD algorithm includes three more free parameters: $w$, $\lambda$ and $\beta$. Parameter $w$ models the amount of noise and outliers in the point sets, while parameters $\lambda$ and $\beta$ control the smoothness of the deformation field.

# 3 Experiments

Registering the fully inflated to exhaled lungs is considered one of the most demanding tasks in medical image registration, which is important for analyzing e.g. local ventilation defects in COPD patients. We use the DIR-Lab COPD data set [5] with 10 inhale-exhale pairs of 3D CT scans for all our experiments. The thorax volumes are resampled to isotropic voxel-sizes of 1 mm and a few thousands keypoints are extracted from inner lung structures with the Foerstner operator. Automatic correspondences to supervise the learning of our DGCNN are established using the discrete and intensity-based registration algorithm of [8], which has an accuracy of ≈1 mm. In all experiments, no CT-based intensity information is used and all processing relies entirely on the geometric keypoint locations.

In our first experiment, we learn point descriptors directly in a supervised metric learning task. Therefore, a triplet loss is employed forcing feature similarity between corresponding keypoint regions in point set pairs. The inhale and exhale point set form the positive pair, while points from the permuted exhale point set yield as negative examples. These learned features can be directly used in a kNN registration. We then investigate the combination of spatial positions and learned descriptors in the feature-based CPD algorithm. Finally, in our concluding experiment, the feature network is trained in an end-to-end manner as described in Sect. 2 to further optimize the pretrained geometric features.

**Implementation details:** Due to the limited number of instances in the used dataset we perform a leave-one-out validation, where we evaluate on one inhale and exhale point set and train our network with the remaining nine pairs. During training we use farthest point sampling to obtain 4096 points from the inhale and exhale point set, respectively. Each evaluation is run ten times and results are averaged to account for the effect of the sampling step. The employed network parameters are specified in Fig. 2. For the CPD algorithm (250 iterations) we use following parameters: $\alpha = 0.05$, $\rho = 0.5$ $w = 0.1$, $\lambda = 5$ and $\beta = 1$. For the end-to-end training we relax parameters $\rho$ and $\beta$ to 0.25 and 0.5, respectively, to allow for further optimization of input features.

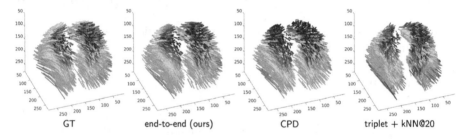

| GT | end-to-end (ours) | CPD | triplet + kNN@20 |

**Fig. 3.** Qualitative results in terms of 3D motion vectors on test case #5. The magnitude is color coded from blue (small motion) to red (large motion). (Color figure online)

## 4    Results and Discussion

Qualitative results are shown in Fig. 3 where our approach demonstrates a good trade-off between the very smooth motion of the CPD and the potential for large correspondences of the features from triplet-learning. Our quantitative results that are evaluated on 300 independent expert landmark pairs for each patient demonstrate that registering the point clouds directly with CPD (3D coordinates as input) yield a relatively large target registration error (TRE) of $6.4 \pm 5.2$ mm (see Table 1). Employing kNN registration based on a DGCNN trained with keypoint correspondences to extract geometric features without regularization is still inferior with a TRE of $9.0 \pm 5.5$ mm highlighting the challenges of this point-based registration task and the difficulties of addressing the deformable alignment with one-to-one correspondence search. Combining the geometric features of a pre-trained DGCNN with the regularizing CPD that is extended to use

**Table 1.** Results for the 10 inhale and exhale CT scan pairs of the DIR-Lab COPD data set [5]. The mean target registration error (TRE) in mm is computed on the 300 expert annotated landmark pairs per case. The $p$-values are obtained by a rank-sum test over all 3000 landmark errors with respect to our best performing approach.

| Case # | Initial | Center-aligned | Triplet + kNN@20 | CPD [10] | Triplet + CPD (ours) | End-to-end (ours) |
|--------|---------|----------------|-------------------|----------|----------------------|-------------------|
| 1 | 26.3 | 17.8 | 8.1 | 5.5 | 4.2 | **3.4** |
| 2 | 21.8 | 14.7 | 15.6 | **8.4** | 9.3 | 8.9 |
| 3 | 12.6 | 10.6 | 6.4 | 2.7 | 2.5 | **2.4** |
| 4 | 29.6 | 19.0 | 8.3 | 4.8 | 3.4 | **3.2** |
| 5 | 30.1 | 18.4 | 7.8 | 8.4 | 5.2 | **4.6** |
| 6 | 28.5 | 16.2 | 7.5 | 14.0 | 5.1 | **4.3** |
| 7 | 21.6 | 10.2 | 6.3 | 3.0 | 2.6 | **2.5** |
| 8 | 26.5 | 17.4 | 6.3 | 6.8 | 4.3 | **3.9** |
| 9 | 14.9 | 14.1 | 9.0 | 3.5 | **3.1** | 3.6 |
| 10 | 21.8 | 19.6 | 14.9 | **7.4** | 7.5 | **7.4** |
| mean | 23.4 | 15.7 | 9.0 | 6.4 | 4.7 | **4.3** |
| std | 11.9 | 7.0 | 5.5 | 5.2 | 4.1 | **3.6** |
| $p$-val | $<10^{-4}$ | $<10^{-4}$ | $<10^{-4}$ | $<10^{-4}$ | $1.4 \cdot 10^{-2}$ | – |

19-dimensional inputs (16 features + 3 coordinates) yields a substantial improvement over each individual method with a TRE of $4.7 \pm 4.1$ mm. Finally, using end-to-end learning to back-propagate the regularized alignment errors through the iterative point drift layers to further improve the feature learning shows another small but significant improvement to $4.3 \pm 3.6$ mm. These alignment errors cannot be directly compared to the large variety of image- and feature-based registration algorithms that reached 3.6 mm [6], 4.7 mm [7] or 1.1 mm [8] for similar datasets, but were based on intensity information, while our comparison is restricted to purely geometric approaches without intensity. In addition, a better outcome would be expected by extending the keypoint extraction to focus on vessel- or airway-based nodes and to include anatomical tree-based edges in the graph model. Nevertheless, the results clearly showed that our models are already able to directly learn semantic geometric features in a data-driven manner based on the inherent correspondence information.

## 5   Conclusion

We have presented a new method for deformable point set registration that learns geometric features from irregular point sets using a dynamic graph CNN (DGCNN) together with a regularizing and fully differentiable high-dimensional coherent point drift (CPD) model. Our results clearly indicate that geometric feature learning, even from relatively uninformative point clouds, is possible with DGCNNs and can be further enhanced when incorporating the CPD model into the optimization. Evaluated on challenging inhale-exhale lung registration of COPD patients we achieve an improvement of 2.1 mm over the classical CPD method and are competitive with many classical image-based registration algorithms despite the fact that no intensity information is used. In addition to these encouraging findings, we believe that alternative regularization models to the CPD, that require fewer iteration steps could have potential to further improve this approach. In future works, many more applications, e.g. surface point shape alignment and analysis, could benefit from deep point registration.

# References

1. Bayer, S., et al.: Intraoperative brain shift compensation using a hybrid mixture model. In: Frangi, A.F., Schnabel, J.A., Davatzikos, C., Alberola-López, C., Fichtinger, G. (eds.) MICCAI 2018. LNCS, vol. 11073, pp. 116–124. Springer, Cham (2018). https://doi.org/10.1007/978-3-030-00937-3_14
2. Bookstein, F.L.: Principal warps: thin-plate splines and the decomposition of deformations. TPAMI **11**(6), 567–585 (1989)
3. Brachmann, E., et al.: DSAC-differentiable RANSAC for camera localization. In: CVPR, pp. 6684–6692 (2017)
4. Bronstein, M.M., Bruna, J., LeCun, Y., Szlam, A., Vandergheynst, P.: Geometric deep learning: going beyond euclidean data. IEEE Signal Process. Mag. **34**(4), 18–42 (2017)
5. Castillo, R., et al.: A reference dataset for deformable image registration spatial accuracy evaluation using the copdgene study archive. Phys. Med. Biol. **58**(9), 2861 (2013)
6. Ehrhardt, J., Werner, R., Schmidt-Richberg, A., Handels, H.: Automatic landmark detection and non-linear landmark-and surface-based registration of lung CT images. In: Medical Image Analysis for the Clinic-A Grand Challenge, MICCAI 2010, pp. 165–174 (2010)
7. Glocker, B., Komodakis, N., Tziritas, G., Navab, N., Paragios, N.: Dense image registration through MRFs and efficient linear programming. Med. Image Anal. **12**(6), 731–741 (2008)
8. Heinrich, M.P., Handels, H., Simpson, I.J.A.: Estimating large lung motion in COPD patients by symmetric regularised correspondence fields. In: Navab, N., Hornegger, J., Wells, W.M., Frangi, A.F. (eds.) MICCAI 2015. LNCS, vol. 9350, pp. 338–345. Springer, Cham (2015). https://doi.org/10.1007/978-3-319-24571-3_41
9. Hu, Y., et al.: Weakly-supervised convolutional neural networks for multimodal image registration. Med. Image Anal. **49**, 1–13 (2018)
10. Myronenko, A., Song, X.: Point set registration: coherent point drift. TPAMI **32**(12), 2262–2275 (2010)
11. Qi, C.R., Su, H., Mo, K., Guibas, L.J.: PointNet: deep learning on point sets for 3d classification and segmentation. In: Proceedings of the Conference on Computer Vision and Pattern Recognition, pp. 652–660 (2017)
12. Ravikumar, N., Gooya, A., Beltrachini, L., Frangi, A.F., Taylor, Z.A.: Generalised coherent point drift for group-wise multi-dimensional analysis of diffusion brain MRI data. Med. Image Anal. **53**, 47–63 (2019)
13. Tschirren, J., McLennan, G., Palágyi, K., Hoffman, E.A., Sonka, M.: Matching and anatomical labeling of human airway tree. TMI **24**(12), 1540–1547 (2005)

14. de Vos, B.D., Berendsen, F.F., Viergever, M.A., Sokooti, H., Staring, M., Išgum, I.: A deep learning framework for unsupervised affine and deformable image registration. Med. Image Anal. **52**, 128–143 (2019)
15. Wang, Y., Sun, Y., Liu, Z., Sarma, S.E., Bronstein, M.M., Solomon, J.M.: Dynamic graph CNN for learning on point clouds. arXiv preprint arXiv:1801.07829 (2018)

# Graph Convolutional Networks for Coronary Artery Segmentation in Cardiac CT Angiography

Jelmer M. Wolterink[1,2]([✉]), Tim Leiner[3], and Ivana Išgum[1,2,4]

[1] Department of Biomedical Engineering and Physics, Amsterdam University
Medical Center, Amsterdam, The Netherlands
j.m.wolterink@amsterdamumc.nl
[2] Image Sciences Institute, University Medical Center Utrecht, Utrecht, The
Netherlands
[3] Department of Radiology, University Medical Center Utrecht, Utrecht, The
Netherlands
[4] Department of Radiology and Nuclear Medicine, Amsterdam University Medical
Center, Amsterdam, The Netherlands

**Abstract.** Detection of coronary artery stenosis in coronary CT angiography (CCTA) requires highly personalized surface meshes enclosing the coronary lumen. In this work, we propose to use graph convolutional networks (GCNs) to predict the spatial location of vertices in a tubular surface mesh that segments the coronary artery lumen. Predictions for individual vertex locations are based on local image features as well as on features of neighboring vertices in the mesh graph. The method was trained and evaluated using the publicly available Coronary Artery Stenoses Detection and Quantification Evaluation Framework. Surface meshes enclosing the full coronary artery tree were automatically extracted. A quantitative evaluation on 78 coronary artery segments showed that these meshes corresponded closely to reference annotations, with a Dice similarity coefficient of 0.75/0.73, a mean surface distance of 0.25/0.28 mm, and a Hausdorff distance of 1.53/1.86 mm in healthy/diseased vessel segments. The results showed that inclusion of mesh information in a GCN improves segmentation overlap and accuracy over a baseline model without interaction on the mesh. The results indicate that GCNs allow efficient extraction of coronary artery surface meshes and that the use of GCNs leads to regular and more accurate meshes.

**Keywords:** Graph convolutional networks · Coronary CT angiography · Coronary arteries · Lumen segmentation

## 1 Introduction

Coronary CT angiography (CCTA) images provide valuable information to determine the anatomical or functional severity of coronary artery stenosis [7].

© Springer Nature Switzerland AG 2019
D. Zhang et al. (Eds.): GLMI 2019, LNCS 11849, pp. 62–69, 2019.
https://doi.org/10.1007/978-3-030-35817-4_8

Methods for stenosis detection [5] and blood flow simulation [12] typically require highly personalized coronary lumen surface meshes with sub-voxel accuracy. Because manual segmentation of the full coronary artery tree in a CCTA image would hardly be feasible, such meshes are typically extracted using automatic or semi-automatic methods [2,8,10]. Deep learning-based segmentation could further improve such methods [9], but widely adopted voxel-based segmentation methods do not meet the requirements of down-stream applications, i.e. sub-voxel accuracy and segmentation of the lumen as a contiguous structure.

An alternative to voxel segmentation is to incorporate a shape prior, i.e. to exploit the fact that an individual vessel or vessel segment has a roughly tubular shape. The wall of this tube can be deformed to match the visible lumen in the CCTA image and obtain an accurate segmentation [6]. In one variant of this approach, a tubular surface mesh along the coronary artery centerline is considered and the spatial location of each mesh vertex is predicted so that the surface closely follows the artery wall. Lugauer et al. [10] used probabilistic boosting trees to predict these locations based on steerable image texture features extracted from 2D cross-sectional images. As predictions were made based on 2D cross-sectional information, additional smoothing of the surface mesh was required through graph-cut optimization. Freiman et al. used a similar approach, but enforced smoothness of the obtained surface by penalizing jumps between neighboring vertices [2].

In this work, we propose to directly optimize the location of the tubular surface mesh vertices using graph convolutional networks (GCNs) [3,4]. GCNs are a recent development in deep learning-based medical image analysis, with high potential for graph-based applications in e.g. airway extraction in chest CT [11] and cortical segmentation in brain MR [1]. We consider the vertices on the coronary lumen surface mesh as graph nodes and solve a regression problem for each of these graph nodes. Predictions for vertices depend on local features as well as on internal representations of adjacent vertices on the mesh. Our experiments show that GCNs are well-suited to accurately predict vertex locations for this natural graph representations, and that direct operation on the tubular mesh reduces the need for additional post-processing.

## 2 Data

We included coronary CT angiography (CCTA) images from the training set of the Coronary Artery Stenoses Detection and Quantification Evaluation Framework [5]. This set contains 18 CCTA images acquired on Philips, Siemens, and Toshiba CT scanners. Images had an in-plane resolution of 0.29–0.43 mm$^2$ and a slice spacing of 0.25–0.45 mm. Within the challenge, reference surface meshes were annotated by three observers in a selection of segments in each data set, for a total of 78 coronary artery segments. For each CCTA volume, we automatically extracted centerlines in all volumes using our previously proposed deep learning-based method [13].

# 3   Methods

We propose to use GCNs to obtain a coronary artery surface mesh based on a CCTA image and an (automatically extracted) coronary artery centerline. Figure 1 provides an overview of the proposed method.

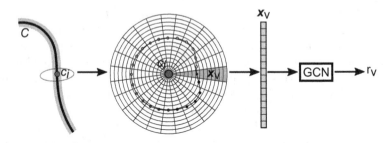

**Fig. 1.** Schematic overview of the proposed method. Given a coronary centerline $C$, rays are cast equiangularly and orthogonally to the centerline at each point $c_i$. Each ray angle corresponds to a vertex $v$ in the luminal surface mesh of which the exact spatial location is determined by $c_i$, an angle $\phi_v$, and the distance $r_v$. Image information along $\mathbf{x}_v$ is used by a GCN that combines this information with that of neighboring vertices to predict $r_v$.

## 3.1   Surface Mesh

The mesh delineating the vessel wall surface is represented by a graph $\mathcal{G}(\mathcal{V}, \mathcal{E})$, with vertices $\mathcal{V}$ and edges $\mathcal{E}$. We assume that the vessel wall is a deformable tube in 3D Euclidean space with known centerline $C$. We constrain the exact spatial location of each vertex to be dependent on only one parameter $r_v$. For each centerline point $c_i$, we determine a 2D cross-sectional plane orthogonal to the centerline direction. Within this cross-sectional plane, equiangularly spaced vertices define a cross-section of the surface mesh. Hence, within the 2D plane, the location of each vertex is defined in polar coordinates $(\phi_v, r_v)$, where $\phi_v$ is fixed. The parameter $r_v$ is defined as the distance to the centerline point $c_i$, and it is this value that we predict using regression.

The combination of all vertices in all cross-sectional planes forms the polygonal lumen surface mesh $\mathcal{G}$. Edges are added between neighboring vertices in cross-sectional planes, and between vertices at the same angle $\phi_v$ in adjacent cross-sectional planes. Four such edges define a quadrilateral mesh face, and each quadrilateral face is further split into two triangular faces. The structure of $\mathcal{G}$ is fixed for a vessel or vessel segment and a GCN is trained to predict the value $r_v$ for each vertex based on information from the image $\mathcal{X}$ encoded in a input vector $\mathbf{x}_v$. In all our experiments, for a vertex $(\phi_v, r_v)$ this input vector contains the image values along a ray cast from the center $c_i$ of the cross-sectional plane at the angle $\phi_v$.

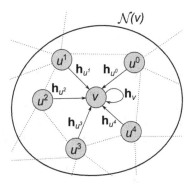

**Fig. 2.** A GCN layer in the proposed method. The graph convolutional network operates on the vertices of the surface mesh and iteratively aggregates information from a vertex $v$ and its neighbors in $\mathcal{N}(v)$ in $\mathbf{h}_v^k$, where $\mathbf{h}_v^0 = \mathbf{x}_v$.

### 3.2 GCN Architecture

We use a graph convolutional network to predict – for each node in the graph – the value of the parameter $r_v$ given the input vector $\mathbf{x}_v$. The GCN consists of layers that aggregate information from neighboring nodes (Fig. 2). By concatenating several such layers, information from a growing neighborhood of nodes in the graph is combined. We use the element-wise mean aggregator as proposed in GraphSAGE [3]. In the $k$-th GCN layer, we aggregate features of vertices $u$ in the neighborhood of vertex $v$, including $v$ itself, to obtain a feature vector $\mathbf{h}_v^k$ for each node. We define $\mathbf{h}_v^0 = \mathbf{x}_v$, i.e. the input to the first GCN layer is the input vector derived from the image $\mathcal{X}$. The aggregation rule is

$$\mathbf{h}_v^k = \sigma \left( \mathbf{W} \cdot \text{MEAN} \left( \{\mathbf{h}_v^{k-1}\} \cup \{\mathbf{h}_u^{k-1}, \forall u \in \mathcal{N}(v)\} \right) \right), \tag{1}$$

where $\sigma$ is an activation function, in our case ReLU. The matrix $\mathbf{W}$ contains trainable weights that determine how features are combined between layers. Different than in GraphSAGE, we do not sample neighbors but use the full available neighborhood. The neighborhood is defined by the edges in $\mathcal{E}$, which are fixed for a given vessel segment or segment.

We use a network with five GCN layers, so that predictions for individual vertices are based on vertices that are at most five steps away on the mesh. The first layer has 32 input features in $\mathbf{x}_v$, while the hidden GCN layers each have 64 nodes. The output layer has 1 node to predict $r_v$. Dropout is used with $p = 0.5$. Given that we train the GCN using individual samples and not with mini-batches, the GCN does not contain batch normalization layers. In total, the GCN network contains 14,567 trainable parameters.

The GCN is trained using a training set consisting of coronary artery segments, each of which is represented by a graph $\mathcal{G}_i$, image information $\mathcal{X}_i$ and reference values $r_v$ for all vertices $v \in V$ in $\mathcal{G}_i$. In each iteration, one segment is randomly selected and the following loss is computed

$$\mathcal{L} = \frac{1}{|\mathcal{V}|} \sum_{v \in \mathcal{V}} |r_v^3 - f(\mathbf{x}_v)^3|, \tag{2}$$

where $\mathcal{V}$ is the set of vertices in $\mathcal{G}_i$ and $f(\mathbf{x}_v)$ is the distance to the centerline predicted by the GCN. Distance values are cubed in the loss function to better guarantee correspondence between automatically segmented and reference vessel volumes. We use no additional regularization on the values of $r_v$. After training, the trained GCN can be applied to a new input graph and image data $(\mathcal{G}', \mathcal{X}')$.

**Table 1.** Quantitative results on the training set of the Coronary Artery Stenoses Detection and Quantification Evaluation Framework. Dice similarity coefficient (DSC), mean surface distance (MSD) and Hausdorff distance (HD) values are shown for human observers as reported in [5], previously proposed methods, the proposed graph convolutional network (GCN), and a multi-layer perceptron (MLP).

| Method | DSC | | MSD (mm) | | HD (mm) | |
|---|---|---|---|---|---|---|
| | Healthy | Diseased | Healthy | Diseased | Healthy | Diseased |
| Expert 1 | 0.74 | 0.79 | 0.26 | 0.26 | 3.61 | 3.29 |
| Expert 2 | 0.66 | 0.73 | 0.25 | 0.31 | 3.00 | 2.70 |
| Expert 3 | 0.80 | 0.76 | 0.23 | 0.24 | 3.25 | 3.07 |
| Lugauer et al. [10] | 0.77 | 0.75 | 0.32 | 0.27 | 2.79 | 1.96 |
| Freiman et al. [2] | 0.69 | 0.74 | 0.49 | 0.28 | 1.69 | 1.22 |
| Mohr et al. [5] | 0.75 | 0.73 | 0.45 | 0.29 | 3.73 | 1.87 |
| Graph convolutional network (GCN) | 0.75 | 0.73 | 0.25 | 0.28 | 1.53 | 1.86 |
| Multi-layer perceptron (MLP) | 0.67 | 0.69 | 0.32 | 0.31 | 1.59 | 1.84 |

## 4   Experiments and Results

The method was implemented in Python using PyTorch and the Deep Graph Library (DGL)[1]. We performed leave-one-patient-out cross-validation experiments on the training set of the Coronary Artery Stenoses Detection and Quantification Evaluation Framework. The networks were trained using annotations by all three observers. Coronary centerlines were automatically extracted using the method proposed in [13] and resampled to 0.5 mm resolution. In all our experiments, we defined 24 discrete values for vertex angles $\phi$ between rays (Fig. 1) and the resolution of input signals $\mathbf{x}_v$ was 0.1 mm. Each ray consisted of 32 input features for a circular field of view of 3.2 mm. Image values were clipped at 0 and 1000 HU to normalize for surrounding low-density tissue, air and hyperdense calcifications. We observed that this circumvents the need for explicit calcium removal steps such as proposed in [10].

Networks were trained end-to-end and parameters were optimized using the Adam optimizer with a learning rate of 0.001. We trained each network for 50,000 iterations. In each iteration, one training sample $(\mathcal{G}_i, \mathcal{X}_i)$ was randomly selected and the loss in Eq. 2 was evaluated. To improve training stability, gradients

---

[1] https://www.dgl.ai/.

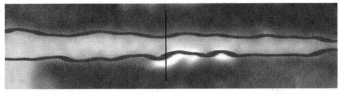

**Fig. 3.** Example segmentation, showing how the GCN has learned to exclude coronary artery calcium from its segmentation. The figure on the left shows the cross-sectional plane indicated by a black line on the straightened multi-planar reconstruction on the right.

were accumulated for 10 iterations, after which the loss was back-propagated and parameters were updated. Experiments were performed using an NVIDIA Titan X GPU with 12 GB of memory. Training of one GCN took around 20 min, while segmentation of all coronary arteries in a CCTA image took around 45 s, including fully automatic coronary centerline extraction [13].

We evaluated the quality of the obtained segmentations using the online platform of the Coronary Artery Stenoses Detection and Quantification Evaluation Framework [5]. Dice similarity coefficients (DSC) were determined based on 2D cross-sectional segmentations obtained along the centerline. In addition, the mean surface distance (MSD) and Hausdorff distance (HD) were computed between automatic and reference meshes. Table 1 lists results the three expert observers in [5], state-of-the-art methods evaluated on the same 78 segments in 18 CCTA images, and the GCN. Results are shown separately for healthy and diseased segments. The results indicate that the GCN obtains results that are comparable to those obtained by other methods in terms of all three metrics, and that like other automatic methods, the GCN outperforms human experts in terms of Hausdorff distance. Figure 3 shows an example segmentation in an artery with coronary artery disease. The segmentation follows the inner vessel wall and excludes coronary artery calcification.

In addition, we performed experiments to determine the value of GCN layers over traditional fully-connected layers. We removed the ability to propagate values between neighboring nodes on the surface mesh from the layer in Eq. 1. The result is a standard fully-connected layer with $\mathbf{h}_v^k = \sigma\left(\mathbf{W} \cdot \mathbf{h}_v^{k-1}\right)$. Like in Eq. 1, this layer only has trainable parameters in $\mathbf{W}$. We built a network which contained only fully-connected layers, i.e. a multi-layer perceptron (MLP) and compared this network to the GCN. Both networks contained 14,567 trainable parameters and both networks were trained in the same manner. Figure 4 shows an example of a left coronary artery tree segmented using the MLP or the GCN. By combining information from neighboring vertices on the surface, the GCN intrinsically leads to smoother segmentations than the MLP. Quantitative results in Table 1 show that the inclusion of GCN layers in the network architecture leads to substantially higher overlap (DSC) and better accuracy (MSD).

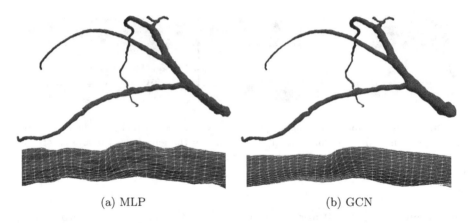

(a) MLP                              (b) GCN

**Fig. 4.** Left coronary artery tree segmented using (a) multi-layer perceptron (MLP) and (b) graph convolutional network (GCN). By including information from neighboring vertices, the GCN leads to a smoother surface than the MLP.

## 5   Discussion and Conclusions

We have proposed a method based on graph convolutional networks for coronary artery segmentation in cardiac CT angiography. Experiments using a publicly available framework showed competitive performance on segmentation of individual artery segments. To the best of our knowledge, this work is among the first applications of GCNs in medical image analysis, following recent works on airway extraction in chest CT [11] and cortical segmentation in brain MR [1]. The method obtained accurate results in both healthy and diseased vessels. Given that segmentations meet requirements of down-stream applications, i.e. contiguous segmentations with sub-voxel accuracy, future work could include validation of the obtained segmentations for anatomical and functional stenosis detection.

We found that when using the same experimental settings on the same data, the inclusion of GCN-layers substantially improved segmentation performance over a baseline network using only fully-connected layers. This indicates that the GCN successfully uses information from a local neighborhood on the surface mesh to predict the location of an individual mesh vertex. Moreover, the method does not require post-processing steps such as conditional random fields, or additional regularization terms to smooth the obtained surface meshes, but directly generates a smooth surface mesh.

A limitation of the mean aggregator used in this work is its invariance to the spatial relation between a vertex and its neighbors. In future work, we will investigate the use of edge features in addition to the node features used in this work. Alternatively, information from neighboring vertices could be combined in different ways, such as convolution in cross-sectional planes. An additional limitation that this work shares with other methods for coronary lumen segmentation [2,6,10] is the dependence on a coronary artery centerline. In preliminary experiments, we found that the exact location of this coronary artery centerline can lead to noticeable differences in segmentation accuracy. We will further investigate this in future work.

In conclusion, GCN-based segmentation of coronary arteries in CCTA is feasible and accurate.

**Acknowledgements.** P15-26, Project 2, Dutch Technology Foundation with participation of Philips Healthcare.

# References

1. Cucurull, G., et al.: Convolutional neural networks for mesh-based parcellation of the cerebral cortex. In: Medical Imaging with Deep Learning (MIDL) (2018)
2. Freiman, M., et al.: Improving CCTA-based lesions' hemodynamic significance assessment by accounting for partial volume modeling in automatic coronary lumen segmentation. Med. Phys. **44**(3), 1040–1049 (2017)
3. Hamilton, W., Ying, Z., Leskovec, J.: Inductive representation learning on large graphs. In: Advances in Neural Information Processing Systems (NIPS), pp. 1024–1034 (2017)
4. Kipf, T.N., Welling, M.: Semi-supervised classification with graph convolutional networks. In: International Conference on Learning Representations (ICLR) (2017)
5. Kirişli, H., et al.: Standardized evaluation framework for evaluating coronary artery stenosis detection, stenosis quantification and lumen segmentation algorithms in computed tomography angiography. Med. Image Anal. **17**(8), 859–876 (2013)
6. Lee, M.C.H., Petersen, K., Pawlowski, N., Glocker, B., Schaap, M.: Tetris: template transformer networks for image segmentation with shape priors. IEEE Trans. Med. Imag. (2019). https://doi.org/10.1109/TMI.2019.2905990
7. Leipsic, J., et al.: SCCT guidelines for the interpretation and reporting of coronary CT angiography: a report of the society of cardiovascular computed tomography guidelines committee. J. Cardiovasc. Comput. Tomogr. **8**(5), 342–358 (2014)
8. Lesage, D., Angelini, E.D., Bloch, I., Funka-Lea, G.: A review of 3D vessel lumen segmentation techniques: models, features and extraction schemes. Med. Image Anal. **13**(6), 819–845 (2009)
9. Litjens, G., et al.: A survey on deep learning in medical image analysis. Med. Image Anal. **42**, 60–88 (2017)
10. Lugauer, F., Zheng, Y., Hornegger, J., Kelm, B.M.: Precise lumen segmentation in coronary computed tomography angiography. In: Menze, B., et al. (eds.) MCV 2014. LNCS, vol. 8848, pp. 137–147. Springer, Cham (2014). https://doi.org/10.1007/978-3-319-13972-2_13
11. Selvan, R., Kipf, T., Welling, M., Pedersen, J.H., Petersen, J., de Bruijne, M.: Extraction of airways using graph neural networks. In: Medical Imaging with Deep Learning (MIDL) (2018)
12. Taylor, C.A., Fonte, T.A., Min, J.K.: Computational fluid dynamics applied to cardiac computed tomography for noninvasive quantification of fractional flow reserve: scientific basis. J. Am. Coll. Cardiol. **61**(22), 2233–2241 (2013)
13. Wolterink, J.M., van Hamersvelt, R.W., Viergever, M.A., Leiner, T., Išgum, I.: Coronary artery centerline extraction in cardiac CT angiography using a CNN-based orientation classifier. Med. Image Anal. **51**, 46–60 (2019)

# Triplet Graph Convolutional Network for Multi-scale Analysis of Functional Connectivity Using Functional MRI

Dongren Yao[1,2,3], Mingxia Liu[3(✉)], Mingliang Wang[3,4], Chunfeng Lian[3], Jie Wei[3,5], Li Sun[6], Jing Sui[1,2(✉)], and Dinggang Shen[3(✉)]

[1] Brainnetome Center & National Laboratory of Pattern Recognition,
Institute of Automation, Chinese Academy of Sciences, Beijing 100190, China
jing.sui@nlpr.ia.ac.cn
[2] University of Chinese Academy of Sciences, Beijing 100049, China
[3] Department of Radiology and BRIC, University of North Carolina at Chapel Hill,
Chapel Hill, NC 27599, USA
{mxliu,dgshen}@med.unc.edu
[4] College of Computer Science and Technology,
Nanjing University of Aeronautics and Astronautics, Nanjing 210016, China
[5] School of Computer Science, Northwestern Polytechnical University,
Xi'an 710072, China
[6] National Clinical Research Center for Mental Disorders &
Key Laboratory of Mental Health, Ministry of Health, Peking University,
Beijing 100191, China

**Abstract.** Brain functional connectivity (FC) derived from resting-state functional MRI (rs-fMRI) data has become a powerful approach to measure and map brain activity. Using fMRI data, graph convolutional network (GCN) has recently shown its superiority in learning discriminative representations of brain FC networks. However, existing studies typically utilize one specific template to partition the brain into multiple regions-of-interest (ROIs) for constructing FCs, which may limit the analysis to a single spatial scale (i.e., a fixed graph) determined by the template. Also, previous methods usually ignore the underlying high-order (e.g., triplet) association among subjects. To this end, we propose a multi-scale triplet graph convolutional network (MTGCN) for brain functional connectivity analysis with rs-fMRI data. Specifically, we first employ multi-scale templates for coarse-to-fine ROI parcellation to construct multi-scale FCs for each subject. We then develop a triplet GCN (TGCN) model to learn multi-scale graph representations of brain FC networks, followed by a weighted fusion scheme for classification. Experimental results on 1,218 subjects suggest the efficacy or our method.

## 1 Introduction

Resting-state functional magnetic resonance imaging (fMRI) provides a powerful tool for capturing brain functional connectivity even between spatially-remote

© Springer Nature Switzerland AG 2019
D. Zhang et al. (Eds.): GLMI 2019, LNCS 11849, pp. 70–78, 2019.
https://doi.org/10.1007/978-3-030-35817-4_9

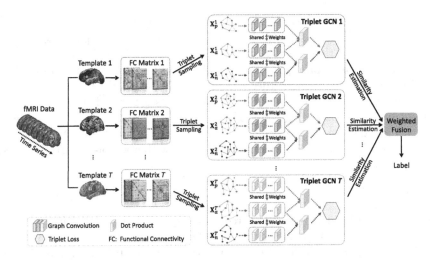

**Fig. 1.** Illustration of our Multi-scale Triplet Graph Convolutional Network (MTGCN). Multiple templates are used for coarse-to-fine parcellation of brain regions and construction of functional connectivity matrices/graphs. Each triplet GCN (TGCN) inputs a triplet of three graphs (e.g., $\mathbf{X}_a^1$, $\mathbf{X}_p^1$, and $\mathbf{X}_n^1$) with the same architecture but different signals, and outputs similarity among the triplet. A weighted fusion scheme is used to combine estimated labels generated from multi-scale TGCNs for classification.

brain regions. Recent studies have shown that fMRI-based analysis of brain connectivity is effective in helping understand the pathology of brain diseases, such as autism spectrum disorder (ASD) and attention-deficit/hyperactivity disorder (ADHD) [1,2]. Since functional disorder (e.g., abnormality or dysfunction between multiple regions) of brain networks has been found in these diseases [3], many studies have focused on using fMRI-based brain connectivity networks to explore potential disorder patterns of brain diseases characterized between patients and healthy controls (HCs). In fMRI-based studies, each brain can be represented as an undirected or directed graph/network containing functionally interconnected regions-of-interests (ROIs), with each ROI treated as a vertex.

Convolutional neural networks (CNNs) have shown their superiority in analyzing functional connectivity (FC) networks [4], but ignoring the important topology information. Graph convolutional neural networks (GCNs) integrate graph convolutional layers to explicitly capture topological information, which can learn useful representations of brain FC networks for brain disease classification [5]. However, existing GCN-based methods usually use one specific template for brain ROI parcellation, which limits the analysis to a single spatial scale (i.e., a fixed graph) determined by the template. Also, previous studies simply model the pairwise relationship between graphs/subjects, without considering the triplet similarity among subjects.

To address these issues, we propose a multi-scale triplet graph convolutional network (MTGCN) for brain functional connectivity analysis with rs-fMRI data, as illustrated in Fig. 1. Specifically, we first apply multi-scale templates to each subject for generating multi-scale FC networks under different spatial scales and ROI definitions. We then develop a triplet GCN (TGCN) model to automatically extract multi-scale graph representations of brain FC networks, incorporated by the triplet similarity among subjects (e.g., $\mathbf{X}_a^1$, $\mathbf{X}_p^1$, and $\mathbf{X}_n^1$). A weighted fusion scheme is finally used to combine estimated labels generated from multi-scale TGCNs for brain disease classification. Experiments results on 1,218 subjects from two real datasets demonstrate the effectiveness of our MTGCN method in ASD and Adult ADHD identification, compared with state-of-the-art methods.

## 2   Method

**Multi-scale FC Network:** To overcome the spatial limitation of using only a single template for ROI parcellation and FC construction, we employ $T$ $(T \geq 2)$ templates (with coarse-to-fine ROI definitions) to generate multi-scale FC networks for each subject. Given a specific template, one can construct a graph (i.e., FC matrix) for each subject, where each node represents an ROI, and the connectivity between a pair of ROIs is represented by the Pearson correlation of their mean time series signals. That is, a *fully-connected* graph can be constructed for each subject, with each vertex connected with all the other vertices.

In this work, we would like to employ spectral GCN for analyzing brain function connectivity. Graph convolution is a type of Laplacian smoothing that computes the new features of a vertex as the weighted average of itself and its neighbors [6]. Using fully-connected network as graph topology, the smoothing operation will make features of those 'connected' vertices similar, thus failing to capture the *node-centralized local topology* via spectral GCNs. Therefore, we propose to construct a KNN graph (other than a fully-connected graph), by connecting each vertex with its $k$-nearest neighbors to model the node-centralized local topology. Also, we aim to capture shared graph topology among all studied subjects, and thus need to construct a KNN graph at the *group-level* (rather than subject-level). Specifically, we first calculate the mean FC matrix of all training subjects in a template space, and then construct a KNN graph by connecting each vertex with its $k$-nearest neighbors (measured by the Pearson correlation). Hence, the graph topology (reflected by vertices and their connectivity) of such a group-level KNN graph is shared by all subjects. For a subject, the signal of each vertex in a KNN graph is represented by an $n$-dimensional vector (i.e., the Pearson correlations between this vertex and all the other ones) corresponding to the $n$-th row of FC matrix, and $n$ is the number of vertices/ROIs defined by the template. Hence, we can represent each subject by both its graph topology and vertex features/signals in specific template space. Given $T$ templates, we can generate $T$ KNN graphs, with each graph denoting the group-level topology of FC networks at a specific spatial scale.

**Triplet GCN:** Graph convolutional network (GCN) generalizes traditional convolutional neural network from Euclidean data (e.g., 2D or 3D images) to the non-Euclidean domain (e.g., graphs and manifolds), and has been emerging as a promising method for graph mining [7]. Denote a graph as $\mathbf{X} = (\mathcal{V}, \mathcal{E})$, where $\mathcal{V}$ is the set of vertices and $\mathcal{E}$ is the set of edges. Also, an adjacency matrix $\mathbf{A} = [a_{ij}] \in \mathbb{R}^{n \times n}$ encodes the connectivity among vertices, with the element $a_{ij}$ indicating whether the $i$-th and $j$-th vertices are connected ($a_{ij} = 1$) or not ($a_{ij} = 0$). Denote $\mathbf{D} = diag(d_1, d_2, \cdots, d_n)$ as a degree matrix, with each element $d_i = \sum_j a_{ij}$ denoting the number of edges connected to the $i$-th vertex. Spectral GCN defines the convolution by decomposing a graph signal $s \in \mathbb{R}^n$ (defined on the vertex of graph $\mathbf{X}$) in the spectral domain. Then the signal $s$ will be processed by a spectral filter $\delta_\theta$ with the first order polynomial of ChebyNet [8], instead of explicitly computing the Laplacian eigenvectors. To reduce the number of parameters (i.e., $\theta_0$ and $\theta_1$), the spectral GCN model assumes that $\theta = \theta_0 = -\theta_1$, and the graph convolution is correspondingly defined as:

$$\delta_\theta * s \approx \theta_0 s - \theta_1 \mathbf{D}^{-\frac{1}{2}} \mathbf{A} \mathbf{D}^{-\frac{1}{2}} s = \theta(\mathbf{I}_n + \mathbf{D}^{-\frac{1}{2}} \mathbf{A} \mathbf{D}^{-\frac{1}{2}})s \qquad (1)$$

where $\mathbf{I} \in \mathbb{R}^{n \times n}$ is an identity matrix. With each convolution defined in Eq. 1 followed by a non-linear activation function (i.e., ReLU), one can generate a simple and flexible spectral GCN by stacking multiple convolutional layers.

Recently, a method based on spectral GCN has been applied to analyze brain FC network for ASD classification, in which two GCN models were constructed to measure the similarity between paired graphs [5]. However, this method only models the pairwise relationship of graphs, ignoring the high-order (e.g., triplet) association among graphs/subjects. To mine the potential high-order similarity between *inter-class* and *intra-class* subjects, we develop a triplet GCN (TGCN) module containing 3 parallel subnetworks (with 3 graph convolutional layers), and these subnetworks share the same network parameters. As shown in Fig. 1, the input of the $t$-th TGCN module is a triplet $\{\mathbf{X}_a^t, \mathbf{X}_p^t, \mathbf{X}_n^t\}$ containing an *anchor* subject $\mathbf{X}_a^t$, a *positive* sample $\mathbf{X}_p$, and a *negative* sample $\mathbf{X}_n^t$, where $\mathbf{X}_a^t$ and $\mathbf{X}_p^t$ are samples from the same category and $\mathbf{X}_n^t$ is selected from a different category. Note that samples in each triplet share the same graph architecture but represented by different vertex signals. Using TGCN, we encourage that the learned graph representations of the anchor and positive samples belonging to the same class (e.g., ASD patient) are similar, while representations of the anchor and negative samples belonging to a different category (e.g., HC) are dissimilar. The loss function to train the $t$-th TGCN module is defined as

$$L_t = \sum_{m=1}^{M} \left[ \| g_t(\mathbf{X}_{a,m}^t) - g_t(\mathbf{X}_{p,m}^t) \|_2^2 - \| g_t(\mathbf{X}_{a,m}^t) - g_t(\mathbf{X}_{n,m}^t) \|_2^2 + \lambda_{trp} \right]_+ \qquad (2)$$

where $M$ is the number of input triplets, $[\cdot]_+ = max\,(s, 0)$, $g_t(\cdot)$ denotes the embedding generated by the $t$-th TGCN module, and the margin $\lambda_{trp}$ is used to enforce the distance between the anchor and negative samples. The output of TGCN is the similarity of the anchor $\mathbf{X}_a$ belonging to a specific category. Given $T$ templates, a multi-scale network containing $T$ TGCN modules can be obtained (see Fig. 1), with each one corresponding to a specific template.

**Weighted Fusion:** With a single-scale TGCN based on a specific template, we can measure the triplet similarity between an anchor sample and two samples from two different categories. In this work, we hypothesize that *similar subjects tend to remain similar in multi-scale template spaces*. With this assumption, the outputs of $T$ TGCN modules are fused via a weighted fusion strategy as follows:

$$L_{Fusion} = \sum\nolimits_{t=1}^{T} \gamma_t L_t \qquad (3)$$

where $\gamma_t = \omega_t / \sum_{t=1}^{T} \omega_t$ represents the weight of the $t$-th TGCN module, and $\omega_t$ is the classification accuracy achieved by the $t$-th TGCN on the training data.

**Implementation:** In the *training* stage, for each training subject (anchor) $\mathbf{X}_a$, we randomly select a pair of positive and negative subjects from training set to generate a triplet set $\{\mathbf{X}_{a,q}, \mathbf{X}_{p,q}, \mathbf{X}_{n,q}\}_{q=1}^{Q}$. Due to limited training subjects, such random selection process is repeated $Q = 25$ to augment samples. In the *testing* stage, for a testing subject (anchor), we first randomly select 5 pairs of positive and negative subjects from training set [9], yielding 5 triplets as the input of MTGCN. The prediction results of these 5 triplets are ensembled to get a final label for the testing subject. Such process is used to suppress the bias introduced by random selection of positive and negative training subjects.

## 3    Experiment and Results

**Subjects and Image Pre-processing:** Two datasets with resting-state fMRI data are used for performance evaluation in this work. The first one is an Autism dataset with 485 ASD patients and 544 healthy controls (HCs) from 34 imaging sites in ABIDE-I and ABIDE-II, with considerable data distribution diversity. The largest site contains 101 subjects, while the smallest one only has 11 subjects. Another is an Attention Hyperactivity Deficit Disorder (ADHD) dataset, containing 112 ADHD patients and 77 age-matched HCs recruited from the Sixth Hospital of Peking University (PKU6).

Each fMRI scan was pre-processed using the Data Processing Assistant for Resting-State fMRI (DPARSFA). The processing pipeline is as follows: (1) discarding the first ten volumes, (2) slice timing correction, (3) head motion correction, (4) normalization with an EPI template in the MNI space, resampling to $3 \times 3 \times 3\,mm^3$ resolution, (5) spatial smoothing using a 4 mm full width half maximum Gaussian kernel, (6) linear detrend and temporal band-pass filtering (0.01 Hz–0.1 Hz), (7) regression out nuisance signals of head motion parameters, white matter, cerebrospinal fluid (CSF), and global signals. The registered fMRI volumes were partitioned into ROIs according to different templates. For the Autism dataset, we use preprocessed data, i.e., FC networks constructed on $T = 3$ predefined templates, including Bootstrap Analysis of Stable Cluster parcellation with 122 ROIs (BASC122) and 197 ROIs (BASC197), and Power Template with 264 ROIs (Power264). For the ADHD dataset, we preprocessed the fMRI time series data using $T = 2$ templates, i.e., Automated Anatomical

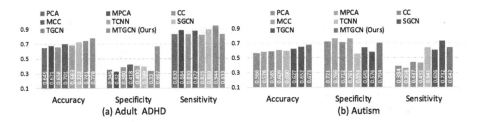

**Fig. 2.** Results achieved by different methods in (a) Adult ADHD vs. HC classification and (b) ASD vs. HC classification.

Labelling (AAL) with 116 ROIs and Brainnetome template (Brainnetome) with 273 ROIs, aiming to partition the brain in a coarse-to-fine manner. In each template space, we extracted the mean time series within each ROI to construct the original FC network/matrix for each subject, and the connectivity was represented by the Pearson correlation coefficient between pairs of ROI-based time series (normalized to $z$ score using Fisher transformation). Then, the constructed FC matrix was used for the construction of multi-scale KNN graphs in MTGCN.

**Experimental Setting:** Two classification tasks are performed in the experiments, i.e., (1) ASD vs. HC classification and (2) Adult ADHD vs. HC classification. We use 60% of the data for training, 10% for validation, and the remaining 30% for testing, and such process is repeated 5 times. Three evaluation metrics are used, including classification accuracy, sensitivity, and specificity. We first compare MTGCN with 2 baseline methods and their multi-template variants, i.e., (1) single-template Principal Component Analysis (**PCA**) with a random forest classifier; (2) single-template clustering coefficient (**CC**) with RF as the classifier; (3) multi-template PCA (**MPCA**); and (4) multi-template CC (**MCC**). In PCA, PCA is used for dimension reduction based on the original FC matrix of each subject in a template space, where the number of components is chosen from 3 to 50, with the step size of 1 via two-fold inner CV. In CC, CC features measure the clustering degree of each node in a graph/matrix in a template space. The number of trees in RF is chosen from [50, 200] (step size: 10), and the depth of each tree is selected from [1, 6] (step size: 1).

We further compare MTGCN with two state-of-the-art methods, i.e., (1) CNN with our proposed triplet representation learning strategy (**TCNN**), and (2) Siamese GCN (**SGCN**) [5]. To validate our multi-scale learning strategy, we further compare MTGCN with its single-scale variant (**TGCN**) using one template. Similar to MTGCN, TCNN inputs the original FC matrix of each subject and aims to learn graph embeddings by measuring the similarity among three subjects, and the network contains 3 convolutional layers and two fully connected layers. These 3 convolutional layers in TCNN have 4, 8, and 8 channels, and the corresponding kernels have the sizes of $5 \times 5$, $4 \times 4$, and $3 \times 3$, respectively. The SGCN method [5] can learn graph representations of brain FC networks. For a fair comparison, both SGCN and TGCN methods share the same GCN architec-

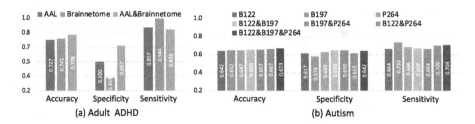

**Fig. 3.** Influence of templates on the performance of our MTGCN method in (a) Adult ADHD vs. HC classification and (b) ASD vs. HC classification. The symbol & represents template combination. B122: BASC122; B197: BASC197; P264: Power264.

ture as MTGCN. Such process is used to suppress the bias introduced by random selection of positive and negative subjects. In MTGCN and TGCN, the $k$ value is chosen from $[5, 30]$ with the step size of 5 for KNN graph construction, and the parameter $\lambda_{trp}$ in Eq. (2) is set as 5 empirically. Four deep methods (i.e., TCNN, SGCN, TGCN and MTGCN) are optimized using the ADAM algorithm (learning rate: 0.001; epoch: 100; mini-batch size: 50). Since five competing methods (i.e., PCA, CC, TCNN, SGCN, and TGCN) can use only one template, we perform template selection on the validation data. For MPCA and MCC, the same multiple templates are used as those in our MTGCN method.

**Results:** The disease classification results are reported in Fig. 2. From Fig. 2, one can find several interesting observations. *First*, four deep learning methods, i.e., TCNN, SGCN, TGCN and MTGCN that learn task-oriented features of FC networks, consistently achieve better performance than four methods (i.e., PCA, CC, MPCA and MCC) using handcrafted features. *Second*, GCN methods (i.e., SGCN, TGCN, and MTGCN) that explicitly model graph topology generally outperform the TCNN method, suggesting the usefulness of mining graph topology of FC networks to boost the classification performance. *Besides*, compared with SGCN based on the pairwise relationship among subjects, our MTGCN method that models the triplet relationship achieves at least 5% improvement (w.r.t., accuracy) in both datasets. It implies that modeling the high-order (e.g., triplet) relationship among subjects boosts the classification results. *Furthermore*, MTGCN usually yields better performance than its single-template variant (i.e., TGCN), while MPCA and MCC using multiple templates outperforms their single-template versions (i.e., PCA and CC). This implies that the efficacy of our multi-scale learning strategy using multiple templates for ROI partition.

**Discussion:** We further analyze the effect of different templates and template combinations used in MTGCN, with results shown in Fig. 3. The Adult ADHD dataset has two templates and 3 combinations, while the Autism dataset has 3 templates and 7 template combinations. Figure 3 suggests that using multi-scale templates in MTGCN usually yields better performance, compared with

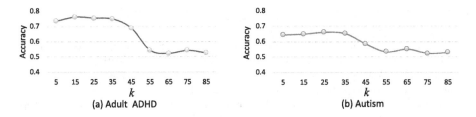

**Fig. 4.** Influence of the parameter $k$ for constructing KNN graphs on the performance of MTGCN in (a) Adult ADHD vs. HC classification and (b) ASD vs. HC classification.

that using a single template. We further analyze the influence of $k$ in KNN graph construction in MTGCN, with results given in Fig. 4. Figure 4 suggests that MTGCN can achieve good results in both datasets when the value of $k$ is within the range $[15, 35]$, and using larger $k$ values (e.g., $>45$) in MTGCN will degrade the performance. The possible reason is that MTGCN cannot focus on the node-centralized local topology when using a too large value of $k$. As the future work, we plan to use unified templates on these 2 datasets for further analysis.

## 4    Conclusion

We proposed a multi-scale triplet graph convolutional network (MTGCN) for fMRI-based brain disease diagnosis. We first constructed multi-scale functional connectivity networks for each subject based on multiple templates (with different ROI partitions). We then designed a multi-scale triplet GCN (TGCN) model to learn graph representation for each subject, followed by a weighted fusion strategy to fuse the outputs of multiple TGCNs for classification. Experimental results on two real fMRI datasets suggest the efficacy of MTGCN.

## References

1. Zhang, D., Huang, J., Jie, B., Du, J., Tu, L., Liu, M.: Ordinal pattern: a new descriptor for brain connectivity networks. IEEE Trans. Med. Imaging **37**(7), 1711–1722 (2018)
2. Lian, C., et al.: Multi-channel multi-scale fully convolutional network for 3D perivascular spaces segmentation in 7T MR images. Med. Image Anal. **46**, 106–117 (2018)
3. Norman, L.J., et al.: Structural and functional brain abnormalities in attention-deficit/hyperactivity disorder and obsessive-compulsive disorder: a comparative meta-analysis. JAMA Psychiatry **73**(8), 815–825 (2016)
4. Zhao, Y., et al.: Automatic recognition of fMRI-derived functional networks using 3-D convolutional neural networks. IEEE Trans. Biomed. Eng. **65**(9), 1975–1984 (2018)
5. Ktena, S.I., et al.: Metric learning with spectral graph convolutions on brain connectivity networks. NeuroImage **169**, 431–442 (2018)

6. Li, Q., Han, Z., Wu, X.M.: Deeper insights into graph convolutional networks for semi-supervised learning. In: AAAI (2018)
7. Wu, Z., Pan, S., Chen, F., Long, G., Zhang, C., Yu, P.S.: A comprehensive survey on graph neural networks. arXiv preprint: arXiv:1901.00596 (2019)
8. Kipf, T.N., Welling, M.: Semi-supervised classification with graph convolutional networks. arXiv preprint: arXiv:1609.02907 (2016)
9. Wu, C.Y., Manmatha, R., Smola, A.J., Krahenbuhl, P.: Sampling matters in deep embedding learning. In: ICCV, pp. 2840–2848 (2017)

# Multi-scale Graph Convolutional Network for Mild Cognitive Impairment Detection

Shuangzhi Yu, Guanghui Yue, Ahmed Elazab, Xuegang Song, Tianfu Wang,
and Baiying Lei[✉]

National-Regional Key Technology Engineering Laboratory for Medical Ultrasound,
Guangdong Key Laboratory for Biomedical Measurements and Ultrasound Imaging,
School of Biomedical Engineering, Health Science Center,
Shenzhen University, Shenzhen 518060, China
leiby@szu.edu.cn

**Abstract.** Mild cognitive impairment (MCI) is an early stage of Alzheimer's disease (AD), which is also the best time for treatment. However, existing methods only consider neuroimaging features learned from group relationships instead of the subjects' individual features. Such methods ignore demographic relationships (i.e., non-image information). In this paper, we propose a novel method based on multi-scale graph convolutional network (MS-GCN) via inception module, which combines image and non-image information for MCI detection. Specifically, since the brain has the characteristics of high-order interactions, we first analyze the dynamic high-order features of resting functional magnetic resonance imaging (rs-fMRI) time series and construct a dynamic high-order brain functional connectivity network (DH-FCN). To get more effective features and further improve the detection performance, we extract the local weighted clustering coefficients from the original DH-FCN. Then, gender and age information are combined with the neuroimaging data to build a graph. Finally, we perform the detection using the MS-GCN, and validate the proposed method on the Alzheimer's Disease Neuroimaging Initiative (ADNI) dataset. The experimental results demonstrate that our proposed method can achieve remarkable MCI detection performance.

**Keywords:** Multi-scale graph convolutional network · Mild cognitive impairment detection · rs-fMRI · Dynamic high-order brain functional connectivity network

## 1 Introduction

Alzheimer's disease (AD) is an irreversible chronic neurodegenerative disorder, characterized by clinical symptom such as memory and cognitive abilities decline. In addition,

This work was supported partly by National Natural Science Foundation of China (Nos. 61871274, 61801305 and 81571758), National Natural Science Foundation of Guangdong Province (No. 2017A030313377), Guangdong Pearl River Talents Plan (2016ZT06S220), Shenzhen Peacock Plan (Nos. KQTD2016053112051497 and KQTD2015033016 104926), and Shenzhen Key Basic Research Project (Nos. JCYJ2017 0413152804728, JCYJ20180507184647636, JCYJ20170818142347251 and JCYJ20170818094109846).

© Springer Nature Switzerland AG 2019
D. Zhang et al. (Eds.): GLMI 2019, LNCS 11849, pp. 79–87, 2019.
https://doi.org/10.1007/978-3-030-35817-4_10

AD causes great suffering to the patient and brings a heavy burden to society [1]. Mild cognitive impairment (MCI) is a prodromal stage of AD, which is also the best time for treatment. A study reports that the annual conversion rate of MCI to AD is as high as 10–15%, while the annual conversion rate of normal control subject to AD is only 1–2% [2]. MCI patients after cognitive training and rehabilitation treatment can delay the progress to AD and some can recover. Therefore, accurate detection of the early MCI is very important to delay the occurrence and development of the disease.

For the MCI detection, resting-state functional MRI (rs-fMRI) [3] has been widely used since it can reflect the activity and connection pattern of brain as well as the topological properties of brain network. Recently, functional connectivity networks (FCNs) have been widely used in analyzing rs-fMRI for the brain diagnosis task. For example, Bullmore et al. [4] constructed FCNs based on rs-fMRI correlation of whole brain time series, it provides a new perspective for brain network analysis. Wee et al. [5] constructed a FCN by group-constrained sparse learning, and achieved good performance in the classification of MCI. Hart et al. [6] built a novel longitudinal FCN model using a variance component approach, which can estimate and draw inference on the group differences in FCNs. However, the conventional FCNs have limitations since it assumed that coupling between brain systems is constant, which fails to consider changes in brain networks over time.

After the brain network construction, the following FCN analysis is of vital for the MCI detection. Recently, graph theory has achieved good performance in FCNs analysis. However, most existing methods fail to accommodate the graph structure and discard information that could be beneficial for further classification or regression analyses based on these similarities. By contrast, graph convolutional networks (GCNs) provide a versatile manner for integration of image and non-image modalities in disease prediction. For example, Parisot et al. [7] exploited GCNs for autism spectrum disorder and AD prediction, and the populations are represented as a sparse graph. GCN's nodes are associated with image-based feature vectors, while phenotypic information is integrated as edge weights. Ktena et al. [8] proposed to learn a graph similarity metric using a siamese GCNs in a supervised setting. However, the above related work usually utilized constant kernel size as filters, which have limited performance due to the uninformative and ineffective features [9].

Motivated by the aforementioned works, in this paper, we construct a novel framework based on MS-GCN for the MCI detection. Compared to the competing works, our method has the following contributions: (1) To reflect the topological properties of brain, we utilize the sub-series rs-fMRI as the input to build the dynamic sub-networks by a sliding window approach. By considering the topographical similarities between each pair of the sub-networks, we can get the dynamic high-order FCNs (DH-FCNs). Meanwhile, we extract the local weighted clustering coefficients from DH-FCNs and combine them with phenotypic data to construct a graph. (2) To increase the width of the network and the adaptability of the network, we utilize the MS-GCNs by designing filters with different kernel sizes (i.e., Inception module) instead of the common GCNs for the MCI detection task. Evaluated on the public Alzheimer's Disease Neuroimaging Initiative (ADNI), our method has achieved an accuracy of 87.5%, 89.02%, 79.27% for the detection tasks of early MCI (EMCI) vs. normal control (NC), late MCI (LMCI) vs. NC and EMCI vs. LMCI, respectively.

## 2   Methodology

The proposed MCI detection framework is shown in Fig. 1. Clearly, it consists of four main steps: (1) Data preprocessing and DH-FCNs construction; (2) Extract feature vectors from FCNs; (3) Build a graph that combines image information (i.e., features) and non-image information (i.e., gender and age); (4) By the Inception module, we get a MS-GCN model for MCI detection. It is worth noting that batch normalization and activation functions are behind each GCN layer, and the activation function is RELU. The following subsection will introduce these parts in detail.

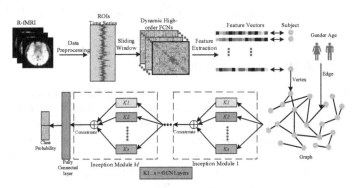

**Fig. 1.** MCI detection framework based on MS-GCN.

### 2.1   Data Preprocessing

In this study, we use a total of 126 subjects, which includes 38 LMCI patients, 44 EMCI patients and 44 NC, each with rs-fMRI data available. All the data are from the ADNI database (adni.loni.usc.edu). The subject's detailed information is shown in Table 1.

**Table 1.** Summary of the subjects' information used in this study.

| Group | LMCI (38) | EMCI (44) | NC (44) |
|---|---|---|---|
| Male/Female | 19 M/19 F | 22 M/22 F | 22 M/22 F |
| Age (mean ± SD) | $76.0 \pm 7.6$ | $76.5 \pm 6.1$ | $76.5 \pm 4.5$ |

All rs-fMRI data is acquired on 3.0 T scanners, each time point is composed of $64 \times 64 \times 48$ voxel, and the size of a single voxel is $3 \times 3 \times 3.4$ mm$^3$. The rs-fMRI data preprocessing procedure is performed using GRETNA toolbox [10], the steps are as follows: (1) To keep magnetization equilibrium, we discard the first 10 acquired rs-fMRI volumes of each subject. (2) The remaining 170 volumes are corrected for the staggered order of slice acquisition during echo-planar scanning by matching all time points to intermediate time points. (3) Afterward, the head motion artifacts in the rs-fMRI time-series are removed by the first volume of each subject as a reference to register all the following volumes. (4) After registration, the volumes are normalized to the Montreal Neurological Institute (MNI) atlas space and resampled to the voxel size of $3 \times 3 \times 3$ mm. (5) After spatial normalization, we spatially smooth the dataset with a 4 mm full width half maximum Gaussian kernel followed by band-pass filtering of frequency interval ($0.01\,\mathrm{Hz} \leq f \leq 0.08\,\mathrm{Hz}$) to minimize the effects of low-frequency drift and high-frequency noise. (6) Each regional mean time series is regressed against the average cerebrospinal fluid and white-matter signals as well as the six parameters from motion correction. (7) A parcellation of the brain space into 90 regions of interest (ROIs) is then performed by warping the automated anatomical labeling (AAL) [11] atlas to the rs-fMRI images.

## 2.2 Dynamic High-Order FCNs Construction

The FCNs are a form of reflecting the interaction between different brain regions. However, the traditional FCNs are based on rs-fMRI correlation of whole brain time series, which does not take into account the dynamic changes between brain regions. Therefore, low-order static brain networks have certain limitations and cannot be directly applied in the diagnosis of brain diseases. To this end, we construct dynamic high order brain networks. Specifically, a sliding window approach is first used to segment the entire rs-fMRI time series into multiple sub-series. Then, Pearson correlation coefficient is used to calculate the correlation of different ROI sub-series and define the correlation coefficient of different ROIs.

Let Q represent the step, B represent sliding window size, and R represent a time series with R time points, and the whole time series is divided into Z sub-time series, where $Z = (R - B)/Q + 1$. Finally, we construct the high-order FCNs based on the topographical similarities between each pair of the sub-networks $c^{(d)}$. The DH-FCNs can then be equivalently written as:

$$\mathbf{h}_n^{(d)} = \left(\mathbf{c}_n^{(d)}\right)^T \mathbf{c}_n^{(d)} \tag{1}$$

## 2.3 Feature Extraction

To improve detection performance, we extract the local weighted clustering coefficients $f_i \in \mathbb{R}^R$ from the original DH-FCNs. In this way, the clustering of each node in the weighted network can be quantified. Compared with the local clustering coefficient, it can represent the network more effectively and the influence of network weight is considered in the calculation process, which makes network representation more effective. Given a network with $K$ vertices, the weight of the edge connecting vertex $i$ and vertex $j$ for each network (i.e., the $i$-th node) is denoted as:

$$f_i = \frac{2\sum_{j:j \in \varepsilon_i}\left(w_{ij}\right)^{\frac{1}{3}}}{|\varepsilon_i|(|\varepsilon_i| - 1)} \tag{2}$$

where $\varepsilon_i$ denotes the set of vertices directly connected to vertex $i$, and $|\varepsilon_i|$ is the number of elements in $\varepsilon_i$. Then, these extracted clustering coefficients are combined as a feature vector.

## 2.4  Graph Construction

The construction of a graph is crucial to accurately model the interactions among the subjects. We construct the undirected graph on the entire data (including training and testing data). Let $G(V, E)$ be a directed graph with a vertex set $v_n \in V$, $(n = 1,2,...,N)$ and edge set $(v_n, v_m) \in E$ where $v_n$ denotes a feature vector from DH-FCNs and $(v_n, v_m) = a_{nm} = a_{mn}$, $a_{nm} \in A$, $A$ is an adjacency matrix that describes the connectivity of vertices. We can obtain the adjacency matrix $A$ through the similarity matrix $S$ of subject's vertex distance measurement, and there are $p$ (i.e. *sex* or *age*) non-image measures $M = \{M_p\}$. The graph is then defined as follows:

$$G_{nm} = S(v_n, v_m)(\mathcal{P}(M_{sex}(v_n), M_{sex}(v_m)) + \mathcal{P}\left(M_{age}(v_n), M_{age}(v_m)\right)) \quad (3)$$

where $S(v_n, v_m)$ represent the similarity between subjects $n$ and $m$, $S(v_n, v_m)$ is defined as follows:

$$S(v_n, v_m) = \frac{(v_n - \bar{v}_n) \odot (v_m - \bar{v}_m)}{\|((v_n - \bar{v}_n))\|_2 \|((v_m - \bar{v}_m))\|_2} \quad (4)$$

$\mathcal{P}(\ )$ represent the distance between $M_p(v_n)$ and $M_p(v_m)$. $\mathcal{P}(\ )$ is defined as

$$\mathcal{P}\left(M_p(v_n), M_p(v_m)\right) = \begin{cases} 1 & if\ |M_{age}(v_n) - M_{age}(v_m)| < \beta\ and\ |M_{sex}(v_n) - M_{sex}(v_m)| = 0 \\ 0 & otherwise \end{cases} \quad (5)$$

where $\beta$ is the standard deviation of the subject's age, $\bar{v}$ is the mean of vector $v$ and $\odot$ is the dot product.

## 2.5  Spectral Convolution

The normalized graph Laplacian matrix is as follows: $L = I_N - D^{-\frac{1}{2}} A D^{-\frac{1}{2}}$, where $D$ is a diagonal matrix $D_{ii} = \sum_j A_{ij}$ and $I_N \in \mathbb{R}^{N \times N}$ is an identity matrix. Since $L$ is a semi-definite matrix, it can be diagonalizable by its eigenvector matrix $U$ such that $L = U \wedge U^T$, where $\wedge$ is a diagonal matrix. The diagonal of each element is its eigenvalue. The graph Fourier transform of a signal $x$ is defined as $\hat{x} = U^T x \in \mathbb{R}^N$, the corresponding inverse Fourier transform is denoted as $x = U\hat{x} \in \mathbb{R}^N$. Therefore, in the Fourier domain, spectral convolution can be defined as the multiplication of signal $x$ with a learnable filter $g_\theta = diag(\theta)$ ($g_\theta$ is a function of the eigenvalues of $L$). The result $y$ of spectral convolution is:

$$y = U g_\theta(\wedge) U^T x = g_\theta(U \wedge U^T) x = g_\theta(L) x \quad (6)$$

Since Eq. (6) is computationally expensive, computational complexity for multiplication with the eigenvector matrix U is $O(N^2)$, we redefine $g_\theta$ using the Chebyshev polynomial parameterization of the filter $g_\theta(\wedge) = \sum_{r=0}^{k} \theta_r T_r(\wedge)$, $\theta \in \mathbb{R}^k$, $K$ is the order of Chebyshev polynomial. The graph convolution can be expressed as $g_\theta * x = \sum_{r=0}^{k} \theta_r T_r(L)x$.

### 2.6  Inception Modules

It is possible to obtain suboptimal detection accuracy for a graph-convolutional network of a filter. We utilize the MS-GCNs by designing filters with different kernel sizes instead of the common GCNs for the MCI detection task. The localization of a filter is defined by taking all the neighbors at a distance of $k$ hops into account for the spectral convolution with a signal $x$. A filter with a fixed $k_s$ used on the full dataset $X$ can be defined as $Y_s = \sum_{r=1}^{k_s} T_r(L)X\theta_{r,s}$. These combined filters are the core of the Inception module, because they consider both the close proximity of a signal $x$ and the broader neighborhood situation, increasing the width of the network and the adaptability of the network to the scale. The receptive fields of different branches are different, and there is multi-scale information in them. Each filter in the module has its own parameter vector $\theta$ and signal $x$, and returns an output vector, which returns an output vector $Y_s$. Finally, the output of each filter passes through an integration function $\mathcal{F}$ to determine the output $\mathcal{Y} = \mathcal{F}(Y_1, Y_2 \ldots Y_s)$ of the Inception module. To merge the output of each inception module we propose two aggregators $\mathcal{F}$, (1) pooling; (2) concatenation; The second method is adopted in this experiment. The Inception module is shown in Fig. 1.

## 3  Experiments and Results

The MCI detection framework is run on the Keras library in Python, and the Tensorflow is the back-end. In this study, the sliding window size is 50, and the stride is 30. In addition, we use 2 inception modules with 4 different sized filters.

To validate the effectiveness and superiority of the proposed method, we compare it with the following methods: (1) Multilayer Perceptron (MLP); (2) First, we construct a DH-FCNs, then use LASSO for feature selection, and finally use support vector machine (SVM) for detection; (3) Two layers of GCNs for detection. It is worth noting that all methods are validated by the leave one-out (LOO) cross-validation. In this study, three kinds of binary detection tasks are performed. The comparison results of different methods are shown in Table 2. Experimental results demonstrate that our method can get better result than competing methods in all detection tasks. In order to verify the effect of Inception module, we remove the Inception module in the proposed architecture, and compare the performance. It is worth noting that the model used the same training hyper-parameters as MS-GCN. The effect of using Inception module of different tasks is shown in Fig. 2. The results show that applying different sized filters on the same input features and graph is beneficial to improve the detection performance. Then, we compare the effect of the number of filters and the number of Inception modules on the detection performance. As shown in Fig. 3, we fix the number of filters and compare the effects of Inception modules with different numbers in terms of detection performance. Then, we fix the number of Inception modules and compare the effects of filters with different numbers. Finally, we select the most important ROIs based on the weight of the brain network, and the connectivity between ROIs is shown in Fig. 4. The Fig. 4 shows that different subjects has different connectivity.

**Table 2.** The comparison results of different methods using different evaluation metrics.

| Data | Method | ACC | SEN | SPEC | YI | F-score |
|------|--------|-----|-----|------|-----|---------|
| EMCI vs. NC | MLP | 0.6230 | 0.6160 | 0.6750 | 0.2910 | 0.6280 |
| | SVM | 0.7830 | 0.7450 | 0.7860 | 0.5310 | 0.7280 |
| | GCNs | 0.7955 | 0.7955 | 0.7955 | 0.5909 | 0.7955 |
| | **MS-GCN** | **0.8750** | **0.8636** | **0.8864** | **0.7500** | **0.8736** |
| LMCI vs. NC | MLP | 0.6364 | 0.6591 | 0.6136 | 0.2727 | 0.6444 |
| | SVM | 0.7960 | 0.7620 | 0.8420 | 0.6120 | 0.8220 |
| | GCNs | 0.8415 | 0.8684 | 0.8182 | 0.6866 | 0.8354 |
| | **MS-GCN** | **0.8902** | **0.8421** | **0.9318** | **0.7739** | **0.8764** |
| LMCI vs. EMCI | MLP | 0.5890 | 0.6620 | 0.6840 | 0.3420 | 0.3440 |
| | SVM | 0.7210 | 0.7350 | 0.7960 | 0.5310 | 0.7430 |
| | GCNs | 0.7195 | 0.6579 | 0.7727 | 0.4306 | 0.6849 |
| | **MS-GCN** | **0.7927** | **0.7368** | **0.8409** | **0.5778** | **0.7671** |

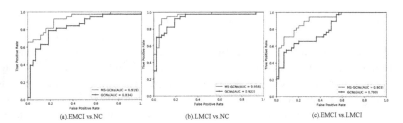

(a).EMCI vs.NC          (b).LMCI vs.NC          (c).EMCI vs.LMCI

**Fig. 2.** Effect of using Inception module on detection performance of different tasks

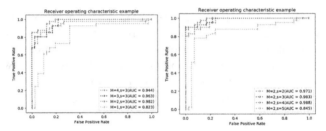

**Fig. 3.** Effect of the number of filters and the number of Inception modules.

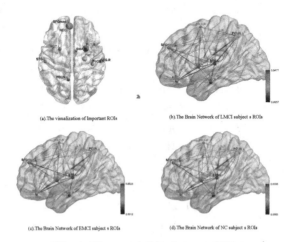

**Fig. 4.** The connectivity between ROIs.

## 4    Conclusion

In this study, we propose a novel MCI detection framework based on MS-GCN. Specifically, we first construct a DH-FCNs by considering the high-order interaction characteristics of the brain. Then, a graph is constructed by combining both image and non-image information. Finally, a graph convolution network model with Inception module is used for detection. The results show that applying different sized filters on the same input features and graph is beneficial to improve detection performance. Our method obtains satisfactory results on ADNI dataset. The method provides a new idea and method for the early computer-aided diagnosis of AD and can be an effective reference for clinical diagnosis. In the future, we will consider more diverse methods to construct brain networks and design more complex network models (e.g., graph generation adversarial network). Furthermore, we will use multi-modal data to further improve the MCI detection performance.

# References

1. Alzheimer's Association: 2018 Alzheimer's disease facts and figures. Alzheimers Dement. **14**(3), 367–425 (2018)
2. Petersen, R.C., et al.: Current concepts in mild cognitive impairment. Arch. Neurol. **58**(12), 1985–1992 (2001)
3. Huettel, S.A., Song, A.W., McCarthy, G.: Sinauer Associates Sunderland. Functional Magnetic Resonance Imaging, MA (2004)
4. Bullmore, E., Sporns, O.: Complex brain networks: graph theoretical analysis of structural and functional systems. Nat. Rev. Neurosci. **10**(3), 186 (2009)
5. Wee, C.-Y., Yap, P.-T., Zhang, D., Wang, L., Shen, D.: Group-constrained sparse fMRI connectivity modeling for mild cognitive impairment identification. Brain Struct. Funct. **219**(2), 641–656 (2014)
6. Hart, B., et al.: A longitudinal model for functional connectivity networks using resting-state fMRI. NeuroImage **178**, 687–701 (2018)
7. Parisot, S., et al.: Disease prediction using graph convolutional networks: application to autism spectrum disorder and Alzheimer's disease. Med. Image Anal. **48**, 117–130 (2018)
8. Ktena, S.I., et al.: Metric learning with spectral graph convolutions on brain connectivity networks. NeuroImage **169**, 431–442 (2018)
9. Kazi, A., et al.: InceptionGCN: receptive field aware graph convolutional network for disease prediction. In: Chung, A.C.S., Gee, J.C., Yushkevich, P.A., Bao, S. (eds.) IPMI 2019. LNCS, vol. 11492, pp. 73–85. Springer, Cham (2019). https://doi.org/10.1007/978-3-030-20351-1_6
10. Wang, J., Wang, X., Xia, M., Liao, X., Evans, A., He, Y.: GRETNA: a graph theoretical network analysis toolbox for imaging connectomics. Front. Hum. Neurosci. **9**, 386 (2015)
11. Tzourio-Mazoyer, N., et al.: Automated anatomical labeling of activations in SPM using a macroscopic anatomical parcellation of the MNI MRI single-subject brain. NeuroImage **15**(1), 273–289 (2002)

# DeepBundle: Fiber Bundle Parcellation with Graph Convolution Neural Networks

Feihong Liu[1,2(✉)], Jun Feng[1], Geng Chen[2], Ye Wu[2], Yoonmi Hong[2], Pew-ThianYap[2(✉)], and Dinggang Shen[2(✉)]

[1] School of Information and Technology, Northwest University, Xi'an, China
fengjun@nwu.edu.cn
[2] Department of Radiology and Biomedical Research Imaging Center (BRIC), University of North Carolina, Chapel Hill, USA
{ptyap,dgshen}@med.unc.edu

**Abstract.** Parcellation of whole-brain tractography streamlines is an important step for tract-based analysis of brain white matter microstructure. Existing fiber parcellation approaches rely on accurate registration between an atlas and the tractograms of an individual, however, due to large individual differences, accurate registration is hard to guarantee in practice. To resolve this issue, we propose a novel deep learning method, called DeepBundle, for registration-free fiber parcellation. Our method utilizes graph convolution neural networks (GCNNs) to predict the parcellation label of each fiber tract. GCNNs are capable of extracting the geometric features of each fiber tract and harnessing the resulting features for accurate fiber parcellation and ultimately avoiding the use of atlases and any registration method. We evaluate DeepBundle using data from the Human Connectome Project. Experimental results demonstrate the advantages of DeepBundle and suggest that the geometric features extracted from each fiber tract can be used to effectively parcellate the fiber tracts.

## 1 Introduction

Diffusion MRI provides valuable insights into the 3D geometric structure of brain neural fiber tracts, allowing tract-based analysis (TBA) of brain white matter microstructure in vivo [1]. TBA usually focuses on specific fiber bundles that are extracted from the whole-brain tractograms. Therefore, effective methods for segmenting whole-brain tractograms into fiber bundles of interest are desirable.

Existing fiber parcellation approaches can be divided into two categories: ROI-based and streamline-based. ROI-based approaches [2,3] first parcellate the brain surface based on an atlas and then use the parcellation ROIs to extract different fiber bundles. Streamline-based approaches [4,5] employ streamline registration methods to directly transfer the fiber parcellation information from an atlas to tractograms of an individual. These methods are directly affected by registration accuracy, which is, however, hard to guarantee in practice due to

© Springer Nature Switzerland AG 2019
D. Zhang et al. (Eds.): GLMI 2019, LNCS 11849, pp. 88–95, 2019.
https://doi.org/10.1007/978-3-030-35817-4_11

factors such as inter-subject variability, noise, and artifacts. Moreover, the registration procedure is usually time-consuming, making it unsuitable for large-scale studies and real-time applications. Recently, Wasserthal et al. [6] proposed to predict the binary mask of a fiber bundle from the whole brain fiber peaks using convolutional neural networks. This method avoids the registration procedure but is limited to generating a binary tract segmentation mask rather than the parcellation labels of the fiber tracts. In addition, this method utilizes the fiber orientation information at each voxel rather than the actual geometries of the fiber tracts.

In this work, we propose a deep-learning approach, called DeepBundle, to parcellate whole-brain tractograms without the time-consuming registration. Specifically, we view the coordinates of the points on each fiber tract as functions defined on a graph. The point coordinates are then fed to a graph convolutional neural networks (GCNN) to extract the latent geometric features of fiber tracts for bundle recognition. Our network is trained end-to-end with the point coordinates as inputs and parcellation labels as outputs, thus avoiding having to manually craft features for the purpose of bundle parcellation. During the testing stage, the point coordinates extracted from fiber tracts of the whole brain are directly fed to the trained networks, thus avoiding the use of atlases and any registration method. Extensive experiments performed using data from the Human Connectome Project (HCP) indicate that DeepBundle yields fiber parcellation labels with remarkably improved accuracy, confirming that the geometric features extracted by GCNNs are effective for fiber bundle parcellation.

## 2    Methods

In this section, we will first show how fiber streamlines can be represented using graphs, and then, introduce the theory of spectral graph convolution and graph pooling. Finally, we will describe our network in detail.

### 2.1    Graph Representation of Fiber Tracts

Considering an undirected graph as $\mathcal{G} = (\mathcal{V}, \mathcal{E}, \mathcal{W})$, $\mathcal{V} = \{v_1, \cdots, v_n\}$ is a set of $n$ vertices, $\mathcal{E} \subseteq \mathcal{V} \times \mathcal{V}$ is the edge set, and $\mathcal{W} = (w_{(i,j)})$ is the $n \times n$ adjacency matrix, which is symmetric, i.e., $w_{(i,j)} = w_{(j,i)}$. We uniformly sample $n$ points on each fiber tract, and the discrete fiber tract can be represented by a graph with edge weights given by

$$w_{i,j} = \begin{cases} 1, & \text{if } i, j \text{ are connected,} \\ 0, & \text{otherwise.} \end{cases} \tag{1}$$

The graph $\mathcal{G}$ now encodes the geometric relationships between sampling points on the fiber tract [7]. We then view the point coordinates extracted from a fiber tract as graph-structured data.

## 2.2  Spectral Graph Convolution

To extract the underlying geometry-invariance features of each fiber tract, we employ spectral graph convolution [8], which generalizes conventional convolution in Euclidean space using graph Fourier transformation. The transformation relies on the eigendecomposition of the graph Laplacian $\Delta$, which is defined as

$$\Delta = \Phi\Lambda\Phi^{\mathrm{T}} = I_n - \mathcal{D}^{-1/2}\mathcal{W}\mathcal{D}^{-1/2}, \tag{2}$$

where $\Phi = (\varphi_1, \cdots, \varphi_n)$ is a matrix of orthonormal eigenvectors ($\Phi^{\mathrm{T}}\Phi = I_n$), $\Lambda = \mathrm{diag}(\lambda_1, \cdots, \lambda_n)$ is a diagonal matrix of corresponding eigenvalues, $I_n$ is an identity matrix, and $\mathcal{D} = \sum_{j \neq i} w_{(i,j)}$ is the degree matrix. Such eigenvectors $(\varphi_1, \cdots, \varphi_n)$ can be interpreted as the Fourier bases, and $\Phi^T$ is used to transform the features from the spatial domain to spectral domain. The graph Fourier transformation is formulated by

$$\mathbf{f} * \mathbf{g} = \Phi\left(\Phi^{\mathrm{T}}\mathbf{g}\right) \odot \left(\Phi^{\mathrm{T}}\mathbf{f}\right) = \Phi\mathrm{diag}\left(\hat{g}_1, \cdots, \hat{g}_n\right)\hat{\mathbf{f}}, \tag{3}$$

where $\mathbf{f} = (f_1, \cdots, f_n)^{\mathrm{T}}$ is the input signal, which denotes the geometric features of one streamline on the vertices of graph $\mathcal{G}$. Its Fourier transformation is given by $\hat{\mathbf{f}} = \left(\Phi^{\mathrm{T}}\mathbf{f}\right)$; $\mathbf{g}$ is a convolutional filter in the spatial domain, and the spectral convolution can be defined as element-wise product $\left(\Phi^{\mathrm{T}}\mathbf{g}\right) \odot \left(\Phi^{\mathrm{T}}\mathbf{f}\right)$, which can also be written by $\mathrm{diag}\left(\hat{g}_1, \cdots, \hat{g}_n\right)\hat{\mathbf{f}}$. Hereby, $\mathrm{diag}\left(\hat{g}_1, \cdots, \hat{g}_n\right)$ is the corresponding convolutional filter in the spectral domain.

Utilizing the spectral definition of the convolution, GCNNs generalize CNNs to graphs. The $\ell$-th spectral convolution layer can be written by

$$\mathbf{f}_k^{(\ell+1)} = \xi\left(\Phi\sum_{k'=1}^{p}\mathrm{diag}\left(\hat{g}_{(k,k',1)}^{(\ell)}, \cdots, \hat{g}_{(k,k',n)}^{(\ell)}\right)\Phi^T\mathbf{f}_{k'}^{(\ell)}\right), \tag{4}$$

where $\mathrm{F}^{(\ell)} = \left(\mathbf{f}_1^{(\ell)}, \cdots, \mathbf{f}_p^{(\ell)}\right)$ and $\mathrm{F}^{(\ell+1)} = \left(\mathbf{f}_1^{(\ell+1)}, \cdots, \mathbf{f}_q^{(\ell+1)}\right)$ are the $n \times p$ and $n \times q$ matrices, representing the input and output features of $\ell$-th spectral convolution layer; $\mathbf{f}_{k'}^{(\ell)}$ and $\mathbf{f}_k^{(\ell+1)}$ denote the $k'$-th column of the input matrix and the $k$-th column of the output matrix. $\Phi = (\varphi_1, \cdots, \varphi_n)$ is an $n \times n$ matrix, and $\mathrm{diag}\left(\hat{g}_{(k,k',1)}^{(\ell)}, \cdots, \hat{g}_{(k,k',n)}^{(\ell)}\right)$ is a $n \times n$ diagonal matrix which denotes learnable filters in the spectral domain; and $\xi$ denotes the nonlinearity, e.g., ReLU.

## 2.3  Fast Graph Pooling

We utilize the Graclus [9,10] to coarsen the input graph into multi-scales, which is similar to the pooling operation in conventional CNNs. In practice, the multi-scale graph is organized as a binary tree, which becomes coarse from the leaf layer to the root layer. When constructing this tree, Graclus introduces fake nodes, rearranges the nodes of the streamline, and thus, we can perform graph pooling using fast 1D spatial pooling. Cousin nodes in one layer are aggregated into one parent node in the upper layer of the binary tree. The pooling process is illustrated in Fig. 1.

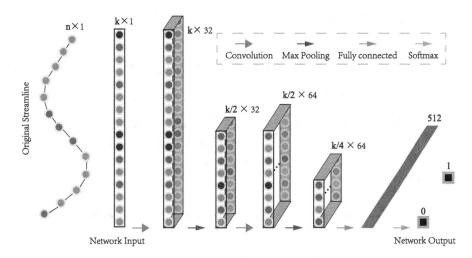

**Fig. 1.** The architecture of the employed spectral GCNNs. Red arrows denote the spectral convolution layers, blue arrows denote the fast max-pooling layers, a green arrow denotes one fully connected layer, and the yellow arrow denotes the softmax layer. (Color figure online)

### 2.4 Network Architecture of DeepBundle

Figure 1 illustrates the network architecture of DeepBundle. We employ a spectral GCNNs with the architecture of GC32-P2-GC64-P2-FC512, where GC$c$ denotes a graph convolution layer which has $c$ filters, P2 denotes a graph pooling layer with a factor 2, and FC512 denotes a fully connected layer with 512 hidden nodes. Each graph convolutional layer is activated by the ReLU function. The last layer is the softmax regression layer, and we employ the cross-entropy loss with an $l_2$ regularization term. We separately trained networks for segmenting different fiber bundles of interest from the whole-brain tracts.

In Fig. 1, the length of the input is increased from $n$ to $k$ due to the introduction of fake nodes (black dots) by Graclus. We employed 32 and 64 filters in the first convolution and the second convolution layer respectively. In the pooling layer, two neighbor nodes are aggregated into one. The input with a length $k$ is reduced to $k/4$ after going through two max-pooling layers.

## 3 Results

### 3.1 Implementation Details

For evaluation, we used the publicly available HCP fiber tract dataset [11]. This dataset contains 105 subjects. Each subject has 72 fiber bundles, containing streamlines of different lengths. We uniformly resampled them to have the same number of points, i.e., 100 points. We then represented all streamlines using a common graph. In our experiments, we randomly selected 25 subjects from

**Table 1.** Classification results for 12 bundles of subject #623844.

| Counts | CST left | CST right | CC 1 | CC 2 | CC 6 | CA |
|---|---|---|---|---|---|---|
| TP | 4755 | 7726 | 4419 | 51967 | 30082 | 1330 |
| FP | 244 | 395 | 143 | 1100 | 602 | 0 |
| FN | 54 | 382 | 29 | 153 | 320 | 0 |
| Counts | UF left | UF right | AF left | AF right | FX left | FX right |
| TP | 3535 | 4916 | 54448 | 42635 | 94 | 123 |
| FP | 0 | 0 | 199 | 495 | 6 | 7 |
| FN | 1 | 3 | 190 | 220 | 1 | 1 |

**Table 2.** Classification performance (mean $\pm$ standard deviation in %) on 12 fiber bundles from 11 subjects.

| | CST left | CST right | CC 1 | CC 2 | CC 6 | CA |
|---|---|---|---|---|---|---|
| Precision | $90.5 \pm 7.1$ | $91.1 \pm 7.9$ | $96.5 \pm 2.1$ | $97.6 \pm 2.2$ | $95.6 \pm 2.3$ | $99.9 \pm 0.1$ |
| Recall | $88.4 \pm 11.6$ | $86.6 \pm 11.6$ | $95.5 \pm 4.3$ | $98.4 \pm 1.3$ | $98.1 \pm 1.8$ | $100 \pm 0.0$ |
| | UF left | UF right | AF left | AF right | FX left | FX right |
| Precision | $99.7 \pm 0.6$ | $99.8 \pm 0.2$ | $99.2 \pm 1.0$ | $99.4 \pm 0.6$ | $87.3 \pm 12.7$ | $90.7 \pm 14.1$ |
| Recall | $99.2 \pm 2.1$ | $99.6 \pm 0.4$ | $99.4 \pm 0.8$ | $96.5 \pm 2.8$ | $97.5 \pm 3.9$ | $96.6 \pm 3.8$ |

the database for training, 2 for validation, and 11 for testing. In preparing the training data, a positive label is assigned to all streamlines from a bundle of interest. The negative samples are collected by (1) selecting streamlines from spatially neighboring bundles, and (2) randomly selecting an equal number of streamlines from all other bundles. For testing, all streamlines of each testing subject were fed separately into the trained network.

### 3.2   Experimental Results

Figure 2 shows the fiber parcellation results of one randomly selected subject (#623844). 12 bundles of interest are parcellated from more than one million whole-brain fiber tracts. Although fiber bundles in the left and right hemispheres may share similar shapes, DeepBundle is able to distinguish between them. For some small-size bundles, e.g., FX, which have only hundreds of streamlines, Deep-Bundle consistently gives promising parcellation results. In addition, we show the quantitative parcellation results of the 12 fiber bundles in Table 1, further confirming the conclusions that can be drawn from Fig. 2.

Table 2 shows the quantitative results computed across 10 testing subjects. A large *precision/recall* value indicates more accurate fiber parcellation. It can be observed that DeepBundle achieves high *precision* and *recall* values for all bundles of interest, indicating promising fiber parcellation accuracy. It is interesting to note that the recall numbers of left CST and right CST are smaller

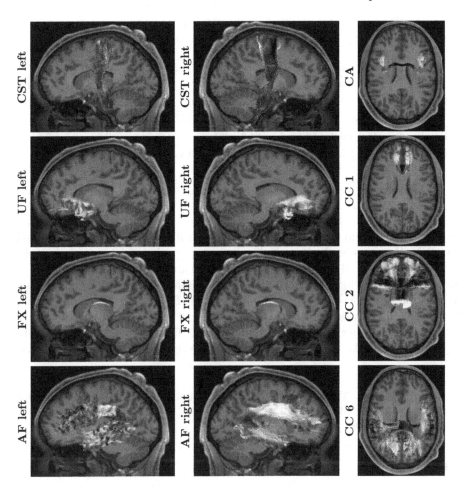

**Fig. 2.** Qualitative results of 12 fiber bundles: Corticospinal tract (CST), Commissure anterior (CA), Corpus callosum (Rostrum (CC 1), Genu (CC 2), Isthmus (CC 6)), Uncinate fascicle (UF), Arcuate fascicle (AF), Fornix (FX). Colored streamlines indicate the true positive (TP) streamlines, whereas black and white denote the false positive (FP) and false negative (FN) streamlines, respectively.

than the other fiber bundles. This is due to the fact their neighboring bundles, such as POPT and FPT, are very similar to CST in shape. Such streamlines induce ambiguities in fiber parcellation, even when performed manually.

We also compared DeepBundle with a popular method called RecoBundles [12]. We mapped all parcellated fiber streamlines to created volumetric visitation maps and computed their Dice scores with respect to the gold standard. The results, shown in Table 3, indicate that DeepBundle significantly improves the Dice score and outperforms RecoBundles for all bundles of interest. RecoBundles gives significantly lower Dice scores CA, left FX, and right FX. DeepBundle yields relatively smaller Dice scores for left CST and right CST, but still significantly outperforms RecoBundles.

**Table 3.** Dice scores (mean ± standard deviation in %) of 12 fiber bundles from 11 testing subjects.

|  | CST left | CST right | CC 1 | CC 2 | CC 6 | CA |
|---|---|---|---|---|---|---|
| RecoBundles | 45.3 ± 9.7 | 40.6 ± 6.1 | 51.3 ± 13.2 | 63.6 ± 8.6 | 60.7 ± 6.31 | 25.2 ± 16.1 |
| DeepBundle | 80.7 ± 10.1 | 86.9 ± 5.1 | 93.0 ± 3.3 | 96.8 ± 1.2 | 97.1 ± 1.4 | 99.1 ± 1.6 |
|  | UF left | UF right | AF left | AF right | FX left | FX right |
| RecoBundles | 46.9 ± 6.3 | 52.1 ± 7.7 | 61.3 ± 9.1 | 63.1 ± 12.7 | 8.1 ± 2.8 | 9.5 ± 3.6 |
| DeepBundle | 96.4 ± 5.1 | 98.1 ± 1.3 | 95.8 ± 3.8 | 96.2 ± 4.0 | 82.4 ± 9.3 | 86.5 ± 8.8 |

## 4    Conclusion

In this paper, we have proposed a framework for fiber bundle parcellation using a GCNN. Our method directly predicts a tract parcellation label from the point coordinates extracted from a fiber tract. GCNNs are capable of extracting robust geometric features for tract parcellation in an end-to-end manner. Experiments on HCP data demonstrate that our method, DeepBundle, yields promising tract bundle parcellation results with high precision and recall rates. DeepBundle also achieves much higher Dice scores compared with RecoBundles. Our results also suggest that DeepBundle is even capable of effectively parcellating small tract bundles.

**Acknowledgment.** This work was supported in part by NIH grant NS093842 and the Xi'an Science and Technology Project funded by the Xi'an Science and Technology Bureau through Grant 201805060ZD11CG44.

## References

1. Ciccarelli, O., Catani, M., Johansen-Berg, H., Clark, C., Thompson, A.: Diffusion-based tractography in neurological disorders: concepts, applications, and future developments. Lancet Neurol. **7**(8), 715–727 (2008)
2. Yendiki, A., et al.: Automated probabilistic reconstruction of white-matter pathways in health and disease using an atlas of the underlying anatomy. Front. Neuroinformatics **5**, 23 (2011)
3. Wassermann, D., et al.: The white matter query language: a novel approach for describing human white matter anatomy. Brain Struct. Funct. **221**(9), 4705–4721 (2016)
4. Garyfallidis, E., Ocegueda, O., Wassermann, D., Descoteaux, M.: Robust and efficient linear registration of white-matter fascicles in the space of streamlines. NeuroImage **117**, 124–140 (2015)
5. Zhang, F., et al.: An anatomically curated fiber clustering white matter atlas for consistent white matter tract parcellation across the lifespan. Neuroimage **179**, 429–447 (2018)
6. Wasserthal, J., Neher, P., Maier-Hein, K.H.: TractSeg - fast and accurate white matter tract segmentation. NeuroImage **183**, 239–253 (2018)

7. Bronstein, M.M., Bruna, J., LeCun, Y., Szlam, A., Vandergheynst, P.: Geometric deep learning: going beyond euclidean data. IEEE Signal Process. Mag. **34**(4), 18–42 (2017)
8. Bruna, J., Zaremba, W., Szlam, A., Lecun, Y.: Spectral networks and locally connected networks on graphs. In: International Conference on Learning Representations (ICLR) (2014)
9. Dhillon, I.S., Guan, Y., Kulis, B.: Weighted graph cuts without eigenvectors: A multilevel approach. IEEE Trans. Pattern Anal. Mach. Intell. (TPAMI) **29**(11), 1944–1957 (2007)
10. Defferrard, M., Bresson, X., Vandergheynst, P.: Convolutional neural networks on graphs with fast localized spectral filtering. In: Advances in Neural Information Processing Systems (NeurIPS), 3844–3852 (2016)
11. Wasserthal, J., Neher, P.F., Maier-Hein, K.H.: Tract orientation mapping for bundle-specific tractography. In: Frangi, A.F., Schnabel, J.A., Davatzikos, C., Alberola-López, C., Fichtinger, G. (eds.) MICCAI 2018. LNCS, vol. 11072, pp. 36–44. Springer, Cham (2018). https://doi.org/10.1007/978-3-030-00931-1_5
12. Garyfallidis, E., et al.: Recognition of white matter bundles using local and global streamline-based registration and clustering. NeuroImage **170**, 283–295 (2018)

# Identification of Functional Connectivity Features in Depression Subtypes Using a Data-Driven Approach

Xingjuan Li[1(✉)] ⓘ, Samantha Burnham[1], Jurgen Fripp[1], Yu Li[2], Xue Li[2], Amir Fazlollahi[1], and Pierrick Bourgeat[1]

[1] CSIRO Australian eHealth Research Centre, Brisbane 4029, Australia
miranda.li@csiro.au
[2] School of Information Technology and Electrical Engineering, The University of Queensland, Brisbane 4067, Australia

**Abstract.** Biomarkers are not well understood in depression, partly because there is no golden rule of what is abnormal in which patients and how neurobiological information can be used to improve diagnosis. The heterogeneity of depression suggests that diverse circuit-level abnormalities in individuals lead to various symptoms. Investigating heterogeneous depression is crucial to understand disease mechanisms and provide personalised medicine. Dynamical functional connectivity (dFC), consisting of spatial-temporal characteristics of brain activity, has been shown to be effective in characterizing the circuit-level abnormalities in depression. However, most of the current studies on dFC are based on one-step mapping while ignoring hierarchical spatial-temporal information, which may leverage the power of diagnosis in depression subtypes. In this study, we propose Brain Network Gated Recurrent Units (BrainNet-GRU) to discover hierarchical resting-state dFC features for the diagnosis of depression subtypes, using data from 770 depressive adults from the UK Biobank. Particularly, we devise diffusion convolutional filters and recurrent units to effectively learn distinctive dynamic brain connectivity for depression subtypes. Experimental results show that BrainNetGRU can identify three types of depression with an accuracy of 72.05%. In addition, BrainNetGRU shows that resting-state functional connections in default mode network (DMN), cingulo-opercular network (CON) and fronto-parietal network (FPN) are important in the diagnosis of depression subtypes.

**Keywords:** Dynamical functional connectivity · Depression subtypes · Resting-state fMRI · Deep learning

## 1 Introduction

Depression is the most common form of mental illness in adults, and is characterized by its heterogeneous nature. It is significantly underdiagnosed due to

D. Zhang et al. (Eds.): GLMI 2019, LNCS 11849, pp. 96–103, 2019.
https://doi.org/10.1007/978-3-030-35817-4_12

the lack of recognition. Particularly, the overlapping nature of depressive sub-type symptoms has been considered as a major factor in the low diagnostic reliability [8]. Identifying a neurological basis associated with depressive sub-type symptoms is of great importance for improving diagnosis [5]. Resting-state functional magnetic resonance imaging (fMRI) is an effective and non-invasive approach to identify depression and has been successfully used to differentiate types of depressive symptoms [12]. Resting-state fMRI (rs-fMRI) measures spontaneous fluctuations of brain activity over time when the subject is at resting state. Dynamical network modelling has been proposed to characterize temporal correlation of rs-fMRI signals in different brain areas [6,7,13]. Resting-state fMRI studies have shown that abnormalities in default-mode network (DMN) are related to depression symptoms [4]. In this study, we propose to identify neural biomarkers for depression subtypes from resting-state dynamic functional connectivity (dFC) data using a data-driven approach.

Recurrent neural network (RNN) is a powerful deep learning model that can automatically learn features from sequence data. Gated recurrent units (GRU) is a simple and powerful variant of RNN [3]. Directly applying GRU on dFC to learn features related to depression subtypes is non-trivial: (1) it is difficult to learn from dFC due to its extensive background noise; (2) the dFC data is complex and characterized by its irregular-structured and temporal properties, which pose a great challenge to deep learning methods; (3) it is difficult to capture features related to depressive subgroups due to the presentation of simlilar symptoms and signs across subjects. Therefore, a general GRU could not be suitable for the study of depression subtypes from resting-state dFC data.

To identify depression subtypes from resting-state dFC data, we propose a novel Brain Network Gated Recurrent Units (BrainNetGRU) to learn dynamic brain connectivity features related to subtypes of depression (Fig. 1). BrainNet-GRU improves traditional GRU in two aspects. First, we use a fully-connected layer as a feature selection layer on the input data. After optimization, fully-connected layer parameters become fixed and can be interpreted as weights on the input dFC before they are connected to BrainNetGRU for the final outcomes. Second, to extract spatial-temporal features from dFC, we use diffusion filters and recurrent units to effectively learn dynamical brain status. BrainNetGRU is trained and optimized to differentiate different depression subtypes. We test the proposed method in the UK Biobank dataset. Experimental results show that the proposed method can predict three types of depression with 72.05% accuracy and discover effective functional connectivity features for identifying three depression subtypes. In particular, experimental results show that resting-state functional connections in DMN, cingulo-opercular network (CON) and fronto-parietal network (FPN) are crucial for identifying subtypes of depression. We are the first to point out that the hierarchical functional network organization is useful and effective features to differentiate depression subtypes. To the best of our knowledge, this paper is the first to identify resting-state dFC features for diagnosing depression subtypes using a data-driven approach.

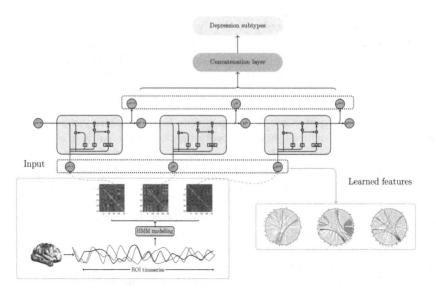

**Fig. 1.** The proposed BrainNetGRU. We first estimate dynamic functional connectivity for all individuals by a hidden Markov model. Then, the estimated functional connectivity matrix are connected to BrainNetGRU to predict depression subtypes. The model is trained to minimize the error between predicted labels and diagnosis labels. After optimization, the model is used to identify network patterns related to depression subtypes.

## 2   Methodology

### 2.1   Data Preprocessing

We include 570 depressive adults and 200 health controls from UK Biobank, with 40.3 % males and 59.6% females, aged 40 years to 70 years (see Table 1). Clinical label for each subject is given by ICD code 10 (UKB filed ID 41202) and information collected at assessment center (UKB field ID 4642, 4653, 6156, 5663, 4598, 4609, 4620, 2090, 2100, 4631, 5375, 5386). The research is conducted under UK Biobank application # 27483. All rs-fMRI scans are acquired using a standard 3T Siemens Skyra scanner (20-channel receiving head coil, duration: 6:10 min, voxel: 2.4 mm × 2.4 mm × 2.4 mm, TE/TR = 39/735 ms, flip angle = 52°, time points = 490.) [1]. Data preprocessing and group independent component analysis (ICA) parcellation have been carried out using FSL software by the UK Biobank. Specifically, all preprocessed fMRI timeseries is projected into the standard space, temporally demeaned and normalised. Group principle component analysis (PCA) is then carried out on all subjects using FSL. The output is fed into ICA using FSL's MELODIC tool, applying spatial-ICA with 25 dimensionalities. The dimensionality determines the number of distinct ICA components. Detailed processing methods can be found elsewhere [1].

**Table 1.** Demographic information.

| Types | Number | Males | Females | Mean age (std. dev) | Age range |
|---|---|---|---|---|---|
| Probable bipolar disorder | 130 | 55 | 75 | 54.5 (7.5) | 41–68 |
| Single probable episode of major depression | 210 | 62 | 148 | 53.8 (7.0) | 40–69 |
| Probable recurrent major depression | 230 | 100 | 130 | 53.1 (7.5) | 40–69 |
| Controls | 200 | 108 | 92 | 55.8 (7.5) | 40–70 |

### 2.2 Estimating Dynamic Functional Connectivity by a HMM

We model dynamics inherent in resting-state fMRI data using a our previously proposed regularized hidden Markov model (HMM) [7] for different subtypes. An HMM is a state-space model that can estimate hidden states from observations in a Markov process. At time point $t$, we want to infer $D$ hidden states representing functional dynamics given a sequence fMRI data as follows:

$$p(s_t = d, \lambda_c) = \sum_l \theta_{l,d} p(s_{t-1} = l, \lambda_c). \tag{1}$$

where $d = \{1, 2, \cdots, D\}$, $\lambda$ denotes parameters, $c$ represents the status of patients, $\theta$ denotes transition probability, $l$ represents influence from other functional connectivity (with $W_d^t \neq W_l^t$).

### 2.3 Spatial Structure Learning

To capture how information flows in a graph, we model the spatial dependencies of graph to a diffusion process. This diffusion process is characterized by a random walk on the brain network $\mathcal{G}$ with restart probability $\alpha \in [0, 1]$, and a state transition matrix $D_O^{-1}W$.

$$\phi = \sum_{k=0}^{\infty} \alpha(1 - \alpha)^k (D_O^{-1}W)^k. \tag{2}$$

The diffusion convolution operation over a graph signal $x$ with graph convolution operator $g_\theta$ on the weighted undirected graph $\mathcal{G}$ is defined as:

$$g_\phi *_{\mathcal{G}} x = \sum_{k=0}^{K-1} (\theta_{k,1}(D_O^{-1}W)^k + \theta_{k,2}(D_I^{-1}W^T)^k)x. \tag{3}$$

where $k$ is the diffusion step, $\theta \in \mathbb{R}^{K \times 2}$ are the parameters for the filter, $D_O^{-1}W$ and $D_I^{-1}W^T$ denote the transition matrix of diffusion process and the reverse one.

## 2.4    Temporal Structure Learning

To model sequential dFC data, we use a RNN as a response model. Particularly, we use the GRU, which have been shown to be extremely successful in tasks involving processing arbitrary input sequences. GRUs use internal memories to capture temporal dependencies of fMRI time series. To make a prediction $Y$, we multiply the hidden state $h$ with a matrix $W$ in GRU. There are two gates controlling information flow and make output prediction. To capture graph features, matrix multiplication is replaced by graph convolution given by Eq. 3. Two gates $gate_r$ and $gate_u$ are given by,

$$
\begin{aligned}
gate_{r,t} &= \sigma(\Theta_{r*\mathcal{G}}[\,X_t, h_{t-1}] + b_{r,t}) \\
gate_{u,t} &= \sigma(\Theta_{u*\mathcal{G}}[\,X_t, h_{t-1}] + b_{u,t}).
\end{aligned}
\tag{4}
$$

where $X_t$ denotes the input at time point $t$, $h_t$ denotes the output from previous time point $t - 1$, $\sigma$ is the sigmoid function and $b$ is a bias term, $\Theta$ are the parameters of a filter.

The next hidden state $h_t$ and the new $\tilde{h}_t$ are given by,

$$
h_t = (1 - gate_{u,t}) \cdot h_{t-1} + gate_{u,t} \cdot \tilde{h}_t.
\tag{5}
$$

$$
\tilde{h}_t = a(\Theta_{h*\mathcal{G}}[X_t,\ gate_{r,t} \cdot h_{t-1}] + b_t).
\tag{6}
$$

# 3    Experimental Results

## 3.1    Experimental Settings

In this study, we use 25-component group ICAs to estimate functional connectivity for depression subtypes. Particularly, we use the recently proposed regularized HMM with 12 states to estimate dynamics from ICA components [7]. Twelve states were chosen by comparing effects of different number of states in HMM.

The BrainNetGRU was trained and evaluated by tensorflow. Data was split into 70% for training, 20% for testing while the remaining 10% data was used for evaluation. Training was stopped when the validation loss ceased to decrease or when the maximum of epochs was executed. BrainNetGRU was trained to minimize cross-entropy loss function using the stochastic gradient descent (SGD) optimizer.

To reduce overfitting problem, we use the following hyper parameters. The learning rate was set as 0.003. The batch size was 32. The weights and biases were initialized randomly. In addition, we used a dropout rate of 0.3 and a small $l2$ norm regularization of 0.0005. Since the dataset is imbalanced, we adopted the class weight strategy during the training process. Specifically, we increased the class weights of bipolar patients relative to other depression types in the loss to balance the distribution. Detailed information on the weighting techniques has been provided elsewhere [2].

## 3.2   Diagnosis of Depression Subtypes

Here, we compare our method against three state-of-the-art of deep learning models using same experimental settings on the same dataset (in Table 2) (1) a fully-connected neural network (FC); (2) a recently proposed graph neural network (GNN) for static brain network analysis [9]; (3) a recently proposed long short-term memory network (LSTM) for dynamic functional network analysis [11], as detailed below. The performance results are shown in Table 2.

**Table 2.** Performances of different models in differentiating depression subtypes.

| Models | ACC (%) | SEN (%) | SPE (%) | f1 (%) |
|---|---|---|---|---|
| FC | 56.08 | 51.09 | 54.44 | 61.43 |
| GNN | 63.88 | 69.39 | 64.38 | 68.33 |
| LSTM | 68.07 | 70.28 | 68.27 | 70.00 |
| **BrainNetGRU** | **72.05** | **71.13** | **73.47** | **73.20** |

## 3.3   Resting-State Functional Connectivity Features of Depression Subtypes

After optimizing the neural network parameters for predicting depression subtypes, the network parameters become fixed and are used for identifying patterns related to subtypes. The first layer parameters are used to study shared features between different types of depression. More specifically, we normalize the first layers features and keep the top 10% of weights for additional analysis. These features represent how input functional connectivity are connected to BrainNetGRU for predicting depression subtypes. To identify the functional networks of interest (NOI) from these selected features, they are compared to five pre-defined functional networks based on definitions given by previous study [10]. Specifically, these five NOIs are default mode network (DMN, component 1, red), left and right cingulo-opercular network(CON, component 13 and 21, green and orange), right and left fronto-parietal network (FPN, component 5 and 6, yellow and blue). It shows that DMN, CON and FPN are strongly related to the prediction depression subtypes. Besides, it has been found that connections in CON-FPN, DMN-CON, DMN-FPN are related to the prediction depression subtypes. This is consistent with previous findings of abnormal functional connections in depression [14]. The results indicate that BrainNetGRU is able to extract crucial and effective features for predicting depression subtypes, Fig. 2 shows selected features from dFC, including DMN, left/right CON, and left/right FPN.

## 4   Conclusion

In this study, we proposed a novel BrainNetGRU, with the novel diffusion operation and a sequence-to-sequence architecture, to identify resting-state dFC features for the diagnosis depression subtypes. We compared the performance of

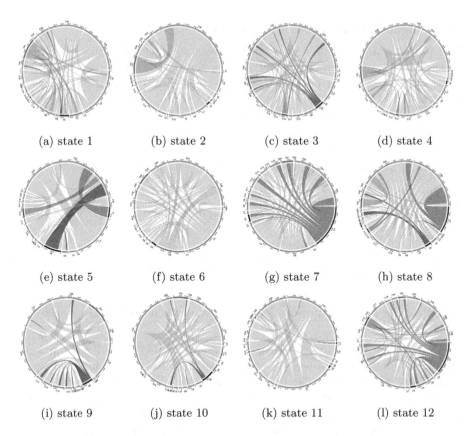

(a) state 1     (b) state 2     (c) state 3     (d) state 4

(e) state 5     (f) state 6     (g) state 7     (h) state 8

(i) state 9     (j) state 10     (k) state 11     (l) state 12

**Fig. 2.** Identified resting-state functional connectivity features for predicting depression subtypes, including DMN (component 1, grid color red), left/right CON (component 13/21, grid color green/orange), right/left FPN (component 5/6, grid color yellow/blue). Note that link shape represents weights on links. (Color figure online)

proposed BrainNetGRU with three state-of-the-art deep learning models. BrainNetGRU gives better performance. To the best of our knowledge, this is the first attempt to propose BrainNetGRU deep learning methodologies to extract features from spatial-temporal varying dFC data. We prove its feasibility and superiority in identifying depression subtypes. Experimental results show that DMN, CON and FPN subnetworks are involved in depression subtypes. Our work suggests the promise of using deep learning to extract meaningful functional connectivity features for the diagnosis of depression subtypes.

## References

1. Alfaro-Almagro, F., et al.: Image processing and quality control for the first 10,000 brain imaging datasets from UK Biobank. Neuroimage **166**, 400–424 (2018)

2. Barua, S., Islam, M.M., Yao, X., Murase, K.: MWMOTE-majority weighted minority oversampling technique for imbalanced data set learning. IEEE Trans. Knowl. Data Eng. **26**(2), 405–425 (2012)
3. Chung, J., Gulcehre, C., Cho, K., Bengio, Y.: Empirical evaluation of gated recurrent neural networks on sequence modeling. arXiv preprint arXiv:1412.3555 (2014)
4. Demirtaş, M., et al.: Dynamic functional connectivity reveals altered variability in functional connectivity among patients with major depressive disorder. Hum. Brain Mapp. **37**(8), 2918–2930 (2016)
5. Drysdale, A.T., et al.: Resting-state connectivity biomarkers define neurophysiological subtypes of depression. Nat. Med. **23**(1), 28 (2017)
6. Khambhati, A.N., Sizemore, A.E., Betzel, R.F., Bassett, D.S.: Modeling and interpreting mesoscale network dynamics. NeuroImage **180**, 337–349 (2018)
7. Li, X., Li, Y., Cui, J.: Estimating interactions of functional brain connectivity by hidden Markov models. In: Gan, G., Li, B., Li, X., Wang, S. (eds.) ADMA 2018. LNCS (LNAI), vol. 11323, pp. 403–412. Springer, Cham (2018). https://doi.org/10.1007/978-3-030-05090-0_34
8. Lieblich, S.M., Castle, D.J., Pantelis, C., Hopwood, M., Young, A.H., Everall, I.P.: High heterogeneity and low reliability in the diagnosis of major depression will impair the development of new drugs. BJPsych open **1**(2), e5–e7 (2015)
9. Parisot, S., et al.: Disease prediction using graph convolutional networks: application to autism spectrum disorder and Alzheimer's disease. Med. Image Anal. **48**, 117–130 (2018)
10. Shen, X., et al.: Resting-state connectivity and its association with cognitive performance, educational attainment, and household income in the UK Biobank. Biol. Psychiatry Cogn. Neurosci. Neuroimaging **3**(10), 878–886 (2018)
11. Yan, W., Zhang, H., Sui, J., Shen, D.: Deep chronnectome learning via full bidirectional long short-term memory networks for MCI diagnosis. In: Frangi, A.F., Schnabel, J.A., Davatzikos, C., Alberola-López, C., Fichtinger, G. (eds.) MICCAI 2018. LNCS, vol. 11072, pp. 249–257. Springer, Cham (2018). https://doi.org/10.1007/978-3-030-00931-1_29
12. Zeng, L.L., et al.: Identifying major depression using whole-brain functional connectivity: a multivariate pattern analysis. Brain **135**(5), 1498–1507 (2012)
13. Zhu, Q., Li, H., Huang, J., Xu, X., Guan, D., Zhang, D.: Hybrid functional brain network with first-order and second-order information for computer-aided diagnosis of schizophrenia. Front. Neurosci. **13**, 603 (2019)
14. Zhu, X., et al.: Evidence of a dissociation pattern in resting-state default mode network connectivity in first-episode, treatment-naive major depression patients. Biol. Psychiatry **71**(7), 611–617 (2012)

# Movie-Watching fMRI Reveals Inter-subject Synchrony Alteration in Functional Brain Activity in ADHD

Chao Tang, Ziyi Huang, Senyu Zhou, Qi Wang, Fa Yi, and Jingxin Nie[✉]

School of Psychology, Center for Studies of Psychological Application, Institution of Cognitive Neuroscience, South China Normal University, Guangzhou 510631, China
niejingxin@gmail.com

**Abstract.** Movie-watching fMRI has been regarded as a novel method to explore the functional brain activity by displaying rich and continuous stimulus. To detect the inter-subject synchrony alteration of brain activity in patients with attention deficit hyperactivity disorder (ADHD), the MRI data of 30 ADHD patients and 30 typically developing (TD) subjects were used in the study, including T1 structural images and functional images (watching the animated film, *The present*). Two movie clips with significant inter-group difference in state consistency (SC) were extracted from the original movie to explore the effect of the different stimulus on the synchrony alteration of functional brain activity. In the three conditions (entire movie, movie clip 1 and movie clip 2), the inter-subject correlation (ISC) and inter-subject functional correlation (ISFC) of each group were calculated and then compared. The results showed: (a) in the three conditions, the ISC of occipital cortex in ADHD was significantly greater than that in TD; (b) ADHD exhibited decreased ISC in the left postcentral gyrus and right orbital frontal cortex during movie clip 1 and decreased ISC in the inferior frontal gyrus during movie clip 2 compared with TD; (c) the significant inter-group ISFC differences were observed in the regions involved in attention, emotion and cognitive control. This study proves the effectiveness of movie-watching fMRI in exploring the inter-subject synchronization of functional brain activity and promotes the exploration of the neural mechanism of ADHD.

**Keywords:** Movie-watching fMRI · ADHD · ISC · ISFC

## 1 Introduction

Movie-watching fMRI is a new way to measure functional brain activity by allowing subjects to freely watch a series of continuous and complex stimulus from the movie [1]. This method provides a variety of rich stimulus, capturing more natural and real brain activity without extra interventions and decreasing head movement [2].

Movie-watching fMRI has been widely applied to explore the functional brain activity of healthy people. By detecting the variability in BOLD-signal based functional connectivity (FC) of 33 healthy people across two different movie conditions and eyes-open

D. Zhang et al. (Eds.): GLMI 2019, LNCS 11849, pp. 104–111, 2019.
https://doi.org/10.1007/978-3-030-35817-4_13

rest, Vanderwal et al. indicated that movies have higher within-subject and between-subject correlations in cluster-wise FC relative to rest [3]. Recently, Simony et al., proposed two measurements, inter-subject correlation (ISC) and inter-subject functional correlation (ISFC), which can separate the stimulus-induced signal from the mixed signal, to detect the dynamic changes in default mode network (DMN) correlation patterns that were locked to the processing of external stimuli [4].

It is known to all that attention deficit hyperactivity disorder (ADHD) is a neurodevelopmental disease with high incidence, but there is still no agreement on its pathogenesis. Therefore, it is of great scientific significance and clinical value to study abnormal brain activity in ADHD patients. In this study, we hypotheses that ADHD patients show the stronger inter-subject correlation in the regions involved in the primary cognition function than healthy people and abnormal asynchrony of functional brain activity in the regions related to advanced cognition function. Thus, 30 ADHD patients and 30 typically developing (TD) subjects were used to explore the inter-subject synchrony alteration in functional brain activities.

## 2   Materials and Methods

### 2.1   Participants

There are 30 ADHD subjects (female: 14, male: 16; mean age: 10.34) and 30 TD subjects (female: 14, male: 16; mean age: 10.46) from the Child Mind Institute Healthy Brain Network (http://fcon_1000.projects.nitrc.org/indi/cmi_healthy_brain_network/index.html). Especially, only the data collected at the Rutgers University Brain Imaging Center were used to reduce the error caused by different scan sites. For all subjects, the inclusion criteria included: (1) 5–20 years of age, (2) no history of neurological disease such as schizophrenia or affective disorder, (3) image at least cover 90% of the brain, (4) IQ scores >90. Finally, four ADHD subjects and four TD subjects were excluded due to the excessive head motion (mean frame-wise displacement >0.2 mm) [5]. A total of 26 ADHD subjects and 26 TD subjects were used in further study. There was no significant group difference in age and gender.

### 2.2   Image Acquisition

All MRI data were acquired on a Siemens 3T Tim Trio scanner. T1 images were obtained with the following parameters: TR = 2500 ms, TE = 3.15 ms, Flip Angle = 8°, Resolution = 0.8 × 0.8 × 0.8 mm$^3$, 224 slices. Functional images were obtained using an echo-planar imaging (EPI) sequence (TR = 800 ms, TE = 30 ms, Flip Angle = 31°, Resolution = 2.4 × 2.4 × 2.4 mm$^3$, 60 slices). Subjects were required to freely watch the animated short, *The present*, during the movie-watching fMRI scanning. The movie lasts for 3 min and 21 s and has a resolution of 720 × 480 pixels. Besides, subjects can hear the movie but no subtitles displayed on the screen during the scanning.

### 2.3  Data Preprocessing

Preprocessing of data was performed with DPARSF v4.3 toolkit [6]. The functional images were first realigned to the middle volume to correct for inter-scan motion artifacts. Then, these images were registered onto the Montreal Neurological Institute (MNI) template and further resampled to $3 \times 3 \times 3$ mm$^3$ resolution. After spatial normalization, the normalized image was detrended and then subjected to temporal band-pass filtering (0.01–0.1 Hz). Finally, nuisance covariates including head motion parameters, white matter signals, and cerebrospinal fluid signals were regressed out.

### 2.4  State Consistency (SC)

To find movie clips revealing the inter-subject variability in functional brain activity, a new measurement, state consistency (SC), was proposed. In brief, the whole brain was first divided into 90 regions of interest (ROI) by AAL atlas [7]. The average time series of each ROI in all subjects were divided into several overlapping windows with a length of 40 s and the step of 1 TR using sliding windows technique [8]. Then, the FC matrix based on each window was calculated. After performing a k-means clustering algorithm on all FC matrices, the FC state in each time window for each subject was assigned. The number of clusters was set as a series of varying values (k = 2, . . . , 10), which was ultimately determined by the minimized ratio of within-cluster similarity and between-clusters similarity. The within-cluster similarity is defined as the average of Euclidean distance between each point in the cluster and the cluster centroid, and the between-clusters similarity refers to the average of Euclidean distance between each cluster centroid. Finally, for each time window, the SC in ADHD and TD could be calculated by the following formula:

$$SC = \sqrt{\frac{N}{N-1}} * \frac{\sqrt{\left((\alpha_1-\overline{\alpha})^2 + (\alpha_2-\overline{\alpha})^2 + \ldots + (\alpha_N-\overline{\alpha})^2\right)}}{\sqrt{\alpha_1^2 + \alpha_2^2 + \ldots + \alpha_N^2}}, \overline{\alpha} = (\alpha_1+\alpha_2 + \ldots +\alpha_N)/N$$

(1)

Where $N$ is the number of FC states. $\alpha_i$ denotes the ratio of the number of subjects in state $i$ to the total number of subjects. SC represents the degree of inter-subject consistency of FC, and its range is between 0 and 1.

### 2.5  Inter-subject Correlation (ISC) and Inter-subject Functional Correlation (ISFC)

There is a hypothesis [4] that the BOLD signal of the brain consists of three parts: (1) the intrinsic neural signal derived from the spontaneous activity of the brain, (2) the stimulus-induced signal caused by external stimuli, and (3) the non-neuronal signal related to physiological noise such as head motion, respiration and heartbeat etcetera. Usually, it is not easy to distinguish the three parts from each other. Recently, Simony et al. have confirmed that intrinsic signals and non-neuronal signals are not relevant between subjects [4]. Therefore, in movie-watching fMRI, by calculating the Pearson correlation coefficient of time series of corresponding brain region between two subjects, ISC describes the similarity of inter-subject functional activity in the same brain region induced by external stimulus and independent of the spontaneous signal and noise signal, as shown in Fig. 1A. Besides, ISFC also provides information about the similarity of functional brain activity between different brain regions [4]. Generally, ISFC includes seed-based ISFC and whole-brain-based ISFC. Seed-based ISFC calculates the Pearson correlation coefficient between the time series of a specific region (seed area) and those of other brain regions (Fig. 1B); whole-brain-based ISFC consists of the seed-based ISFC of each brain region over the whole brain and the diagonal of the ISFC matrix is ISC (Fig. 1C). Furthermore, the parts above and below the diagonal of the ISFC matrix were averaged to facilitate further statistical analysis and interpretation of the results.

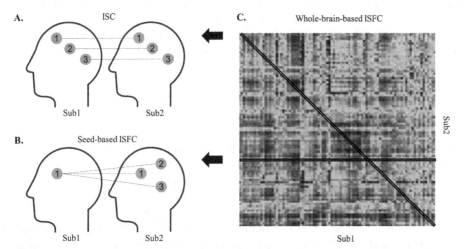

**Fig. 1.** ISC and ISFC. (A) ISC calculates the Pearson correlation coefficient of time series of the corresponding brain area between two subjects. (B) Seed-based ISFC represents the similarity of functional brain activity of a subject's seed area and those of the other subject's brain areas across the whole brain. (C) Whole-brain-based ISFC indicates the inter-regional functional correlation across the whole brain between two subjects.

## 2.6  Statistics Analysis

A permutation test (100,000 times) was performed on the SC to determine movie clips which could reveal significant inter-group difference in inter-subject functional activity, taking a significance threshold of $P < 0.01$, and two movie clips were found. The clip 1 (*The present*: 0:32–1:22) is from window 48 to window 59 and the clip 2 (*The present*: 02:17–02:59) is from window 179 to window 181.

Finally, to analyze the effect of the different stimulus on synchrony alteration of the functional activity in ADHD and TD, for the three conditions, including watching (1) the entire film, (2) the movie clip1, (3) the movie clip2, the ISC and ISFC of each group were calculated, and the inter-group ISC and ISFC differences between ADHD patients and TD subjects were analyzed by two-sample t tests ($P < 0.01$), corrected for multiple comparisons with familywise error correction (FWE) at the cluster level.

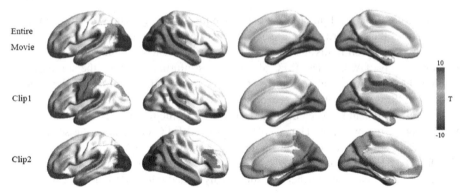

**Fig. 2.** The ISC difference between ADHD and TD in the three conditions. The red indicates the ISC of ADHD is significantly greater than that of TD and the blue means the opposite. Entire Movie represents watching the whole animated short film; Clip 1 denotes watching the movie clip 1; Clip 2 denotes watching the movie clip 2. (Color figure online)

## 3    Results

### 3.1    Between-Group Differences in ISC

In the entire movie, as shown in Fig. 2, ADHD showed increased ISC in the bilateral hippocampus (HIP), cuneus, lingual gyrus (LG), occipital lobe, fusiform gyrus (FFG), angular gyrus (AG), superior temporal gyrus (STG), heschl gyrus (HG) and right middle temporal gyrus (MTG) than TD. There was no significant decreased ISC in ADHD.

In movie clip 1, the ISC in the bilateral cuneus, LG, STG, right HG, left superior occipital gyrus (SOG) and right superior temporal pole (TP) in ADHD increased than that in TD. In addition, the ISC in the left precentral gyrus (preCG), the right superior orbital frontal cortex (OFC), the left cingulate cortex (CC), and the left postcentral gyrus (postCG) in ADHD significantly decreased than that in TD.

In movie clip 2, compared with TD, the increased ISC of the bilateral superior OFC, posterior cingulate cortex (PCC), parahippocampal (paraHIP), cuneus, LG, occipital lobe, FFG, right superior parietal gyrus (SPG), right AG, bilateral precuneus, STG, right MTG and right inferior temporal gyrus (ITG) was observed in ADHD, and the decreased ISC of the inferior frontal gyrus (IFG) was found in ADHD.

Overall, the ISC difference between ADHD and TD varied in the movie clips. For example, the significant inter-group ISC difference in the postCG existed in the movie clip 1, which did not appear in the entire movie or movie clip 2. In addition, the ISC in the occipital and temporal lobe in ADHD was significantly greater than that in TD in the three conditions.

### 3.2    Between-Group Differences in ISFC

In the entire movie, ADHD showed the most significant increased ISFC within the visual network (occipital lobe, FFG, and LG) compared with TD. Besides, the ISFC between the visual network and STG, amygdala (AMG), and the ISFC between superior OFC and insular, AMG in ADHD were greater than that in TD. Compared with TD, ADHD showed the decreased ISFC between anterior cingulate gyrus (ACC) and SOG, supramarginal gyrus (SMG), SPG, the decreased ISFC between SPG and medial superior frontal gyrus (SFG), middle OFC, the decreased ISFC between superior OFC and SMG, and the decreased ISFC between medial SFG and SMG, insular. More details were shown in Fig. 3.

ADHD>TD                                      ADHD<TD

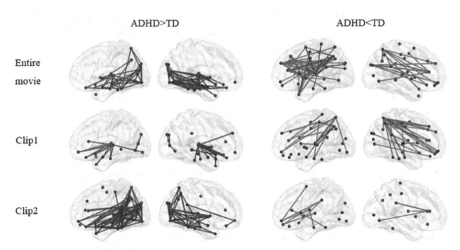

Entire
movie

Clip1

Clip2

**Fig. 3.** The ISFC difference between ADHD and TD in the three conditions. The red line indicates the ISFC of ADHD is significantly greater than that of TD and the blue means the opposite. Entire Movie represents watching the whole animated short film; Clip 1 denotes watching the movie clip 1; Clip 2 denotes watching the movie clip 2. (Color figure online)

Like the entire movie, the ISFC within the visual network in ADHD were also obviously greater than that in TD during the movie clip 1. Furthermore, ADHD also showed the increased ISFC within the auditory network, and the increased ISFC between the auditory network and olfactory cortex, paraHIP, AMG, insular, inferior occipital gyrus (IOG), putamen than TD. However, compared with TD, the decreased ISFC between SPG and OFC, olfactory cortex, ACC, HIP, AMG, FFG, AG, precuneus, putamen, thalamus, ITG, HG, and the decreased ISFC between postCG and lateral SFG, OFC, middle frontal gyrus (MFG), ACC, paraHIP were found in ADHD. Compared with TD, for the movie clip 2, the ISFC within the visual network, the ISFC between the visual network and preCG, supplementary motor areas (SMA), PCC, HIP, AMG, putamen, pallium, superior OFC, SPG, temporal lobe, the ISFC within DMN, the ISFC between DMN and superior OFC, IFG, SPG, ACC, putamen, MTG in ADHD were greater than that in TD. Furthermore, ADHD showed the decreased ISFC between SMG and superior OFC, olfactory cortex, ACC, the decreased ISFC between olfactory cortex and postCG, paracentral lobule, the decreased ISFC between LG and IFG, ACC, and the decreased ISFC between caudate and FFG than TD.

Clearly, there were significant inter-group ISFC differences in the three conditions. For example, compared with TD, the decreased ISFC of ADHD in the movie clip 1 was significantly greater than that in the movie clip 2. In addition, whether in the entire movie or in the two movie clips, the inter-group ISFC difference within the visual network was obvious, and the ISFC between the brain regions involved in attention, emotion, and cognitive control was significantly different between ADHD and TD.

## 4   Conclusion and Discussion

This study first takes advantage of the two measurements (ISC and ISFC) to explore the inter-subject synchrony alteration of the functional brain activity in ADHD and TD. The results indicated that ADHD patients showed stronger inter-subject consistency of functional activity in the occipital lobe, temporal lobe, AMG and insular than TD subjects, which mainly involve in audiovisual attention and emotion perception [9, 10], but weaker inter-subject synchrony in some regions, such as ACC and SPG, which involve in the process of cognitive control [11].

To explore the effect of the different stimulus on ISC and ISFC, two movie clips with significant inter-group SC difference were selected. The movie clip 1 describes the boy's emotional changes, from the curiosity of receiving a gift to the joy of seeing a puppy, finally turning into a disgust to the one-leg puppy. The movie clip 2 depicts that the little boy changes his attitude to the puppy and intends to play with the puppy. Whether in the entire movie or in the two movie clips, the brain areas involved in the visual and auditory network [12], such as occipital lobe, STG and SPG, were exhibited significant ISC inter-group differences. Nonetheless, compared with the TD group, the decreased ISFC between the regions related to cognitive control (e.g. ACC) [11] and the regions within the visual network (e.g. SOG) [12] were found in ADHD, which is related to the cognitive control deficit of ADHD patients who often fail to control the visual attention to the external stimulus [13]. More interesting, the increased ISFC between the regions related to emotional response (e.g. amygdala and insular) [9] and the regions within the visual and auditory network [14] in ADHD was found in the two movie clips, which imply ADHD patients have a stronger emotional response when they notice the scene with intense emotion. The result is roughly in line with the previous study that ADHD showed significant impairment compared to controls in regulating all emotions [15]. There is still something to improve in the future. For instance, demographic information such as the subtypes of ADHD, the diagnostic score could further apply to the correlation analysis of behavior and brain activity.

## References

1. Campbell, K.L., Shafto, M.A., Wright, P., et al.: Idiosyncratic responding during movie-watching predicted by age differences in attentional control. Neurobiol. Aging **36**(11), 3045–3055 (2015)
2. Huijbers, W., Van Dijk, K.R.A., Boenniger, M.M., et al.: Less head motion during MRI under task than resting-state conditions. Neuroimage **147**, 111–120 (2017)
3. Vanderwal, T., Eilbott, J., Finn, E.S., et al.: Individual differences in functional connectivity during naturalistic viewing conditions. Neuroimage **157**, 521–530 (2017)
4. Simony, E., Honey, C.J., Chen, J., et al.: Dynamic reconfiguration of the default mode network during narrative comprehension. Nat. Commun. **7**, 12141 (2016)

5. Jenkinson, M., Bannister, P., Brady, M., et al.: Improved optimization for the robust and accurate linear registration and motion correction of brain images. Neuroimage **17**(2), 825–841 (2002)
6. Yan, C.G., Wang, X.D., Zuo, X.N., et al.: DPABI: data processing & analysis for (resting-state) brain imaging. Neuroinformatics **14**(3), 339–351 (2016)
7. Tzourio-Mazoyer, N., Landeau, B., Papathanassiou, D., et al.: Automated anatomical labeling of activations in SPM using a macroscopic anatomical parcellation of the MNI MRI single-subject brain. Neuroimage **15**(1), 273–289 (2002)
8. Tang, C., Wei, Y., Zhao, J., Nie, J.: The dynamic measurements of regional brain activity for resting-state fMRI: d-ALFF, d-fALFF and d-ReHo. In: Frangi, A.F., Schnabel, J.A., Davatzikos, C., Alberola-López, C., Fichtinger, G. (eds.) MICCAI 2018. LNCS, vol. 11072, pp. 190–197. Springer, Cham (2018). https://doi.org/10.1007/978-3-030-00931-1_22
9. LeDoux, J.E.: Emotion circuits in the brain. Annu. Rev. Neurosci. **23**, 155–184 (2000)
10. Vossel, S., Geng, J.J., Fink, G.R.: Dorsal and ventral attention systems: distinct neural circuits but collaborative roles. The Neurosci. **20**(2), 150–159 (2014)
11. Fan, J.: An information theory account of cognitive control. Front. Hum. Neurosci. **8**, 680 (2014)
12. Heine, L., Soddu, A., Gomez, F., et al.: Resting state networks and consciousness: alterations of multiple resting state network connectivity in physiological, pharmacological, and pathological consciousness States. Front. Psychol. **3**, 295 (2012)
13. Silk, T., Vance, A., Rinehart, N., et al.: Fronto-parietal activation in attention-deficit hyperactivity disorder, combined type: functional magnetic resonance imaging study. Brit. J. Psychiatry **187**(3), 282–283 (2005)
14. Sjowall, D., Roth, L., Lindqvist, S., et al.: Multiple deficits in ADHD: executive dysfunction, delay aversion, reaction time variability, and emotional deficits. J. Child Psychol. Psychiatry **54**(6), 619–627 (2013)
15. Davies, J., Gander, P.E., Andrews, M., et al.: Auditory network connectivity in tinnitus patients: a resting-state fMRI study. Int. J. Audiol. **53**(3), 192–198 (2014)

# Weakly- and Semi-supervised Graph CNN for Identifying Basal Cell Carcinoma on Pathological Images

Junyan Wu[1], Jia-Xing Zhong[2], Eric Z. Chen[3], Jingwei Zhang[4], Jay J. Ye[5], and Limin Yu[6(✉)]

[1] Cleerly Inc., New York City, NY, USA
mylotarg1989@gmail.com
[2] School of Electronic and Computer Engineering, Peking University, Beijing, China
jxzhong@pku.edu.cn
[3] Dana-Farber Cancer Institute, Boston, USA
chvlyl@gmail.com
[4] Carolinas Dermatology Group, Florence, USA
caroderm@gmail.com
[5] Dahl-Chase Pathology Associates, Bangor, USA
jye@dahlchase.com
[6] Beaumont Health, Royal Oak, USA
juatgeneit@gmail.com

**Abstract.** Deep learning has been used to identify Basal Cell Carcinoma (BCC) from pathology images. The traditional patch-based strategy has the problem of integrating patch level information into the whole image level prediction. Also, it is often difficult to obtain sufficient high-quality patch labels such as pixel-wise segmentation masks. Benefiting from the recent development of Graph-CNN (GCN), we propose a new weakly- and semi-supervised GCN architecture to model patch-patch relation and provide patch-aware interpretability. Integrating prior knowledge and structure information, without relying on pixel-wise segmentation labels, our whole image level prediction achieves state-of-art performance with mAP 0.9556 and AUC 0.9502. Further visualization demonstrates that our model is implicitly consistent with the pixel-wise segmentation labels, which indicates our model can identify the region of interests without relying on the pixel-wise labels.

**Keywords:** Basal Cell Carcinoma · Graph-CNN · Pathology

## 1 Introduction

Recent years, deep learning has been broadly used in medical image analysis. Several studies have proven that it has the ability to classify Basal Cell Carcinoma (BCC) based on pathological images. Cruz-Roa *et al.* [2] proposed a

---

J. Wu and J.-X. Zhong—These authors contributed equally.

© Springer Nature Switzerland AG 2019
D. Zhang et al. (Eds.): GLMI 2019, LNCS 11849, pp. 112–119, 2019.
https://doi.org/10.1007/978-3-030-35817-4_14

deep learning architecture for BCC detection. Their work utilized an autoencoder to extract the patch features and used a single average pooling layer plus softmax classifier to generate the prediction. Another research used the concept of bag of features for representing image-level information [1]. Both approaches directly aggregated the patch features inside a fixed amount of neighbor patches. The methods lack the learnability for structure information based on inter-patch topological information. Traditional patch-based method for processing pathology image has certain challenges: 1. the patch-wise training relies on segmentation labeling which takes lots of human efforts; 2. The traditional convolutional neural network cannot directly learn the inter-patch structure for delivering convincing whole image-wise prediction. 3. It's hard to interpret entire image-wise output based on patch-wise information. One of latest research embed the clustering concept into the multiple instance learning (MIL) to solve the above problems [8].

In this paper, we proposed a graph convolutional neural network (GCN) to *predict the BCC on pathological images, and output corresponding interpretations in the form of a probability score for each patch.* To make full use of supervision on various levels, our model allows two types of supervisions, *i.e.* weakly- and semi-supervised formulations. The *weakly-supervision* refers to the setting that only image-level labels are available, and the *semi-supervision* means that the pixel-wise segmentation labels are also provided in several images.

Our key idea is to *combine prior knowledge from humans and structural information between patches into a graph-based model.* Based upon a GCN module, we aggregate patch-level predictions into the whole image level output and utilize the image level supervision to enhance the patch level interpretability in turn.

In a nutshell, our contribution is three-fold:

- Involving prior knowledge and structural information, we design a classifier to identify the BCC on pathological images and to output corresponding patch-level interpretations.
- Our model flexibly works under both semi- and weakly-supervisions. To the best of our knowledge, it is the first GCN model to support both two supervised formulations simultaneously.
- Both theoretical proofs and experimental results demonstrate the efficacy of our model. Remarkably, the image-level classification performance achieves 95.56% mAP with 0.0347 patch level MSE even under the weak supervision.

## 2    Methodology

Given a pathology image $\mathbf{I}$, we divide it into $M \times N$ equal-size patches. First, the patch-level features are extracted with a Resnet-50 [4] pre-trained on Imagenet [3]. Denote the $D-$dimensional feature vector of a certain patch $\mathbf{I}_{(m,n)}$ as $\mathbf{F}_{(m,n)} \in \mathbb{R}^D$, where $(m,n)$ is the position tuple.

Based on these patches, our target is to predict the image-level category $Y \in \{0,1\}$ as well as the patch-level cancer probabilities $\mathbf{p}_{patch}$, indicating

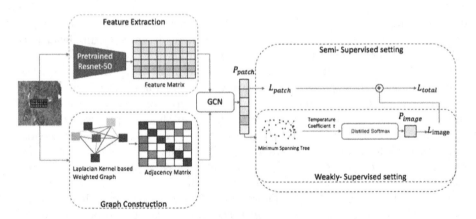

**Fig. 1.** Framework of our model. The GCN module propagates supervisory signals amongst patches and outputs the patch-level interpretation, while the structure-aware aggregator makes an image-level prediction over patches.

whether the patch contains cancer cells. During the training process, only the image-level annotation is available under our weakly-supervised settings. Therefore, we are facing two major challenges: *how to integrate the patch-level predictions into an image-level predictions, and how to provide convincing patch-aware interpretability under only the image-level supervision.*

As Fig. 1 depicts, our framework consists of two modules, *i.e.*, a graph convolutional module and an aggregation function. These two modules attempt to address the aforementioned challenges. The former propagates supervisory information over patches to learn patch-aware interpretability, while the latter bridges the gap between patch-level predictions and image-level predictions by utilizing prior knowledge.

## 2.1  Graph Convolutional Module

In the case of the curse of dimensionality, the pre-trained features $\mathbf{F} \in \mathbb{R}^{M \times N \times D}$ are first compressed with two fully connected layers. We leverage the topological information of these patches via an attribute graph $G = (V, E, \mathbf{F})$, where $V$ is the vertex set of $G$ and $E$ is the edge set. In this problem, $V$ is composed of patches, and $E$ describes their topological relationship. Similar to previous researches, the graphical information $(V, E)$ is specified with the corresponding adjacency matrix $\mathbf{A}$ in this paper.

Since no patch-level supervision is provided under the weakly-supervised setting, we would like to introduce topology information to improve the patch-level predictive performance. First of all, we establish the adjacency matrix $\mathbf{A} \in \mathbb{R}^{|M \times N| \times |M \times N|}$ as:

$$\mathbf{A}_{(i,j)} = \phi(i, j), \tag{1}$$

where $\phi$ is a kernel function, and $\mathbf{A}_{(i,j)}$ reflects the topological relationship between the $i^{th}$ and the $j^{th}$ image amongst all of these $M \times N$ patches. To distinguish patches in different distances, we utilize an exponential kernel in practice:

$$\phi(i,j) = \exp(-(|m_i - m_j| + |n_i - n_j|)).    \quad (2)$$

To drive nearby patches potentially from the same cluster to assign similar categories, the graph-Laplacian operation is naturally exerted over this graph structure. Following Kipf and Welling [6], we apply the renormalization trick for numeric stability:

$$\hat{\mathbf{A}} = \tilde{\mathbf{D}}^{-\frac{1}{2}} \tilde{\mathbf{A}} \tilde{\mathbf{D}}^{-\frac{1}{2}},    \quad (3)$$

where the self-loop adjacency $\tilde{\mathbf{A}} = \mathbf{A} + \mathbf{I_n}$ is obtained with an identity matrix $\mathbf{I_n} \in \mathbb{R}^{N \times N}$, and $\tilde{\mathbf{D}}$ is the corresponding degree matrix:

$$\tilde{\mathbf{D}}_{(i,i)} = \sum_j \tilde{\mathbf{A}}_{(i,j)}.    \quad (4)$$

The output $\mathbf{H}$ of this layer is an approximation of graph-Laplacian:

$$\mathbf{H} = \alpha(\hat{\mathbf{A}}\mathbf{X}\mathbf{W}),    \quad (5)$$

where $\mathbf{W}$ is a learnable parametric matrix, and $\alpha$ is an activation function. Our graph convolution is fully differentiable. Thus it is convenient to incorporate the stacked graph convolution into neural networks.

To interpret the patch-level likelihood of containing cancer cells, the last output of our graph convolutional module is a probabilistic vector $\mathbf{p}_{patch} \in \mathbb{R}^{|M \times N|}$:

$$\mathbf{p}_{patch} = Sigmoid(\mathbf{H}_{last}),    \quad (6)$$

where $\mathbf{H}_{last} \in \mathbb{R}^{|M \times N|}$ is the feature map of the last graph convolutional layer. Under the weakly supervised setting, it is directly forwarded to our aggregator. Under the semi-supervised setting, we can seamlessly append an auxiliary loss for these patch-level probabilities:

$$L_{patch}(\mathbf{p}_{patch}, \mathbf{s}) = CE(\mathbf{p}_{patch}, \mathbf{s}),    \quad (7)$$

where the patch-level ground truth $\mathbf{s}$ is defined as an area proportion of cancer cells with respect to the certain patch, and $CE$ is a cross-entropy loss. Since segmentation labels are available under the semi-supervised setting, $\mathbf{s}$ can be easily calculated.

## 2.2   Aggregation Function

The goal of our aggregation function is to predict the image category over patch-level predictions integrating structure information and prior knowledge. Our aggregator is based upon two observations:

(a) The denser patches with predictive cancer cells, the more possible there is really a cluster of cancer cells within the patches.
(b) The more patches with high probabilities, the more possible the corresponding image is positive.

We measure the density of patches from different images with the average weight of a minimum spanning tree (MST) of the graph $G$ with respect to high-probability patches, and compute the image-level prediction via a distilling softmax [5]:

$$p_{image} = \sum_{i \in H} \frac{\exp(\mathbf{p}_{patch(i)}/\tau)}{\sum_{i \in H} \exp(\mathbf{p}_{patch(i)}/\tau)} \times \mathbf{p}_{patch(i)}, \tag{8}$$

where the temperature coefficient $\tau = \frac{\sum_{i \in H} w_i}{|H|} = \bar{w}_{i \in H}$ is defined upon the MST weights $w_i$ of the high-probability patch set $H \subseteq V$, and $\tau$ is the mean weight $\bar{w}_{i \in H}$ with respect to the MST. By propagating information from $H$ to $V - H$ through our graph convolutional module, all of the patches can be incorporated into the training process. Based on the aggregation function, we provide two theoretical guarantees as follows:

**Theorem 1.** *Given fixed patch-level probabilistic estimations* $\mathbf{p}_{patch}$, $p_{image}$ *is a monotone decreasing function of the average weight* $\bar{w}_{i \in H}$.

**Theorem 2.** *Given a fixed average weight* $\bar{w}_{i \in H}$ *with respect to the MST over* $G$, $p_{image}$ *is a monotone increasing function of the mean patch-level probabilistic estimation* $\bar{\mathbf{p}}_{patch}$.

The proof is provided in **Appendix**. Intuitively, Theorem 1 means that our model tends to highlight an image with *denser high-probability patches*, while Theorem 2 means that an image deemed as a positive example should have *more patches with higher predictive cancerness probabilities*. Finally, the image-level cost function is a cross-entropy loss between $p_{image}$ and the category label of this image:

$$L_{image}(p_{image}, y) = CE(p_{image}, y). \tag{9}$$

Obviously, it is flexible for our model to switch between weakly- and semi-supervised formulations by utilizing different loss functions: $L_{semi} = L_{patch} + L_{image}$ and $L_{weakly} = L_{image}$.

## 3   Experiments

### 3.1   Dataset

There are 1,241 images in our whole BCC dataset, including 598 positive and 643 negative examples. The images were captured by smartphones during frozen section including BCC and normal tissues at 100x and 200x magnifications. It's a private database collecting from 2 different hospitals. The image samples contain 4 major types of BCC: superficial, nodular, micronodular and infiltrative. The image labels were generated by 3 dermatopathologists. We partitioned the dataset into two portions: 830 for training and 411 for testing. The enlargement factor of these images are from 10x to 20x. In accordance with the resolution of images, we divide each image into from $11 \times 13$ to $12 \times 16$ patches and obtain 228,704 patches in total. For the weakly-supervised setting, all of the 824 training images only have image-level category annotations. For the semi-supervised formulation, segmentation labels of 200 images, about 25% of the training data are provided to obtain the **s** in Eq. 7.

## 3.2   Experiment Settings

We implement our model with Pytorch [7] on an Nvidia Tesla V100 GPU. The feature vector is extracted from the last global average pooling layer of the pre-trained Resnet-50, and the output dimensions of the first two fully connected layers are 512 and 128 respectively, at the 60% dropout rate. The graph convolutional module has two convolutional layers: a 32-unit hidden layer activated by ReLu and the last 1-unit output layers. We optimize the GCN via SGD with the following hyper-parameters: initial learning rate = 0.0001, momentum = 0.9 and weight decay = 0.0001. The set $H$ in Eq. 8 is composed of the top 10% highest-score patches of an image. Since our model is the only known interpretable classifier to allow the two supervisions simultaneously with respect to BCC diagnoses, we compare our model with [2] under the weak supervision. For a fair comparison, we replace the original feature extractor in [2] with the Resnet-50.

## 4   Results

**Table 1.** Performance on patch-level interpretation.

| Metric/value | Weakly-supervised Cruz-Roa *et al.* [2] | Weakly-supervised ours | Semi-supervised ours |
|---|---|---|---|
| SSIM | 0.1998 | 0.5570 | **0.6658** |
| PSNR | 7.1097 | 23.229 | **30.0569** |
| MSE | 0.2338 | 0.0347 | **0.0296** |
| MAE | 0.2962 | 0.0780 | **0.0636** |

**Quantitative Performance on Patch-Level Interpretation.** As far as we know, there is no specific measurements to evaluate the patch-level interpretation. In this paper, we take inspiration from crowd counting problems to measure the interpretation performance. The goal of crowd counting is to estimate the number of crowd within certain regions of an image. This resembles our target to some extent: we want to validate the predictive score of cancer cells within certain patches of an image. Therefore, we leverage 4 typical metrics, *i.e.* SSIM, PSNR, MSE and MAE. The specific definitions of these metrics are provided in **Appendix**. As shown in Table 1, semi-supervised model with only 25% labeled patches obviously surpasses the weakly-supervised counterpart. This observation reflects two facts: the extra patch-level supervision is beneficial for acquiring interpretability, and our model can take advantage of such a supervision. Without patch-level supervisory signals, our model still has a descent interpretability of 0.0347 MSE, which outperforms the BCC classifier in [2] by a large margin.

**Qualitative Analysis on Patch-Level Interpretation.** For further analysis on patch-level interpretation, we visualize the results under both supervisions. As depicted in Fig. 2, although no patch-level supervision is available under the weakly-supervised formulation, our model still approximately localizes the cancerness regions. Nevertheless, it is possible to underestimate several small cancerness regions (*e.g.* the right part of the $3^{rd}$ column in Fig. 2) since our aggregator may regard such fragmentary patches as noises. Under the semi-supervised setting, the boundary of a cancerness region becomes more accurate, and the small positive region can be more noticeable.

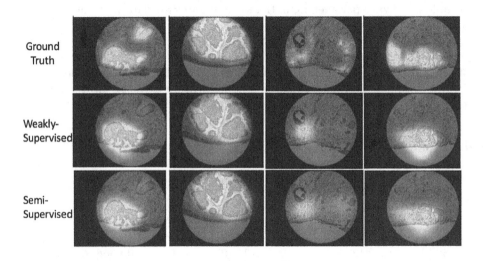

**Fig. 2.** Patch-level interpretation.

**Quantitative Performance on Image-Level Classification.** When it comes to image-level classification, we measure the performance upon ROC-AUC, mAP, *etc.* ROC-AUC is the area under the receiver operating characteristics curve. A larger frame-level AUC implies higher diagnostic ability. The mAP is short for mean average precision, and a higher mAP indicates better performance. Besides the two primary metrics, we also make comparison upon others. Please refer to **Appendix** for the other metrics in more detail. As shown in Table 2, our weakly-supervised model significantly surpasses the model in [2,8], achieving an excellent performance of 95.02% ROC-AUC and 95.56% mAP. The extra patch-level supervision slightly boosts the performance to 95.38% ROC-AUC and 95.83% mAP. Both of our models are consistently superior to the other BCC classifier with respect to all the metrics.

**Table 2.** Performance on image-level classification.

| Metric/value | Weakly-supervised MCIL-Boost [8] | Weakly-supervised Cruz-Roa *et al.* [2] | Weakly-supervised ours | Semi-supervised ours |
|---|---|---|---|---|
| ROC-AUC | 0.9256 | 0.8821 | 0.9502 | **0.9538** |
| mAP | 0.9296 | 0.8850 | 0.9556 | **0.9583** |
| Accuracy | 0.8516 | 0.7956 | 0.8856 | **0.9027** |
| Precision | 0.8674 | 0.8365 | 0.8962 | **0.9037** |
| Sensitivity | 0.8093 | 0.6963 | 0.8586 | **0.8848** |
| Specificity | 0.8894 | 0.8818 | 0.9136 | **0.9182** |

## 5   Conclusion

In this paper, we focus on the interpretable BCC identification under weakly- and semi- supervisions. By integrating prior knowledge and structure information, the performance get significantly improved on both image-level classification and patch-level interpretation. Extensive experiments demonstrate the proposed model obtains satisfactory results under the two supervised settings.

## References

1. Arevalo, J., Cruz-Roa, A., González, F.A.: Hybrid image representation learning model with invariant features for Basal Cell Carcinoma detection. In: IX International Seminar on Medical Information Processing and Analysis, vol. 8922, p. 89220M. International Society for Optics and Photonics (2013)
2. Cruz-Roa, A.A., Arevalo Ovalle, J.E., Madabhushi, A., González Osorio, F.A.: A deep learning architecture for image representation, visual interpretability and automated basal-cell carcinoma cancer detection. In: Mori, K., Sakuma, I., Sato, Y., Barillot, C., Navab, N. (eds.) MICCAI 2013. LNCS, vol. 8150, pp. 403–410. Springer, Heidelberg (2013). https://doi.org/10.1007/978-3-642-40763-5_50
3. Deng, J., Dong, W., Socher, R., Li, L.J., Li, K., Fei-Fei, L.: ImageNet: a large-scale hierarchical image database. In: CVPR (2009)
4. He, K., Zhang, X., Ren, S., Sun, J.: Deep residual learning for image recognition. In: CVPR, pp. 770–778 (2016)
5. Hinton, G., Vinyals, O., Dean, J.: Distilling the knowledge in a neural network. In: NIPS Deep Learning and Representation Learning Workshop (2015)
6. Kipf, T.N., Welling, M.: Semi-supervised classification with graph convolutional networks. In: ICLR (2017)
7. Paszke, A., et al.: Automatic differentiation in PyTorch (2017)
8. Xu, Y., Zhu, J.Y., Eric, I., Chang, C., Lai, M., Tu, Z.: Weakly supervised histopathology cancer image segmentation and classification. Med. Image Anal. **18**(3), 591–604 (2014)

# Geometric Brain Surface Network for Brain Cortical Parcellation

Wen Zhang$^{(\boxtimes)}$ and Yalin Wang

School of Computing, Informatics and Decision Systems Engineering,
Arizona State University, Tempe, AZ, USA
wenzhang.ccm@gmail.com

**Abstract.** A large number of surface-based analyses on brain imaging data adopt some specific brain atlases to better assess structural and functional changes in one or more brain regions. In these analyses, it is necessary to obtain an anatomically correct surface parcellation scheme in an individual brain by referring to the given atlas. Traditional ways to accomplish this goal are through a designed surface-based registration or hand-crafted surface features, although both of them are time-consuming. A recent deep learning approach depends on a regular spherical parameterization of the mesh, which is computationally prohibitive in some cases and may also demand further post-processing to refine the network output. Therefore, an accurate and fully-automatic cortical surface parcellation scheme directly working on the original brain surfaces would be highly advantageous. In this study, we propose an end-to-end deep brain cortical parcellation network, called **DBPN**. Through intrinsic and extrinsic graph convolution kernels, DBPN dynamically deciphers neighborhood graph topology around each vertex and encodes the deciphered knowledge into node features. Eventually, a non-linear mapping between the node features and parcellation labels is constructed. Our model is a two-stage deep network which contains a coarse parcellation network with a U-shape structure and a refinement network to fine-tune the coarse results. We evaluate our model in a large public dataset and our work achieves superior performance than state-of-the-art baseline methods in both accuracy and efficiency.

**Keywords:** Brain cortical surface · Deep learning · Geometry · Parcellation

## 1 Introduction

Brain cortical surface, delineating the shape of the cerebral cortex, is highly folded and consists of a large number of functionally and structurally different regions [2]. Identifying these regions demands a consistent parcellation map of the cortical surface among a group of subjects. Generally, a brain atlas would be defined beforehand according to an anatomical protocol and then parcellation schemes in the individual brain shall be drawn by following the given

© Springer Nature Switzerland AG 2019
D. Zhang et al. (Eds.): GLMI 2019, LNCS 11849, pp. 120–129, 2019.
https://doi.org/10.1007/978-3-030-35817-4_15

atlas. However, the conventional ways to do this such as manual labeling [6] or registration-based mapping [13] are inefficient due to the requirements of expert guidance and heavy computation. Therefore, an automatic pipeline which effectively generates a projection from the atlas to an individual brain surface is much needed. However, it is challenging because of the diversity of brain shapes owing to different genetic and environmental affection [8]. As a result, it is extremely difficult to locate boundaries of the brain regions. It is a common belief that a plausible solution shall collectively analyze brain surface features, e.g. cortical thickness and area, together with their embedded geometry structures, e.g. local surface structure.

Deep learning is a powerful tool for geometric feature learning on the non-Euclidean structured data, such as graphs and triangular meshes [1]. Efforts to generalize the conventional image-based convolutional operators to these irregular data can be categorized into spectral [5] and spatial [7] approaches. Here, we favor the latter approach to encode both intrinsic and extrinsic surface structures. Until recently, only a few studies applied deep models to process brain cortical surfaces [10,11]. However, there are some limitations in previous work. For example, inputs of their models are feature patches based on the intrinsic structure of the brain surface while the extrinsic structures are ignored. Another drawback of the patch-based study is that it is unable to change patch size dynamically according to the complexity of local shapes. Besides, these methods require a time-consuming parameterization of brain surfaces, i.e. a regular metric in a sphere. However, deformation from the brain surface to a sphere might introduce distortions and sometimes is difficult to achieve if there are topological defects on the original surface, e.g. holes or triangle flips. In addition, existing deep models designed for brain parcellation require post-processing on the network outputs.

To overcome the aforementioned limitations, we propose an automatic and end-to-end deep brain parcellation network (DBPN). To fully describe brain surfaces, we use two surface-based convolution kernels, i.e. intrinsic and extrinsic kernels, to aggregate local vertex features. The intrinsic kernel uses a polar coordinate system depending on the geodesic distance while the extrinsic kernel uses a Cartesian coordinate system which is embedded in the local Euclidean space around each vertex. The convolutional operation in these two kernels is carried out by referring a continuous B-spline kernel [4] which is efficient to compute. We design a two-step learning framework for the brain parcellation. The first learning is a coarse parcellation built with a U-shape deep network and relies on both intrinsic and extrinsic geometry features. The second is a refinement learning built upon the coarse parcellation scheme. This network depends on the intrinsic kernel to remove disconnected clusters and smooth the regional boundaries. We test our model in a large dataset containing 101 normal subjects and manually-created labels. The experimental results demonstrate the effectiveness and efficiency of our model. The main contributions of this work are 4 folds: (1) proposing an end-to-end deep model for surface-based brain parcellation; (2) directly working on the original brain surfaces without a sphere parameterization; (3) using graph convolution with the intrinsic and extrinsic kernels to capture local geometry structures; (4) designing a two-step learning scheme to construct a smooth parcellation map.

## 2    Methods

In this section, we first introduce two surface convolution kernels which capture intrinsic and extrinsic geometrical properties of human cortical surfaces. After that, based on these kernels, a two-stage deep network is proposed. In the first stage, we design a U-shape network to gather clustering information in the deep layers. The vertex clustering pattern, to a large extent, relies on the surface extrinsic properties. Then, we construct the second stage of parcellation with a refinement network. It removes cluster noises caused by the spatial down/up-sampling in the first stage. This network only uses the intrinsic surface kernel to guarantee the smoothness of parcellation scheme on the surface.

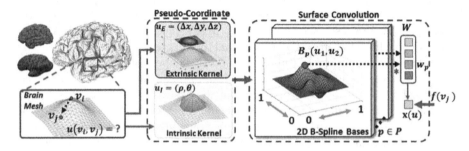

**Fig. 1.** B-spline-based intrinsic and extrinsic convolution kernels. In these kernels, aggregation of local vertex features is regulated by the learned edge weight $x(u)$ which is determined by the intrinsic and extrinsic geometry structures, i.e., expressions of pseudo-coordinate $u(v_i, v_j)$. Here, we show an example of 2-dimensional B-Spline convolution (the right block).

### 2.1    Surface-Based Convolution Kernels

A surface can be realized from two aspects, i.e., extrinsic and intrinsic structures, and they are geometrically associated. The extrinsic structure of a surface depends on a coordinate system in an embedding space of that surface. Therefore, different coordinate systems might lead to distinct expressions of the extrinsic structures. The most common coordinate system for meshes and point clouds is the Cartesian coordinate in the Euclidean space. In contrast, the intrinsic structure is independent of the embedding space, meaning it can be measured within a surface itself without any reference to a specific coordinate system. An intrinsic structure example is the geodesic distance between two points in a surface. To have a comprehensive awareness of a brain surface, both of these geometry structures are indispensable.

A brain surface is generally represented as a local connected graph $G = \{V, E, X, F\}$, where $V = \{v_i\}_{i=1}^{N}$ is the set of nodes, i.e. vertices, $E = \{\epsilon_{i,j}\}$ is the set of edges and $X = \{x_{i,j}\}$ is the corresponding edge weights. Generally, $G$ is sparse meaning the number of edges $|E| \ll N^2$. A function $F = \{f(v_i) \in \mathbb{R}^M\}$ is defined on each vertex $v_i$, which can be regarded as node signals or features. The neighbourhood graph of $v$ is denoted by $\mathcal{N}(v)$.

In this study, the convolution kernel encodes the local mesh geometry around a given node and meanwhile aggregates the neighboring node features such as cortical thickness and surface area. The output of this kernel is the new node features. We understand the aggregation mechanism as an analogy of image-based convolutional operation but differs on the definition of aggregation weights, i.e. $x_{i,j}$, which are defined on edges rather than nodes. The aggregation is mathematically formulated as:

$$AGG(v_i) = \delta(\frac{1}{|\mathcal{N}(v_i)|} \sum_{v_j \in \mathcal{N}(v_i)} x_{i,j} * f(v_j) * W), \qquad (1)$$

where $W \in \mathbb{R}^{M_{in} \times M_{out}}$ is a trainable weight matrix controlling the feature dimension and $\delta$ is a non-linear activation. In Eq. 1, we want $x_{i,j}$ to be a function based on the local geometry properties on edges via the pseudo-coordinates [1], $u(v_i, v_j) \in \mathbb{R}^k$, and thus kernel value $x(u)$ is learned dynamically (Fig. 1). For the extrinsic geometric property, we use a 3-dimensional Cartesian coordinate system to reflect a shift from a source node $v_i = (x_i, y_i, z_i)$ to a target node $v_j = (x_j, y_j, z_j)$ in the Euclidean space, as $u_E(v_i, v_j) = (x_i - x_j, y_i - y_j, z_i - z_j)$. For the intrinsic geometric property, we use a 2-dimensional polar coordinates denoted by $u_I(v_i, v_j) = (\rho, \theta)$, where $\rho$ is the geodesic distance between $v_i$ and $v_j$, $\theta$ is the rotation angle in the tangent plane with respect to the maximal curvature direction. Noting that the pseudo-coordinates will scaled to a range $[0,1]$ in each dimension.

Since the brain surface is geometrically complex and its shape is diverse subject-to-subject, optimal $x(u)$ fitting to various geometry patterns is hard to specify. In this study, we use a spline-based convolution kernel [4] to automatically encode it. The idea is to generate a set of feature manifolds as B-spline surfaces and learn their combination weights as parameters. Mathematically, suppose that the pseudo-coordinates used in this kernel is $k$-dimensional, i.e. $k = 2$ or 3, we define $k$ B-spline bases of degree $m$ as $(\{N_{i,j}^m\}_{j=1}^{d_i})_{i=1}^{k}$, based on equidistant knot vectors. $d_i$ is the kernel size defined in the $i$-th dimension of $u$. The larger $d_i$, the more control points in the B-spline surface. By referring the B-spline composition, we give the convolution kernel as:

$$x(u) = \sum_{p \in \mathcal{P}} w_p * B_p(u). \qquad (2)$$

$w_p$ is a trainable control weight for each element $p$ from the Cartesian product $\mathcal{P} = N_{1,i}^m \times ... \times N_{k,i}^m$ and $B_p(u)$ is the product of the basis functions, $B_p(u) = \prod_{i=1}^{k} N_{i,p_i}^m(u_i)$. We can interpret $B_p(u)$ as a B-spline surface in the feature space depend on $u(v_i, v_j)$ and the corresponding $w_p$ controls the weight of this surface. There are a total of $D = \prod_{i=1}^{k} d_i$ such kind of surfaces in $\mathcal{P}$ for each $u$ and thus the computation has a fixed time complexity for searching the $B_p(u)$ value in a B-spline surface.

## 2.2 Coarse Parcellation Network

This network serves as a coarse parcellation of brain surfaces, which projects 3 vertical features, e.g. surface area, mean curvature, and cortical thickness, to the label space. We have two parallel sub-networks (Fig. 2). One uses the intrinsic convolution kernel to aggregates local vertex features up to k-hops in the surface graph. The other is built with the extrinsic convolution kernel and has a U-shape structure for node clustering.

The U-net structure has a good performance in brain segmentation tasks [9]. For the U-shape structure in our model, two key components are down-sampling and up-sampling operations on the surface graph. The down-sampling operation pools similar vertices together by searching meaningful neighborhoods on graphs. The pooled patterns are stored for the later up-sampling process which restores the original vertex order. Since clustering on the general graph is NP-hard, here, we use a multi-level graph clustering algorithm, called Graclus [3], to approximate the graph clustering. This method has been proved to be effectively dealing with large graphs with thousands of vertices. It avoids eigenvector computation which is painful and prohibitive for large graphs but, instead,

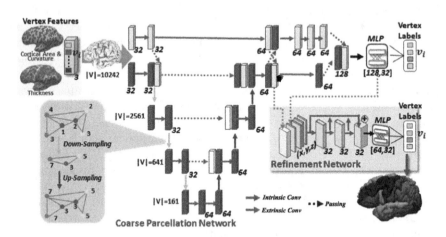

**Fig. 2.** Pipeline of DBPN. We design the extrinsic and intrinsic convolutional kernels based on B-spline functions to encode local geometry patterns and aggregate node features. With these kernels, a two-stage parcellation is proposed. In the coarse parcellation network, intrinsic and extrinsic encoding is conducted concurrently, which accommodates a U-shape structure with graph spatial down/up-samplings. The refinement network further modifies the coarse results with intrinsic kernels. DBPN learns a projection from the vertex-wise features to the parcellation labels.

directly optimizes a weighted graph clustering objective, e.g. normalized cut. Each round of clustering groups vertices by pairs. The node value in the coarsened graph is the sum of grouped nodes while the new pseudo-coordinate is their average. The edge is the union of connection patterns (shown in the gray block, Fig. 2). For each down-sampling layer in our model, we perform graph clustering twice that divides the number of vertices by four. The up-sampling works in the opposite way by reversing the coarsening scheme. During this reverse operation, the value of a vertex in the coarser level will be passed back to and shared by all of its elements in the finer level. It is worth noting that we only deploy the U-shape network in the extrinsic sub-network. Since each of the down-sampling and up-sampling operations would change local graph topology, it is time-consuming to recompute the intrinsic pseudo-coordinates but the extrinsic kernels.

In the end, we combine node features generated from the intrinsic and extrinsic sub-networks respectively and feed them into a multilayer perceptron (MLP) with a softmax in the last layer. The output of this coarse parcellation network is the probability of each vertex belonging to the given parcellation label. The object function of this network is the negative log-likelihood which is extensively utilized in multi-label classification.

### 2.3 Refinement Parcellation Network

The output of coarse parcellation might contain several discontinued clusters due to the down-sampling on the local extrinsic geometry rather than intrinsic structures. Therefore, we create a refinement network based on the surface intrinsic structure to removes noises in each parcellated region and meanwhile fine-tune the boundary of those regions. We add two additional vertex-wise information to the feature vector generated before the last softmax layer in the coarse parcellation network. One additional information is a copy of encoded vertex features in the middle of the intrinsic sub-network. The other is the vertex spatial coordinate vector $(x, y, z)$. In this refinement network, we add a skip method [12] which let the network dynamically adopt various sizes of the neighborhood in aggregation. After 3 intrinsic convolutional layers, we use an MLP to obtain the vertex-wise probability. Here, in addition to the negative log-likelihood, we add n multi-class Dice score weighted by $\lambda$ to the vertex-wise loss function.

$$D(g, \tilde{g}) = \frac{1}{|\mathbf{L}|} \sum_{l \in \mathbf{L}} \frac{2 \sum_i g_l^i \tilde{g}_l^i}{\sum_i (g_l^i + \tilde{g}_l^i)}, \tag{3}$$

where $\{g_l^i\}_{i \in Y, l \in \mathbf{L}}$, $\{\tilde{g}_l^i\}_{i \in Y, l \in \mathbf{L}}$ are the set of label probability vectors for all vertices for the ground truth and the prediction label. $|\mathbf{L}|$ is the number of brain regions.

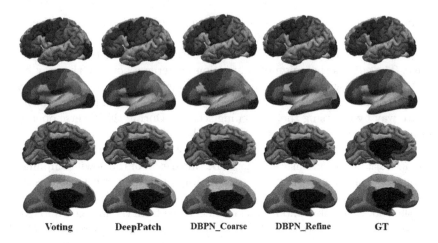

| Voting | DeepPatch | DBPN_Coarse | DBPN_Refine | GT |

**Fig. 3.** Visualization of brain surface parcellation. Along with the baseline methods, i.e., Voting and DeepPatch, we present our coarse (DBPN_Coarse) and refined (DBPN_Refine) parcellation results and compare them with the ground truth (GT) data.

## 3  Experimental Results

### 3.1  Dataset and Settings

We evaluate our model on a large public dataset[1], named Mindboggle-101, which contains a surface-based brain atlas drawn by following the Desikan–Killiany–Tourville protocol [6]. Only the left brain surfaces are evaluated and each surface is manually parcellated into 32 sub-regions. The brain surface is reconstructed by using the standard computation pipeline in FreeSurfer package[2] and 3 vertex-wise structural features, i.e. cortical thickness, surface area, and curvature, are measured. The 5-fold cross-validation is carried out in this study. Since each subject brain contains 10424 vertices, the total training samples are 833920 vertices (from 80 subjects). To assess model performance, we compute the average regional Dice score for each subject and report statistics for the group of testing. The hyper-parameter $\lambda$ in the refinement network is empirically set to 10. For the two-stage learning, we first train the coarse parcellation network with a learning rate $r = 0.01$ and then reduce it to $r = 0.0001$ when training the refinement network which has a learning rate $r = 0.005$. The strategy of learning decay is added.

Here, we pick two baseline methods for brain cortical parcellation. The first one, termed as Voting, is a multi-atlas based parcellation method which use majority voting to combine parcellation scheme in the training data [6]. Specifically, surface-based registrations project label information in the training data

---

[1] https://mindboggle.info/data.html.
[2] http://surfer.nmr.mgh.harvard.edu/.

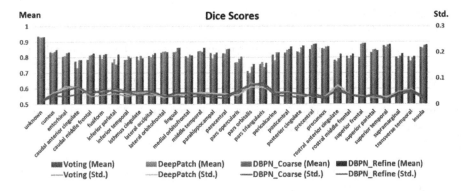

**Fig. 4.** Comparison of brain regional Dice scores.

to the surface of the testing data. Then we do majority voting vertex-wisely to determine parcellation scheme in each subject and compute the statistics. The second one, termed as DeepPatch, is a deep learning model based on multi-channel feature images in local intrinsic patches [11]. We extract vertex patches based on the local polar coordinate in the spherical domain and follow the network settings reported in the paper. Note that we do not include the post-process to remove noise in this method to have a fair comparison as a deep model.

## 3.2 Results

We show the parcellation scheme of a randomly selected sample in Fig. 3. Both of the original and inflated brain surfaces overlaid with predicted labels are presented. Our method outperforms other baselines with the closest consistency to the ground truth and achieves a Dice score of $0.846 \pm 0.034$ after refinement and $0.831 \pm 0.037$ in the coarse parcellation, while the method with majority voting obtains $0.817 \pm 0.038$ and the deep model with spherical patches achieves $0.821 \pm 0.037$. Besides, we observe that, compared with the result from the coarse parcellation network, refinement network prominently remove discontinued clusters and improve the boundary prediction by adding smoothness. When considering the computational efficiency, our DBPN significantly outperforms the others. Since our method is an end-to-end framework, once the model has been well trained, testing on a subject will complete in a few seconds. In contrast, due to the burden computation of surface-based registration or spherical parameterization, other baseline methods might need hours to process.

To further quantitatively address parcellation results in details, we compute the Dice score for each of the 32 subregions and report the statistics in Fig. 4. Compared to majority voting method and the deep model with spherical patches, DBPN achieves better results in 27 out of 32 brain subregions and most of them have a clear boundary locating at the stable cortical landmarks, i.e. gyrus and sulci.

## 4  Conclusion and Future Works

We describes a novel surface-based deep learning model for brain parcellation. Two graph convolution kernels is designed based on the intrinsic and extrinsic geometric properties. Built on these kernels, a two-stage network parcellates cortical surface to a coarse map and then refines it. There are several interesting directions that are warranted for further investigation. For example, vertex features extracted from multimodal neuroimaging data can potentially improve parcellation accuracy.

**Acknowledgments.** The research was supported by NIH (R21AG043760, R21AG049-216, and U54EB020403).

## References

1. Bronstein, M.M., Bruna, J., LeCun, Y., Szlam, A., Vandergheynst, P.: Geometric deep learning: going beyond Euclidean data. IEEE Signal Process. Mag. **34**(4), 18–42 (2017)
2. Dale, A.M., Fischl, B., Sereno, M.I.: Cortical surface-based analysis: I. Segmentation and surface reconstruction. Neuroimage **9**(2), 179–194 (1999)
3. Dhillon, I.S., Guan, Y., Kulis, B.: Weighted graph cuts without eigenvectors a multilevel approach. IEEE Trans. Pattern Anal. Mach. Intell. **29**(11), 1944–1957 (2007)
4. Fey, M., Eric Lenssen, J., Weichert, F., Müller, H.: SplineCNN: fast geometric deep learning with continuous B-spline kernels. In: CVPR, pp. 869–877 (2018)
5. Kipf, T.N., Welling, M.: Semi-supervised classification with graph convolutional networks. arXiv preprint arXiv:1609.02907 (2016)
6. Klein, A., Tourville, J.: 101 labeled brain images and a consistent human cortical labeling protocol. Front. Neurosci. **6**, 171 (2012)
7. Monti, F., Boscaini, D., Masci, J., Rodola, E., Svoboda, J., Bronstein, M.M.: Geometric deep learning on graphs and manifolds using mixture model CNNs. In: CVPR, pp. 5115–5124 (2017)
8. Paus, T.: How environment and genes shape the adolescent brain. Horm. Behav. **64**(2), 195–202 (2013)
9. Ronneberger, O., Fischer, P., Brox, T.: U-net: convolutional networks for biomedical image segmentation. In: Navab, N., Hornegger, J., Wells, W.M., Frangi, A.F. (eds.) MICCAI 2015. LNCS, vol. 9351, pp. 234–241. Springer, Cham (2015). https://doi.org/10.1007/978-3-319-24574-4_28
10. Seong, S.B., Pae, C., Park, H.J.: Geometric convolutional neural network for analyzing surface-based neuroimaging data. Front. Neuroinform. **12**, 42 (2018)
11. Wu, Z., Li, G., Wang, L., Shi, F., Lin, W., Gilmore, J.H., Shen, D.: Registration-free infant cortical surface parcellation using deep convolutional neural networks. In: Frangi, A.F., Schnabel, J.A., Davatzikos, C., Alberola-López, C., Fichtinger, G. (eds.) MICCAI 2018. LNCS, vol. 11072, pp. 672–680. Springer, Cham (2018). https://doi.org/10.1007/978-3-030-00931-1_77

12. Xu, K., Li, C., Tian, Y., Sonobe, T., Kawarabayashi, K.i., Jegelka, S.: Representation learning on graphs with jumping knowledge networks. arXiv preprint arXiv:1806.03536 (2018)
13. Zhang, W., Wang, J., Fan, L., Zhang, Y., Fox, P.T., Eickhoff, S.B., Yu, C., Jiang, T.: Functional organization of the fusiform gyrus revealed with connectivity profiles. Hum. Brain Mapp. **37**(8), 3003–3016 (2016)

# Automatic Detection of Craniomaxillofacial Anatomical Landmarks on CBCT Images Using 3D Mask R-CNN

Yankun Lang[1], Li Wang[1], Pew-Thian Yap[1], Chunfeng Lian[1], Hannah Deng[2], Kim-Han Thung[1], Deqiang Xiao[1], Peng Yuan[2], Steve G. F. Shen[4], Jaime Gateno[2,3], Tianshu Kuang[2], David M. Alfi[2,3], James J. Xia[2,3(✉)], and Dinggang Shen[1(✉)]

[1] BRIC and Department of Radiology, University of North Carolina at Chapel Hill, Chapel Hill, USA
dgshen@med.unc.edu
[2] Department of Oral and Maxillofacial Surgery, Houston Methodist Hospital, Houston, TX, USA
jxia@houstonmethodist.org
[3] Department of Surgery (Oral and Maxillofacial Surgery), Weill Medical College, Cornell University, New York, NY, USA
[4] Department of Oral and Craniofacial Surgery, Shanghai 9th Hospital, Shanghai Jiaotong University College of Medicine, Shanghai, China

**Abstract.** Craniomaxillofacial (CMF) landmark localization is an important step for characterizing jaw deformities and designing surgical plans. However, due to the complexity of facial structure and the deformities of CMF patients, it is still difficult to accurately localize a large scale of landmarks simultaneously. In this work, we propose a three-stage coarse-to-fine deep learning method for digitizing 105 anatomical craniomaxillofacial landmarks on cone-beam computed tomography (CBCT) images. The first stage outputs a coarse location of each landmark from a low-resolution image, which is gradually refined in the next two stages using the corresponding higher resolution images. Our method is implemented using Mask R-CNN, by also incorporating a new loss function that learns the geometrical relationships between the landmarks in the form of a root/leaf structure. We evaluate our approach on 49 CBCT scans of patients and achieve an average detection error of $1.75 \pm 0.91$ mm. Experimental results show that our approach overperforms the related methods in the term of accuracy.

## 1 Introduction

Craniomaxillofacial (CMF) surgery aims to correct congenital or acquired deformities of the head and face. Due to complex head anatomy, it requires a detailed surgical plan, which is typically based on cone-beam computed tomography

© Springer Nature Switzerland AG 2019
D. Zhang et al. (Eds.): GLMI 2019, LNCS 11849, pp. 130–137, 2019.
https://doi.org/10.1007/978-3-030-35817-4_16

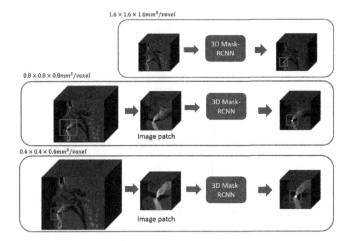

**Fig. 1.** Our coarse-to-fine 3-stage training strategy. Image resolution: first $1.6 \times 1.6 \times 1.6\,\mathrm{mm}^3$, then $0.8 \times 0.8 \times 0.8\,\mathrm{mm}^3$, and finally $0.4 \times 0.4 \times 0.4\,\mathrm{mm}^3$.

(CBCT). CMF landmark localization (also called "landmark digitization") is an important step to characterize jaw deformities and design surgical plans. The landmark detection is typically formulated as a classification or regression problem based on discriminative image features [1,2]. Different from conventional methods that designing handcrafted features, deep learning methods can automatically learn discriminative features for landmark detection [3,4]. For example, Payer et al. [3] used a fully convolutional network (FCN) to localize multiple anatomical landmarks simultaneously. The FCN learns a non-linear mapping between an image and the landmarks, which are represented as heat maps. Zhang et al. [4] employed a cascade of two FCNs to detect large-scale anatomical landmarks simultaneously. The first FCN is a regression model that learns a 3D displacement map which records a displacement from the current voxel location to a respective landmark in a specific axis. The second FCN shares the same weights and architecture as the first FCN, but with extra layers to localize landmarks.

Using image patches to train a network may result in mis-detection due to the ignorance of global information [10,11]. It happens even more frequently in temporomandibular joints and the areas without prominent anatomical structures, where the landmarks have the similar appearances and structural features, making them undistinguishable without global information. In this paper, we propose a coarse-to-fine three-stage approach to gradually detect CMF landmarks from low-to-high resolution CBCT images (Fig. 1). In the first stage, a simple network is trained using down-sampled 3D images, to output a coarse location for each landmark. Then, in the second and third stages, we refine landmark locations by training our network using patches sampled from medium- and high-resolution 3D images, respectively, around the landmark locations that are estimated in the previous stage. In addition, we employ Mask Region-based Convolutional

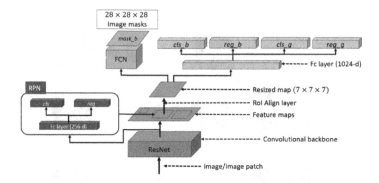

**Fig. 2.** The proposed Mask R-CNN used for detecting landmarks. Two tasks are added to learn (1) the region where the landmark is and (2) the geometrical relationship to its corresponding root node.

Neural Networks (Mask R-CNN) [6] in all stages to predict the location of each landmark based on a 3D bounding box in which it is centered. Furthermore, we group all the landmarks into 9 pre-defined anatomical regions as shown in Fig. 3(a). Landmarks in each region are defined to follow a root/leaf structure that describes the relative location between a leaf node to its root node. This geometrical relationship is leveraged for localizing the landmarks in the region where the anatomical structures are not prominent. Finally, we develop a new loss function that encodes the relationship describing the relative location between the predicted landmark and its corresponding root node.

The contribution of our paper is thus two-fold, i.e., we propose a coarse-to-fine landmark localization framework, and we introduce a new loss function that considers root/leaf structure of landmark locations into the Mask R-CNN, to automatically identify CMF landmarks.

## 2 Method

### 2.1 Mask R-CNN

Similar to Mask R-CNN, our network consists of a region proposal network (RPN) and a bounding box recognition network (Fig. 2). The backbone in this network is a ResNet consisting of three convolutional blocks in the form of two $3 \times 3 \times 3$ conv (convolutional layer) with a ReLU (Rectified Linear Units) activation layer and a BN (Batch Normalization) layer, followed by a pooling layer. The output channel of each block is 32, 64, 128, respectively. The output features are shared by the RPN and the bounding box recognition network.

**Region Proposal Networks (RPN).** The aim of RPN is to generate a number of proposals indicating foreground/background for landmarks. To generate such bounding boxes, a sliding window with size of $3 \times 3 \times 3$ is run spatially on the input feature maps. For each sliding window, a group of anchors, which has the same center but different aspect ratios and scales, are generated. Finally, the feature maps after the sliding window are fed into a small network with two tasks: (1) a bounding box regression head ($reg$) determining the coordinates of the proposal region, and (2) a classification head ($cls$) indicating if the corresponding proposal region contains a landmark or not. The training loss is defined as:

$$L^{RPN}(c_i, p_i) = L_{cls}{}^{RPN}(c_i, c_i{}^*) + \lambda L_{reg}{}^{RPN}(\mathbf{p}_i, \mathbf{p}_i{}^*) \tag{1}$$

where $L_{cls}{}^{RPN}$ is a binary classification loss. $c_i$ is the predicted score of anchor $i$ being a landmark contained object. The ground truth $c^*$ is defined as:

$$c^* = \begin{cases} 1, & \text{if } IoU > 0.5 \\ -1, & \text{if } 0.3 \le IoU \le 0.5 \\ 0, & \text{Otherwise} \end{cases} \tag{2}$$

where $IoU$ (Intersection over Union) is the overlap of ground-truth boxes with anchors. Anchors assigned with $-1$ do not contribute to the training. The regression term $L_{reg}{}^{RPN}$ is defined as a $l1$-smooth loss in [7]. $\mathbf{p}_i$ is a 6-dimensional vector representing the offset parameters of the predicted 3D bounding box, and $\mathbf{p}_i^*$ is that of the ground-truth box associated with a positive anchor. $\lambda$ is a weight to balance these two terms.

**Bounding Box Recognition Network.** After RPN, a small feature map is cropped from the shared feature maps according to each positive proposal region. Then Region of Interest Align (RoIAlign) [5] layer is applied to resize the cropped feature maps to a certain size $7 \times 7 \times 7$ through bilinear interpolation. In the original Mask R-CNN, each fixed feature map is shared by 3 tasks. (1) A classification task ($cls\_b$): it learns a discrete probability distribution $c^b$ over all landmark labels. (2) A bounding box regression task ($reg\_b$): it is the same as the one in RPN, which predicts the parameters $\mathbf{p}^b$ for refining the proposal region to the ground-truth box. To get more accurate result, we only refine the center of bounding boxes rather than the coordinates. (3) A mask task ($mask\_b$): it is constructed as a small FCN that outputs the mask of the proposal region $l^b$, representing the distribution of bones around landmarks there. Considering geometrical relationship between the landmarks, we add two auxiliary tasks ($cls\_g$ and $reg\_g$) that will be discussed next.

**Root/leaf Structure.** Landmarks are grouped into 9 regions/classes (denoted as $c^g$): left-midface (LMI), upper-midface (UMI), right midface (RMI), mid-midface (MMI), tooth-midface (TMI), left-mandible (LMA), right-mandible (RMA), mid-mandible (MMA), tooth-mandible (TMA), as shown in Fig. 3(a). The landmarks located in the same region follow a tree structure: one landmark is defined as the root node, while the others are defined as the leaf nodes (Fig. 3(b)). As shown in Fig. 3(c), the geometrical relationship between a predicted landmark and its corresponding leaf and root nodes is defined by a 6-dimentional vector as:

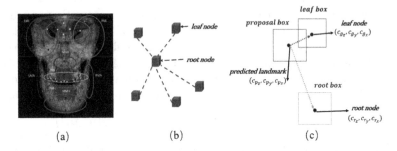

**Fig. 3.** (a) shows the predefined regions. (b) shows an example of the root/leaf structure and (c) shows an example of the geometrical relationship between a predicted landmark and its corresponding leaf and root nodes.

$$\mathbf{p}^g = [\delta_{z_g}, \delta_{y_g}, \delta_{x_g}, \delta_{z_r}, \delta_{y_r}, \delta_{x_r}] \tag{3}$$

where the first three and the last three values denote the displacement vectors from the proposal landmark to the target (leaf node) and the root landmark (root node), respectively. Also, another task is added to predict the label of the landmark's region. The final loss function of our bounding box recognition network is thus given as:

$$
\begin{aligned}
L^b(c^b, \mathbf{p}^b, l^b, \mathbf{p}^g, c^g) = {L_{cls}}^b(c^b, c^{b*}) + {L_{reg}}^b(\mathbf{p}^b, \mathbf{p}^{b*}) + {L_{seg}}^b(l^b, l^{b*}) \\
+ L_{reg}^g(\mathbf{p}^g, \mathbf{p}^{g*}) + L_{cls}^g(c^g, c^{g*})
\end{aligned}
\tag{4}
$$

where $c^{b*}$, $\mathbf{p}^{b*}$, $l^{b*}$, $\mathbf{p}^{g*}$, and $c^{g*}$ are the corresponding ground-truths. Furthermore, we employ multi-class classification losses for $L_{cls}^b$, $L_{seg}^b$ and $L_{cls}^g$, and $l1$-smooth losses for $L_{reg}^b$ and $L_{reg}^g$.

## 2.2   Implementation

To train the model in the 1st-stage, each image is down-sampled to $1.6 \times 1.6 \times 1.6 \, \mathrm{mm}^3$ and padded to a dimension of $128 \times 128 \times 128$ voxels. The size of basic anchor is set to $64 \times 64 \times 64$ voxels to make each landmark have at least one positive anchor associated with it. Image resolution in the 2nd and 3rd refinement stages is $0.8 \times 0.8 \times 0.8 \, \mathrm{mm}^3$ and $0.4 \times 0.4 \times 0.4 \, \mathrm{mm}^3$, respectively, and 100 image patches with the size of $64 \times 64 \times 64$ voxels are sampled around each landmark position obtained from the previous stage. We reduce the basic anchor size to $48 \times 48 \times 48$ voxels and $40 \times 40 \times 40$ voxels, respectively. This is because only one landmark needs to be detected from an image patch. We reduce the size of bounding box along the resolutions (from $1.6 \times 1.6 \times 1.6 \, \mathrm{mm}^3$, then $0.8 \times 0.8 \times 0.8 \, \mathrm{mm}^3$ and $0.4 \times 0.4 \times 0.4 \, \mathrm{mm}^3$) to gradually localize the landmarks. Furthermore, we only use the patches around possible locations so that the training computation can be greatly reduced. It takes 3 days to train each model under an environment of Intel Core i7-8700K CPU with a 12 GB GeForce GTX 1080Ti graphic memory card.

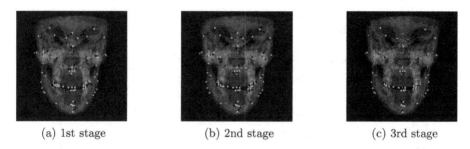

(a) 1st stage                    (b) 2nd stage                    (c) 3rd stage

**Fig. 4.** Results of the three stages on a randomly selected testing subject. Predicted landmarks and ground truth are illustrated in red and green, respectively.

Our model is trained by back-propagation and stochastic gradient descend (SGD) in an end-to-end manner. The initial learning rate is set to 0.001, decaying by 20% after each 5 epochs. The total number of training epoch is 20, each with 12000 iteration steps. To simplify the training, at the first 5 epochs, we use a large weight assigned for RPN losses to train the networks for giving more stable and reliable proposal regions. After that, we lower the RPN weights and increase the weights for bounding box recognition losses.

# 3   Experimental Results

## 3.1   Materials and Methods

Our approach was tested on 49 sets of CBCT images ($0.4 \times 0.4 \times 0.4 \, mm^3$ or $0.3 \times 0.3 \times 0.3 \, mm^3$) of patients with non-syndromic jaw deformities, where 10 sets were used for testing, 34 for training, and 5 for validation. Due to low contrast and artifacts in CBCTs, we first pre-trained our models using randomly selected 20 sets of normal spiral CT images (scanning matrix: $0.488 \times 0.488 \, mm^2$; and slice thickness: $1.25 \, mm$) that were previously collected for a different purpose [8]. After the pre-training, we subsequently trained our network using CBCT images of patient subjects. Prior to the training, each image was resampled to a common resolution of $0.4 \times 0.4 \times 0.4 \, mm^3$, and the intensities of each image were normalized to the same distribution by histogram matching and Gaussian normalization constant (GNC). Data augmentation, including rotation, flipping, and adding noise, was used to increase the training set and the robustness of our models. For each image, the midface and the mandible were segmented, and 105 landmarks (59 on the midface and 46 on the mandible) were jointly digitized by two experienced CMF surgeons using AnatomicAligner system [9], which are served as the ground truth. For our three-stage coarse-to-fine approach, the results of each stage were compared to the ground truth using mean square errors (MSEs).

In addition, we compared our approach to two U-net based methods: (1) a basic U-net that only used image patch as input [3]; and (2) a dual-input U-net that uses both the segmentation map and image patch as input. In both

**Table 1.** Comparison results of mean square error (mm) in 9 anatomical regions. U-net 1 and U-net 2 refer to basic U-net and dual-input U-net 2, respectively.

|  | U-net (basic) | U-net (dual-input) | Mask R-CNN | Our approach |
|---|---|---|---|---|
| LMI | $2.86 \pm 1.35$ | $2.53 \pm 1.32$ | $2.41 \pm 0.75$ | $\mathbf{1.33 \pm 0.46}$ |
| UMI | $1.75 \pm 1.25$ | $1.68 \pm 1.27$ | $1.65 \pm 1.23$ | $\mathbf{1.58 \pm 0.98}$ |
| RMI | $2.71 \pm 1.28$ | $2.31 \pm 1.25$ | $1.75 \pm 0.68$ | $\mathbf{1.31 \pm 0.56}$ |
| MMI | $2.14 \pm 1.32$ | $2.04 \pm 1.34$ | $1.78 \pm 1.12$ | $\mathbf{1.57 \pm 0.79}$ |
| TMI | $2.65 \pm 1.75$ | $2.35 \pm 1.28$ | $2.35 \pm 1.21$ | $\mathbf{2.05 \pm 1.12}$ |
| LMA | $2.76 \pm 1.68$ | $2.55 \pm 1.64$ | $1.98 \pm 1.32$ | $\mathbf{1.71 \pm 1.11}$ |
| RMA | $2.95 \pm 1.72$ | $2.25 \pm 1.59$ | $1.95 \pm 1.48$ | $\mathbf{1.67 \pm 1.16}$ |
| MMA | $2.32 \pm 1.21$ | $2.12 \pm 1.11$ | $2.03 \pm 1.30$ | $\mathbf{1.65 \pm 1.26}$ |
| TMA | $2.85 \pm 1.64$ | $2.43 \pm 1.31$ | $2.05 \pm 1.17$ | $\mathbf{1.76 \pm 0.76}$ |

methods, each landmark was represented as a heat map. Moreover, to evaluate the specific contribution of the proposed root/leaf structure, we also compared our method to the original Mask R-CNN.

### 3.2 Comparison Results

Figure 4(a–c) show the coarse-to-fine results of landmark localization obtained from the first to the third stages, respectively. The MSEs were gradually reduced from 3.32 mm at the first stage, down to 2.11 mm at the second stage, and further reduced to 1.75 mm at the third stage.

The MSEs of different methods are presented in Table 1. Results by basic U-net showed the largest MSE error (2.86 mm). Mis-detection was more frequently occurred in regions with relatively smooth surface (e.g., LMI/RMI, LMA/RMA), where anatomical structures were not prominent. In addition, the results in tooth area were not consistent, leading to a large standard deviation. The results by the dual-input U-net using segmentation map as an additional input showed a significantly improved result of 2.34 mm. The segmentation map provided prior knowledge for landmark feature difference between the midface and the mandible. However, large errors still existed in smooth surface regions. The results achieved with the original Mask R-CNN showed the average detection error was reduced to 2.08 mm. This implies that the three learning tasks used by Mask R-CNN (i.e., $cls\_b$, $reg\_b$, and $mask\_b$) are effective in localizing the landmark locations. In particular, the generated mask in the 3D bounding box of the corresponding landmark provides useful bony surface information that can facilitate the landmark localization. Finally, our proposed approach further improved over the original Mask R-CNN. The introduction of additional root/leaf auxiliary tasks could eliminate the locational uncertainty for the landmarks on the smooth surfaces. In addition, our proposed approach also improved the landmark detection accuracy by considering the relative relationship between the root landmark and its corresponding leaf landmarks. Overall, our approach further reduced the landmark detection error by 0.48 mm when compared to Mask R-CNN, and ultimately achieved the highest detection accuracy with an average MSE of $1.75 \pm 0.91$ mm. Our approach took about 20 min to finish the test due to the high number of network parameters, which is slower than the compared methods (about 10 min) but significantly improved accuracy.

## 4 Conclusion

In this work, we have proposed a three-stage coarse-to-fine training strategy to gradually localize 105 anatomical CMF landmarks from CBCT images. Improved localization accuracy is achieved by using a modified Mask R-CNN with two additional tasks that learn landmark relationships through a root/leaf structure. Experimental results showed that our approach can accurately detect a large number of landmarks simultaneously.

**Acknowledgment.** This work was supported in part by NIDCR grants (DE022676 and DE027251).

## References

1. Zhan, Y., et al.: Robust automatic knee MR slice positioning through redundant and hierarchical anatomy detection. IEEE TMI **30**(12), 2087–2100 (2011)
2. Criminisi, A., et al.: Regression forests for efficient anatomy detection and localization in computed tomography scans. MedIA **17**(8), 1293–1303 (2013)
3. Payer, C., Štern, D., Bischof, H., Urschler, M.: Regressing heatmaps for multiple landmark localization using CNNs. In: Ourselin, S., Joskowicz, L., Sabuncu, M.R., Unal, G., Wells, W. (eds.) MICCAI 2016. LNCS, vol. 9901, pp. 230–238. Springer, Cham (2016). https://doi.org/10.1007/978-3-319-46723-8_27
4. Zhang, J., et al.: Joint craniomaxillofacial bone segmentation and landmark digitization by context-guided fully convolutional networks. In: Descoteaux, M., Maier-Hein, L., Franz, A., Jannin, P., Collins, D.L., Duchesne, S. (eds.) MICCAI 2017. LNCS, vol. 10434, pp. 720–728. Springer, Cham (2017). https://doi.org/10.1007/978-3-319-66185-8_81
5. Ren, S., et al.: Faster R-CNN: towards real-time object detection with region proposal networks. In: Advances in Neural Information Processing Systems, pp. 91–99 (2015)
6. He, K., et al.: Mask R-CNN. arXiv Preprint (2017)
7. Girshick, R.: Fast R-CNN. arXiv:1504.08083 (2015)
8. Yan, J., et al.: Three-dimensional CT measurement for the craniomaxillofacial structure of normal occlusion adults in Jiangsu, Zhejiang and Shanghai Area. China J. Oral Maxillofac. Surg. **8**, 2–9 (2010)
9. Yuan, P., et al.: Design, development and clinical validation of computer-aided surgical simulation system for streamlined orthognathic surgical planning. Int. J. Comput. Assist. Radiol. Surg. **12**, 2129–2143 (2017)
10. Lian, C., et al.: Multi-channel multi-scale fully convolutional network for 3D perivascular spaces segmentation in 7T MR images. MedIA **46**, 106–117 (2018)
11. Lian, C., et al.: Hierarchical fully convolutional network for joint atrophy localization and Alzheimer's disease diagnosis using structural MRI. IEEE TPAMI (2019)

# Discriminative-Region-Aware Residual Network for Adolescent Brain Structure and Cognitive Development Analysis

Yongsheng Pan[1,2], Mingxia Liu[2(✉)], Li Wang[2], Yong Xia[1(✉)],
and Dinggang Shen[2(✉)]

[1] School of Computer Science and Engineering,
Northwestern Polytechnical University, Xi'an 710072, China
yxia@nwpu.edu.cn
[2] Department of Radiology and BRIC,
University of North Carolina at Chapel Hill, Chapel Hill, NC 27599, USA
{mxliu,dgshen}@med.unc.edu

**Abstract.** The brains of adolescents undergo profound cognitive development, especially the development of fluid intelligence (FI) that is the ability to reason and think logically (independent of acquired knowledge). Such development may be influenced by many factors, such as changes in the brain structure caused by neurodevelopment. Unfortunately, the association between brain structure and fluid intelligence is not well understood. Cross-sectional structural MRI data released by the Adolescent Brain Cognitive Development (ABCD) study pave a way to investigate adolescents' brain structure via MRIs, but each 3D volume may contain irrelevant or even noisy information, thus degrading the learning performance of computer-aided analysis systems. To this end, we propose a discriminative-region-aware residual network (DRNet) to jointly predict FI scores and identify discriminative regions in brain MRIs. Specifically, we first develop a *feature extraction module* (containing several convolutional layers and ResNet blocks) to learn MRI features in a data-driven manner. Based on the learned feature maps, we then propose a *discriminative region identification module* to explicitly determine the weights of different regions in the brain, followed by a *regression module* to predict FI scores. Experimental results on $4,154$ subjects with T1-weighted MRIs from ABCD suggest that our method can *not only* predict fluid intelligence scores based on structural MRIs *but also* explicitly specify those discriminative regions in the brain.

## 1 Introduction

The brains of adolescents undergo profound cognitive development, especially the development of fluid intelligence. Independent of acquired knowledge, fluid intelligence or fluid reasoning is the ability to reason and think logically [1,2],

© Springer Nature Switzerland AG 2019
D. Zhang et al. (Eds.): GLMI 2019, LNCS 11849, pp. 138–146, 2019.
https://doi.org/10.1007/978-3-030-35817-4_17

such as analyzing and solving novel problems, identifying patterns and relationships that underpin these problems and the extrapolation of these using logic. Recent studies are finding that aerobic conditioning, hand-eye coordination, motor skills, and daily physicality are important for maintaining fluid intelligence. With the neurodevelopment in adolescent brains, the resulting changes in brain structure may also influence the development of fluid intelligence. Previous studies have shown that changes in the brain structure can lead to changes in behavior and thinking [3,4]. As an example, many neuroscience studies on children and young adults with autism spectrum disorder demonstrate abnormalities in several brain regions (*e.g.*, hippocampus and precentral gyrus), while studies on old adults with Alzheimer's disease find structural changes in different brain regions (such as hippocampus and amygdala) [5,6]. Unfortunately, the association between adolescent brain structure and fluid intelligence has not been well understood currently. Therefore, bridging this gap is very meaningful for analyzing adolescent brain cognitive development.

Magnetic resonance (MR) examination allows clinicians and researchers to examine brain anatomy in a non-invasive manner. Especially, structural MR imaging (MRI) has been widely used to investigate brain morphology because of its high spatial resolution and contrast sensitivity [7]. Recently, the Adolescent Brain Cognitive Development (ABCD) study [8] released cross-sectional structural MRI data, paving a way to investigate the anatomical structure of adolescent brains via MRIs. Since each 3D volume contains a large number of regions, directly using the whole MR image may degrade the learning performance of computer-aided analysis systems due to those irrelevant or noisy regions.

To address this issue, various MRI-based machine/deep learning methods have been developed, by relying on prior anatomical knowledge or learn discriminative brain regions in a data-driven manner. For example, Zhang *et al.* [9] first defined multiple anatomical landmarks in brain MR images via group comparison, and then extracted image patches based on these landmarks for automated brain disease diagnosis. Li *et al.* [10] developed a multi-channel convolutional neural network (CNN) for identifying autism spectrum disorder, by first detecting anatomical landmarks and then training a CNN model for classification. However, these two methods employed handcrafted MRI features that may not well coordinated the subsequent classifier and treated landmark definition and classifier training as two standalone steps, thus leading to sub-optimal performance. Lian *et al.* [6] proposed a hierarchical fully convolutional network to automatically identify discriminative local patches and regions in the whole brain MRI, upon which task-driven MRI features were then jointly learned and fused to construct hierarchical classification models for disease identification, achieving state-of-the-art performance. However, this method cannot explicitly uncover the importance of different brain regions. Most importantly, existing methods generally focus on adult brains [6,9] or infant brains [10], and hence cannot be directly applied to adolescent brains due to differences in data distribution.

In this paper, we propose a discriminative-region-aware residual network (DRNet) to jointly predict fluid intelligence (FI) scores and identify

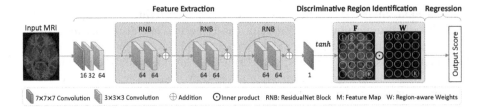

**Fig. 1.** Illustration of the proposed discriminative-region-aware residual network (DRNet) for joint fluid intelligence (FI) prediction and discriminative brain region identification. Three major components are included in DRNet: (1) a *feature extraction module* with 3 convolutional layers and 3 ResNet blocks (RNB) to learn MRI features, (2) a *discriminative region identification module* to explicitly learn the weights of different brain regions in each MRI, and (3) a *regression module* to estimate the FI score of the input MRI. The learned FI map (*e.g.*, **F** containing $K$ regions) are further weighted by the to-be-learned *region-aware weight map* **W** (with the same size as **F**) to automatically discover those discriminative regions for FI score prediction.

discriminative regions in brain MRIs. As shown in Fig. 1, given an input MR image, we first resort to a *feature extraction module* (containing several convolutional layers and ResNet blocks) to learn its features automatically. Based on the learned feature maps, we then design a *discriminative region identification module* to explicitly learn the weights of different regions in each brain MRI, followed by a *regression module* to predict FI scores. To the best of our knowledge, this is almost the first attempts to investigate the association of adolescent brain structure and fluid intelligence using structure MRIs and deep residual networks. Experimental results on 4,154 subjects from ABCD suggest that our method achieves promising results, in comparison to several state-of-the-art methods.

## 2    Method

**Feature Extraction Module:** As shown in Fig. 1, the proposed feature extraction contains a backbone with three convolutional layers (with 16, 32, and 64 channels, respectively) and three ResNet Blocks (RNBs) to extract MRI features, as well as a fully-connected layer (with 1 channel) to predict an FI map for all brain regions. In each RNB, there are two subsequent convolutional layers (with 32 channels) and an addition operation. Relu is used as the activation function for all convolutional layers, while *tanh* is used for the fully-connected layer. The strides are set to 2 for the second and third convolutional layers, and 1 for all the other layers. Since the resolution of all images is $1 \times 1 \times 1 \text{mm}^3$, the resolution of the output FI maps is $4 \times 4 \times 4$. Given an MR image with the size of $144 \times 176 \times 144$, the output $N$-channel FI map (denoted as $\mathbf{F} = \{f_1, f_2, \cdots, f_N\}$) is sized of $36 \times 44 \times 36$ (*i.e.*, $K = 51840$ in Fig. 1), with each element corresponding to a specific region around a center location in the original brain MRI.

**Discriminative Region Identification Module:** It's worth noting that not all of those $K$ regions in the FI maps are related to the task of FI prediction. To select the most discriminative regions, we employ a *region-aware weight map* (denoted as $\mathbf{W} = \{w_1, w_2, \cdots, w_N\}$) to encourage that the output FI maps (*i.e.*, $\mathbf{F}$) should focus on those discriminative regions. The sum of the element-wise product of $\mathbf{W}$ and $\mathbf{F}$ is considered as the final FI score $S_{FI}$ of the input MR image, which could be represented as

$$S_{FI} = \mathbf{W} \odot \mathbf{F} = \Sigma_{n=1}^{N} w_n f_n; \Sigma_{l=1}^{N} w_n = 1. \tag{1}$$

Using Eq. 1, we encourage that those most discriminative regions will contribute more to the final FI prediction result, while the influence of those uninformative brain regions will be suppressed. Another advantage of the proposed discriminative region identification module is that the weights of different brain regions in MRI can be explicitly captured by the region-aware weight map $\mathbf{W}$, and the learning of $\mathbf{W}$ is seamlessly incorporated into the network training process. Such a region-aware weight learning strategy can be flexibly applied to other neuroimage-based deep networks, thus potentially helping reduce the negative influence of uninformative regions in 3D volumes.

**Implementation:** The proposed network is implemented in Python with TensorFlow. The Adam solver [11] is used with a batch size of 1 and a learning rate of $2 \times 10^{-3}$. In the *training* stage, we first pre-train the network without updating the weight matrix (*e.g.*, $\mathbf{W}$) for brain regions, based on all training subjects. We then train the entire DRNet in an end-to-end manner for joint FI score prediction and region weight learning. In the *testing* stage, the structural MR image of an unseen testing subject is fed into the DRNet, and the predicted FI score will be obtained for this subject.

## 3  Experiment

### 3.1  Materials and Image Pre-processing

A cross-section of T1-weighted MR imaging data and the corresponding fluid intelligence scores for children aged 9–10 years were downloaded online (https://nda.nih.gov/edit_collection.html?id=2573). These subjects were partitioned into two subsets, including (1) training set with 3, 739 subjects, and (2) validation set with 415 subjects. Fluid intelligence scores of all subjects were measured by the ABCD study using the NIH Toolbox Neurocognition battery [12].

We employed our in-house tools to pre-process all T1-weighted MR images. A standard pipeline for image pre-processing include the following eight procedures, including (1) anterior commissure (AC)-posterior commissure (PC) alignment; (2) skull stripping; (3) intensity correction; (4) cerebellum removal; (5) linear alignment to the Colin27 template; (6) re-sampling all images to have the same size of $181 \times 217 \times 181 \, mm^3$ (with a spatial resolution of $1 \times 1 \times 1 \, mm^3$); (7) cropping each image to $144 \times 176 \times 144 \, mm^3$ to remove the background; and (8) performing intensity inhomogeneity correction by using N3 algorithm.

**Table 1.** Results of FI score prediction achieved by five different methods on the training data using 5-fold cross-validation.

| Method | Fold #1 | | Fold #2 | | Fold #3 | | Fold #4 | | Fold #5 | |
|---|---|---|---|---|---|---|---|---|---|---|
| | MAE | MSE | MAE | MSE | MAE | MSE | MAE | MSE | MAE | MSE |
| RVR [13] | 7.09 | 78.32 | 7.24 | 83.38 | 7.35 | 88.74 | 7.33 | 84.90 | 7.17 | 85.63 |
| CNN [14] | 7.10 | 79.55 | 7.22 | 83.38 | 7.37 | 89.28 | 7.38 | 85.86 | 7.19 | 86.41 |
| DSNN [15] | 7.10 | 77.84 | 7.26 | 83.67 | 7.34 | 88.64 | 7.32 | 84.71 | 7.18 | 85.51 |
| DRNet_now | 7.09 | 77.97 | 7.27 | 83.80 | 7.43 | 90.36 | 7.33 | 84.97 | 7.19 | 85.54 |
| DRNet (Ours) | 7.05 | 77.37 | 7.24 | 83.16 | 7.33 | 88.16 | 7.29 | 84.37 | 7.13 | 85.37 |

## 3.2   Experimental Setup

We compared the proposed DRNet with two baseline methods and a state-of-the-art method for MRI-based regression, including (1) region-based volumetric representation (RVR) [13], (2) a conventional convolutional neural network (CNN) [14], and (3) disease-image specific neural network (DSNN) [15]. To evaluate the effect of the proposed discriminative region identification module, we further compare DRNet with its variant that does not contain the region-aware weight map (i.e., $\mathbf{W}$), and call this method as "DRNet_now". For the fair comparison, our DRNet and four competing methods share the same input MRIs and output FI scores. The details of the competing methods are listed as follows.

(1) **RVR** [13]. In this method, each brain MRI is first segmented into three tissue types, i.e., gray matter (GM), white matter (WM) and cerebrospinal fluid (CSF). The AAL template with 90 pre-defined regions-of-interest in cortical and sub-cortical regions was further aligned to each MR image via nonlinear image registration. Finally, normalized volumes of GM tissue inside those 90 ROIs are concatenated to be the feature representation of each MRI, followed by a linear support vector regressor (with default parameters) for FI score regression.

(2) **CNN** [14]. In this method, each input MR image is fed to a sequence of 9 convolutional layers, with the channel numbers of 16, 32, 64, 64, 64, 64, 64, 64, 64, respectively. The generated feature maps are further fed into a fully-connected layer (with 1 channel) to predict the FI score of each subject. Similar to our DRNet, all convolutional layers employ the Relu activation function, while the fully-connected layer use *tanh* as the activation function.

(3) **DSNN** [15]. The DSNN method contains a feature extraction module and a spatial cosine module. There are 5 convolutional layers in the feature extraction module, with 16, 32, 64, 64, and 64 channels, respectively. Among these five layers, the first 4 and the last Conv layers are respectively followed by the max-pooling and average-pooling with the stride of 2 and the size of $3 \times 3$. The spatial cosine module in DSNN was used to $l_2$-normalize the feature vectors in feature map of the $5^{th}$ convolutional layer and concatenates them to be spatial representation, followed by a fully-connected layer with cosine kernel to estimate the FI score of a subject.

(4) **DRNet_now**. The network architecture of DRNet_now is similar to that of our DRNet. Specifically, each input MRI is fed into the feature extraction module (see Fig. 1), followed by a fully-connected layer (with *tanh* activation function) for predicting the FI score. That is, DRNet_now cannot explicitly learn the region weights from data.

In the experiments, we used two evaluation metrics to measure the quality of predicted FI scores generated by different methods, including (1) the mean absolute error (MAE), and (2) the mean square error (MSE).

### 3.3    Cross-validation Results on Training Data

In the first group of experiments, we compared the proposed DRNet with four competing methods using a five-fold cross-validation strategy on the training data. Specifically, we randomly partitioned the training data to five folds (with roughly equal size). Each time, one fold was used as the testing set and the remaining folds were combined to be the training set for training a specific regression model.

The MAE and MSE results of the predicted FI scores achieved by five methods are shown in Table 1. From this table, one may have the following observations. *First*, four deep learning methods (*i.e.*, CNN, DSNN, DRNet_now and DRNet) that learn task-specific MRI features usually perform better than RVR that use handcrafted features. *Second*, the overall performance of our DRNet is slightly better than that of the other methods. This implies that explicitly considering the weights of different brain regions (as we do in DRNet) is useful to promote the prediction results for FI scores. *Besides*, our DRNet consistently outperforms its variant DRNet_now among all five folds, suggesting the effectiveness of the proposed region-aware weight learning strategy.

### 3.4    Results on Validation Data

In the second group of experiments, we first trained five models (*i.e.*, RVR, CNN, DSNN, DRNet_now and DRNet) on all training data and evaluated them on 415 subjects in the validation set. The MAE and MSE results achieved by these five methods are reported in Table 2. Results in Table 2 verify again that our DRNet generally outperforms four competing methods in MRI-based FI score prediction. On the other hand, from Tables 1 and 2, we can see that the overall performance achieved by five methods on the validation data is better than that on the training data (using cross-validation). The possible reason is that the models in Table 2 are trained using all subjects in the training set to produce more powerful predictive models, while those in Table 2 are trained only using 80% training data in each fold. This demonstrates that using more data could further improve the robustness of the trained models.

### 3.5    Identified Discriminative Regions

We now show the learned region-aware weight map (*i.e.*, **W**) in Fig. 2. From this figure, one can observe that different brain regions do contribute differently to the

**Table 2.** Results of FI score prediction achieved by five different methods on validation data (with models learned on the training data).

| Method | RVR [13] | | CNN [14] | | DSNN [15] | | DRNet_now | | DRNet (Ours) | |
|--------|------|------|------|------|------|------|------|------|------|------|
| | MAE | MSE | MAE | MSE | MAE | MSE | MAE | MSE | MAE | MSE |
| Result | 6.48 | 71.58 | 6.81 | 75.70 | 6.47 | 70.81 | 6.46 | 70.88 | 6.45 | 70.79 |

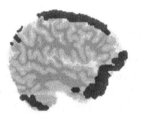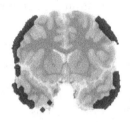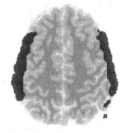

**Fig. 2.** Region-aware weight map (*i.e.*, **W** in Eq. 1) learned by our proposed DRNet for structural MRIs in ABCD, where the green region is discriminative to FI.

task of FI score prediction. This further validates the rationality of our proposed region-aware weight learning strategy in DRNet. Also, this figure suggests that the most discriminative regions located in the parietal cortex and the frontal cortex, which is consistent with previous studies [16].

## 3.6   Limitations and Future Work

There are still several limitations to be addressed, listed in the following. *First*, in the current work, we don't consider data distribution differences among different imaging sites, *e.g.*, caused by different populations, while those MRIs in ABCD were acquired from 21 different sites. It is desirable to develop an efficient data harmonization strategy to explicitly alleviate the negative influence of different data distributions in multiple sites. *Second*, we simply employ T1-weighted MR images in the experiments, while subjects in ABCD have multi-modal neuroimages (*e.g.*, T2-weighted MRI and functional MRI). In the future, we plan to take advantage of these multi-modal neuroimaging data to further improve the learning performance, by extending our DRNet to a multi-modal framework. *Besides*, we only consider imaging data in the current network, while demographic information (*e.g.*, age and gender) of subjects may also be associated with brain status. Therefore, it's reasonable to incorporate the demographic information to the model learning process to further improve the prediction results, which will also be our future work.

# 4    Conclusion

In this paper, we proposed a discriminative-region-aware residual network (DRNet), based on which one can jointly predict FI scores and identify discriminative regions in brain MRIs. Specifically, a feature extraction module was designed to learn MRI features from data automatically. A discriminative region identification module was further designed to explicitly learn the weights of different regions in each brain MRI, followed by a regression module to predict the FI score of the input MR image. Experimental results on 4,154 subjects from the ABCD study suggest the efficacy of our method in both tasks of fluid intelligence prediction and discriminative brain region identification.

# References

1. Carroll, J.B., et al.: Human Cognitive Abilities: A Survey of Factor-analytic Studies. Cambridge University Press, Cambridge (1993)
2. Jaeggi, S.M., Buschkuehl, M., Jonides, J., Perrig, W.J.: Improving fluid intelligence with training on working memory. Proc. Nat. Acad. Sci. U.S.A. **105**(19), 6829–6833 (2008)
3. Casey, B., Giedd, J.N., Thomas, K.M.: Structural and functional brain development and its relation to cognitive development. Biol. Psychol. **54**(1–3), 241–257 (2000)
4. Casey, B., Getz, S., Galvan, A.: The adolescent brain. Dev. Rev. **28**(1), 62–77 (2008)
5. Baron, J., Chetelat, G., Desgranges, B., Perchey, G., Landeau, B., De La Sayette, V., Eustache, F.: In vivo mapping of gray matter loss with voxel-based morphometry in mild Alzheimer's disease. NeuroImage **14**(2), 298–309 (2001)
6. Lian, C., Liu, M., Zhang, J., Shen, D.: Hierarchical fully convolutional network for joint atrophy localization and Alzheimer's disease diagnosis using structural MRI. IEEE Trans. Pattern Anal. Mach. Intell. (2018)
7. Giedd, J.N., et al.: Brain development during childhood and adolescence: a longitudinal MRI study. Nat. Neurosci. **2**(10), 861 (1999)
8. Volkow, N.D., Koob, G.F., Croyle, R.T., Bianchi, D.W., Gordon, J.A., Koroshetz, W.J., Pérez-Stable, E.J., Riley, W.T., Bloch, M.H., Conway, K., et al.: The conception of the ABCD study: from substance use to a broad NIH collaboration. Dev. Cogn. Neurosci. **32**, 4–7 (2018)
9. Zhang, J., Gao, Y., Gao, Y., Munsell, B.C., Shen, D.: Detecting anatomical landmarks for fast Alzheimer's disease diagnosis. IEEE Trans. Med. Imaging **35**(12), 2524–2533 (2016)
10. Li, G., Liu, M., Sun, Q., Shen, D., Wang, L.: Early diagnosis of autism disease by multi-channel CNNs. In: Shi, Y., Suk, H.-I., Liu, M. (eds.) MLMI 2018. LNCS, vol. 11046, pp. 303–309. Springer, Cham (2018). https://doi.org/10.1007/978-3-030-00919-9_35
11. Kingma, D.P., Ba, J.: Adam: a method for stochastic optimization. arXiv preprint arXiv:1412.6980 (2014)
12. Akshoomoff, N., et al.: NIH toolbox cognitive function battery (NIHTB-CFB): measuring executive function and attention. Monogr. Soc. Res. Child. Dev. **78**, 119–132 (2013)

13. Liu, M., Zhang, J., Yap, P.T., Shen, D.: View-aligned hypergraph learning for Alzheimer's disease diagnosis with incomplete multi-modality data. Med. Image Anal. **36**, 123–134 (2017)
14. Krizhevsky, A., Sutskever, I., Hinton, G.E.: Imagenet classification with deep convolutional neural networks. In: NIPS, pp. 1097–1105 (2012)
15. Pan, Y., Liu, M., Lian, C., Xia, Y., Shen, D.: Disease-image specific generative adversarial network for brain disease diagnosis with incomplete multi-modal neuroimages. In: Shen, D., et al. (eds.) MICCAI 2019. LNCS, vol. 11766, pp. 137–145. Springer, Cham (2019)
16. Jung, R.E., Haier, R.J.: The parieto-frontal integration theory (P-FIT) of intelligence: converging neuroimaging evidence. Behav. Brain Sci. **30**(2), 135–154 (2007)

# Graph Modeling for Identifying Breast Tumor Located in Dense Background of a Mammogram

Shelda Sajeev$^{(\boxtimes)}$, Mariusz Bajger$^{(\boxtimes)}$, and Gobert Lee$^{(\boxtimes)}$

College of Science and Engineering, Flinders University, Adelaide, SA 5001, Australia
{shelda.sajeev,mariusz.bajger,gobert.lee}@flinders.edu.au

**Abstract.** Identifying breast tumor in a mammogram is a challenging task even for experienced radiologists if the tumor is located in a dense tissue. In this study, a novel superpixel based graph modeling technique is proposed to extract texture features from the computer identified suspicious regions of mammograms. Graph models are constructed from specific structured superpixel patterns and used to generate feature vectors used for classifications of regions of mammograms. Two mammographic datasets were used to evaluate the effectiveness of the proposed approach: the publicly available Digital Database for Screening Mammography (DDSM), and a local database of mammograms (BSSA). Using Linear Discriminant Analysis (LDA) classifier, an AUC score of 0.910 was achieved for DDSM and 0.893 for BSSA. The results indicate that graph models can capture texture features capable of identifying masses located in dense tissues, and help improve computer-aided detection systems.

**Keywords:** Graph modeling · Superpixel tessellation · Mass localization · Dense background · Mammography

## 1 Introduction

In literature, numerous graph based approaches can be seen in histopathological image analysis where the spatial connectivity relationship between the cells is measured to distinguish between cancerous and healthy tissues [1,2,13]. Segmentation and detection of cell nucleus is the initial step for most of the cell graph based studies. The centroids of the cell nuclei forms the graph nodes and edges are formed based on the spatial proximity between the nuclei. Different topological properties are captured based on the cell graph features and classification of tissues is performed based on these graph features. Early studies on cell graphs were based on graph techniques like Voronoi tessellation and Delaunay triangulation [17]. However, these conventional graph techniques (Voronoi and Delaunay) construct global graph which connects every node. Hence, from these graphs, only global information like edge length statistics can be extracted. Later, cell graph approaches were generalized by introducing/allowing arbitrary

© Springer Nature Switzerland AG 2019
D. Zhang et al. (Eds.): GLMI 2019, LNCS 11849, pp. 147–154, 2019.
https://doi.org/10.1007/978-3-030-35817-4_18

edges based on the pairwise distance relationship between the nodes [1,2,13]. Cells or cell nuclei form the graph nodes and an edge between a pair of nodes exists based on the spatial proximity/distance between them. Both local and global graph features can be extracted from these approaches.

In the field of mammography, graph methods were used for pectoral muscle identification [10], breast segmentation [6] and temporal analysis of mammograms [9]. Recently, Chen et al. [4] used spatial connectivity graphs (similar to cell graph approaches) for classification of microcalcifications. However, graph based approaches for mammographic mass texture analysis have not been explored in the literature so far except the preliminary study [15]. The current study significantly extends [15] in several aspects. This approach is fully automatic and is applied to two different datasets with large number of ROIs to fully evaluate its potential (only a very small number of manually selected ROIs from one dataset was used in [15] to demonstrate the concept). Additionally, a hybrid feature vector comprising both graph and non-graph based features is utilized for tumor identification with a rigorous feature selection process conducted to optimize the feature vector. Two linear classifiers are trained in two ways and yield comparable outcome demonstrating the robustness of the framework.

Female breast is made of different types of parenchymal patterns. Organization of these patterns are not random but are linked with their underlying function or functional state. The presence of cancer/masses can change the normal organization of the tissue patterns. Hence, understanding the tissue structure organization and their relationships can be used to predict malfunctioning when the patterns start changing. From these observations, it can be hypothesized that the spatial relationships between the structured superpixel patterns found in mass regions may differ from those found in normal dense regions. Hence, graph theoretical features extracted from the superpixel pattern graph that reflect their topological properties could be used to distinguish mass regions from normal dense regions. This study was motivated by the above hypothesis and related literature [1,2,4,13].

In the proposed approach, first, the suspicious regions of interests (ROIs) are identified from each mammogram using techniques like breast region extraction, contrast enhancement and breast segmentation, described in Sect. 2. Then each ROI is transformed into its superpixel representation using Statistical Region Merging (SRM) technique [11]. Using Superpixel-based Local Binary Pattern (SLBP) analysis, described in [16], nine structured superpixel patterns are generated. Subsequently, superpixel pattern graphs are constructed based on these nine patterns. Finally, the spatial connectivity of these nine superpixel pattern graphs is used to extract feature vectors for discriminating cancer and non cancer ROIs. The class discrimination capability of features generated from the structured superpixel patterns graphs are evaluated using AUC, sensitivity and specificity.

## 2 Materials and Methods

The proposed mass localization approach consists of six stages: breast region extraction using Otsu thresholding [12], contrast enhancement using adaptive

CLAHE [14], segmentation based on Fuzzy C-means (FCM) clustering, selection of ROIs, feature extraction using graph modeling, and classification.

## 2.1   Dataset

The data used in this study are taken from two databases. The publicly available Digital Database for Screening Mammography (DDSM) [8] and BreastScreen SA (BSSA), a local screening archive in Adelaide, South Australia. The dense background in this study refers to density of the immediate background environment of the mass and not the overall density of the breast, as used in the Breast Imaging Report and Data System (BI-RADS). This is because a mass may be located in a non-dense area of a breast despite the mammogram having high BI-RADS density score and similarly, low BI-RADS breast density score does not exclude masses located in dense tissues. The mammograms in DDSM were acquired using four scanners: Lumisys 200 Laser (50 μm pixel size, 12 bits), DBA M2100 ImageClear (42 μm pixel size, 16 bits), Howtek 960 (43.5 μm pixel size, 12 bits) and Howtek Multi-Rad850 (43.5 μm pixel size, 12 bits). The mammograms in BSSA were acquired using a Vidar Diagnostic Pro Advantage digitiser (48 μm pixel size, 12 bit). We selected all the malignant cases satisfying our criteria (malignant masses located in dense background). This resulted in 41 cases (all from different women) from DDSM and 29 cases (all from different women) from BSSA. The original mass contours provided with the DDSM and BSSA data are very generous and in this study more tight ones, provided by an experienced radiologist (more than 10 years clinical practice), were used.

## 2.2   Breast Region Extraction and Contrast Enhancement

Otsu thresholding method [12] was used to separate the foreground regions with high intensity from the dark background region. After thresholding the background intensity values were changed to zero. Morphological opening operation with a disk shaped structuring element with size 10 was applied to remove small objects from mammograms and filling was used to obtain a smooth breast border. Then the region with largest area was selected as the breast region. Contrast enhancement was applied using adaptive CLAHE based on entropy [14]. The objective of this step was to enhance the contrast between the masses and their background in order to improve the FCM segmentation.

## 2.3   Breast Segmentation and Suspicious Mass Regions Selection

FCM clustering, with 10 clusters, was used for segmentation. The number of clusters was chosen based on the results from our previous study [14]. The segmented mammograms were further processed by applying morphological filing of holes, followed by morphological opening operation, with the size 2 structuring element of disk type. The opening operation smooths contours, breaks narrow isthmuses and eliminates small islands. All connected components with the area bigger than 50px were considered for further analysis.

In FCM, lower clusters have regions with low intensity values and top clusters have regions with high intensity values. For finding the suspicious mass regions, we considered only top clusters as mass regions have higher intensity compared to others. The top four clusters, in case of DDSM, and the top three clusters, in case of the BSSA data, were considered. Removing the lower clusters resulted in 1905 regions for 41 mammograms collected from the DDSM database, and 1757 regions for 29 mammograms from BSSA.

Each of those regions was used to automatically generate an ROI. A MAT-LAB script finding the smallest rectangle containing the region was utilized. This rectangular region is referred to as ROI in this study. The automatically generated ROI was considered to be a true mass ROI if it met two criteria: (1) the centroid of a segmented region was included in the expert annotated area and (2) more than 25% of the segmented region intersected with the true mass region (expert annotated region) [5]. The details of ROIs in each dataset are provided in Table 1. None of the true masses were missed in the process.

**Table 1.** Number of ROIs extracted from each dataset. The number underneath each dataset shows the number of mammograms in each set.

|  | BSSA (29) | DDSM (41) |
|---|---|---|
| No. of mass regions | 49 | 75 |
| No. of normal regions | 1708 | 1830 |
| ROIs/image ratio | 60.5 | 46.5 |

### 2.4 Feature Extraction Using Superpixel Pattern-Based Graph Modeling

The graph modeling approach consists of the following steps: superpixel generation using Statistical Region Merging (SRM) technique, superpixel pattern extraction, morphological operation, superpixel pattern graph generation and graph features extraction. Figure 1 shows an example of graph modeling approach.

SRM technique was used to generate superpixel tessellation from each ROI. The superpixel size of 9 pixels was used for this study, based on our previous analysis [16]. Superpixel Local Binary Pattern (SLBP) [16], an extension of local binary patterns onto an irregular grid superpixel structure, was used to generate SLBP patterns. For graph modeling, for each ROI, nine binary images corresponding to the nine uniform rotational invariant SLBP patterns were generated. The nine SLBP are: $P_0$ (00000000), $P_1$ (00000001), $P_3$ (00000011), $P_7$ (00000111), $P_{15}$ (00001111), $P_{31}$ (00011111), $P_{63}$ (00111111), $P_{127}$ (01111111) and $P_{255}$ (11111111). Figure 1b shows an example of SLBP construction and 1c shows an example of binary image for pattern $P_1$.

The superpixel pattern graph was generated based on the spatial connectivity between the patterns in the binary image. The connectivity was established by

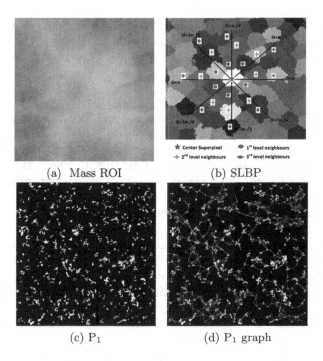

(a)  Mass ROI                  (b) SLBP

(c) P$_1$                      (d) P$_1$ graph

**Fig. 1.** An example showing mass ROI, SLBP approach, binary image for superpixel pattern P$_1$ and the graph for superpixel pattern P$_1$ (at scale 2) for the selected mass ROI ([15]).

means of morphological dilation (with a disk shaped structural element) applied to individual superpixels at two scales: scale 1 - using one superpixel size as radius (9 pixels), and scale 2 - using two superpixel size as radius (18 pixels). In the graph, each node represents the structured superpixel, and an edge is added between two nodes if the two corresponding superpixels are connected or overlap with each other in the binary image plane.

The adjacency matrix was used to encode the superpixel pattern graph. Let $M$ be the adjacency matrix, then $M_{xy} \in \{0, 1\}$, $x, y = 1, 2, \ldots k$, where $k$ is the number of nodes in graph and $M_{xy} = 1$ if two nodes $i$ and $j$ are connected, otherwise $M_{xy} = 0$. In this study, four graph theoretical features: average vertex degree, cluster coefficient, percentage of isolated nodes and giant connected component ratio are investigated. Here, $G(V, E)$ is used to represent a graph where $V$ is the vertex set and $E$ is the edge set. The cardinality of $V$ and $E$ is represented by $|V|$ and $|E|$, respectively. The average vertex degree is calculated as $\sum_{k \in V} d(k)/|V|$, where $d(k)$ is the number of edges incident on vertex $k$. The average clustering coefficient is defined by $\sum_{k \in V} c(k)/|V|$, where $c(k)$ is the ratio between number of edges adjacent to vertex $k$ and the number of all possible edges between $k's$ neighbors. The percentage of isolated vertices is the ratio of the number of isolated vertices (vertex with degree of zero) to the total number of vertices in $G$. Finally, the giant connected component ratio is the ratio of the number of vertices in the giant connected component (largest set of vertices that are reachable from any other) to the total number of vertices in $|V|$.

### 2.5   Feature Selection and Classification

The maximum dimensionality of the feature space is 72 (9 structured superpixel patterns, 2 scales, 4 graph features = $9 \times 2 \times 4 = 72$). Feature selection was conducted exclusively using DDSM dataset utilizing correlation based feature selection method and the best fit search method [7] with 10-fold cross validation. This reduced the feature dimensionality to 22. Linear Discriminant Analysis (LDA) and Support Vector Machine with linear kernel (SVM-L) were used to validate the classification power of selected features.

As the data for classification was highly unbalanced (see Table 1), for training, minority class was over sampled using SMOTE (Synthetic Minority Over-Sampling Technique) [3]. Based on the features of the original dataset, this technique generates new instances of minority class from the nearest neighbors of line joining the minority class samples. In our study, SMOTE was used to generate similar number of mass samples as normal ones to have a balanced dataset for training the classifier. Due to very small dataset, leave one out cross validation was used.

## 3   Results

The proposed approach was evaluated on DDSM dataset and again on unseen BSSA dataset and the performance of the classifiers was assessed using three widely-used medical diagnostic metrics: area under the ROC curve (AUC), sensitivity and specificity. Table 2 presents the experimental results for the graph features for DDSM and BSSA using LDA and SVM-L classifiers. The highest AUC score of 0.835 was achieved using the LDA. To investigate the effects of combining additional features with the proposed graph features, three basic mass features: mean intensity, area and eccentricity, were also extracted and included in the feature set. Table 3 show the combined results for LDA and SVM-L classifiers. The proposed method achieved an AUC score up to 0.910 and 0.894 for DDSM and BSSA respectively. The same feature set was used with both datasets. When tested on BSSA dataset an AUC score of 0.903 was achieved, with a model trained on DDSM dataset, and an AUC score of 0.905 was achieved when tested on DDSM dataset, with a model trained on BSSA dataset. The results are summarized in Table 4.

## 4   Conclusion and Discussion

In this study, a novel method is proposed based on the topology of structured superpixel patterns. Graph models are constructed on structured superpixel patterns using morphological dilation to represent the spatial connectivity relationship between the structured superpixel patterns within a ROI. A set of graph

**Table 2.** Classification results using leave-one-out method for the proposed superpixel based graph features.

| Database | DDSM | | | BSSA | | |
|---|---|---|---|---|---|---|
| | AUC | Sensitivity | Specificity | AUC | Sensitivity | Specificity |
| LDA | 0.835 | 0.789 | 0.778 | 0.810 | 0.744 | 0.767 |
| SVM - L | 0.812 | 0.725 | 0.825 | 0.809 | 0.780 | 0.714 |

**Table 3.** Classification results using leave-one-out method for proposed superpixel based graph features *combined* along with basic mass features.

| Database | DDSM | | | BSSA | | |
|---|---|---|---|---|---|---|
| | AUC | Sensitivity | Specificity | AUC | Sensitivity | Specificity |
| LDA | 0.910 | 0.903 | 0.801 | 0.894 | 0.886 | 0.792 |
| SVM - L | 0.900 | 0.760 | 0.850 | 0.892 | 0.780 | 0.870 |

**Table 4.** Classification results: DDSM used for training and BSSA used for testing (DDSM/BSSA), and BSSA used for training and DDSM used for testing (BSSA/DDSM). The combined feature set was used.

| Database | DDSM/BSSA | | | BSSA/DDSM | | |
|---|---|---|---|---|---|---|
| | AUC | Sensitivity | Specificity | AUC | Sensitivity | Specificity |
| LDA | 0.903 | 0.867 | 0.810 | 0.905 | 0.790 | 0.849 |
| SVM-L | 0.881 | 0.848 | 0.847 | 0.908 | 0.770 | 0.875 |

features are generated from the proposed graph models and classification is performed based on these features. Performance of the proposed system was evaluated using ROC curve. The combined feature set resulted in the highest AUC scores for mass classification on DDSM and BSSA: 0.910 and 0.894, respectively. This high mass discrimination capability of the proposed features shows that the framework could be used in the clinical setting for identification of masses in dense tissues, which is a particularly challenging task for radiologists.

**Acknowledgments.** The authors would like to thank Dr. Peter Downey, clinical radiologist of BreastScreen SA for validating the core mass contours and valuable comments and discussions.

# References

1. Bilgin, C., Demir, C., Nagi, C., et al.: Cell-graph mining for breast tissue modeling and classification. In: 29th Annual International Conference of the IEEE on Engineering in Medicine and Biology Society, EMBS 2007, pp. 5311–5314 (2007)

2. Bilgin, C.C., Bullough, P., Plopper, G.E., et al.: ECM-aware cell-graph mining for bone tissue modeling and classification. Data Min. Knowl. Disc. **20**(3), 416–438 (2010)

3. Chawla, N.V., Bowyer, K.W., Hall, L.O., et al.: SMOTE: synthetic minority over-sampling technique. J. Artif. Intell. Res. **16**(2002), 321–357 (2002)

4. Chen, Z., Strange, H., Oliver, A., et al.: Topological modeling and classification of mammographic microcalcification clusters. IEEE Trans. Biomed. Eng. **62**(4), 1203–1214 (2015)

5. Choi, J., Ro, Y.M.: Multiresolution local binary pattern texture analysis combined with variable selection for application to false-positive reduction in computer-aided detection of breast masses on mammograms. Phys. Med. Biol. **57**(21), 7029–7052 (2012)

6. Don, S., Choi, E., Min, D.: Breast mass segmentation in digital mammography using graph cuts. In: Lee, G., Howard, D., Ślęzak, D. (eds.) ICHIT 2011. CCIS, vol. 206, pp. 88–96. Springer, Heidelberg (2011). https://doi.org/10.1007/978-3-642-24106-2_12

7. Hall, M.A.: Correlation-based feature selection for machine learning (1999)

8. Heath, M., Bowyer, K., Kopans, D., et al.: The digital database for screening mammography. In: Proceedings of the Fifth International Workshop on Digital Mammography, pp. 212–218. Medical Physics Publishing (2001)

9. Ma, F., Bajger, M., Bottema, M.J.: A graph matching based automatic regional registration method for sequential mammogram analysis. In: Proceedings of SPIE, vol. 6915, p. 6915-11 (2008)

10. Ma, F., Bajger, M., Slavotinek, J.P., et al.: Two graph theory based methods for identifying the pectoral muscle in mammograms. Pattern Recogn. **40**(9), 2592–2602 (2007)

11. Nock, R., Nielsen, F.: Statistical region merging. IEEE Trans. Pattern Anal. Mach. Intell. **26**(11), 1452–1458 (2004)

12. Otsu, N.: A threshold selection method from gray-level histograms. IEEE Trans. Syst. Man Cybern. **9**(1), 62–66 (1979)

13. Oztan, B., Shubert, K.R., Bjornsson, C.S., et al.: Biologically-driven cell-graphs for breast tissue grading. In: 2013 IEEE 10th International Symposium on Biomedical Imaging (ISBI), pp. 137–140. IEEE (2013)

14. Sajeev, S., Bajger, M., Lee, G.: Segmentation of breast masses in local dense background using adaptive clip limit-CLAHE. In: 2015 International Conference on Digital Image Computing: Techniques and Applications (DICTA), pp. 1–8, November 2015

15. Sajeev, S., Bajger, M., Lee, G.: Superpixel pattern graphs for identifying breast mass ROIs in dense background: a preliminary study. In: 14th International Workshop on Breast Imaging (IWBI 2018). Proc. SPIE. vol. 10718 (2018)

16. Sajeev, S., Bajger, M., Lee, G.: Superpixel texture analysis for classification of breast masses in dense background. IET Comput. Vision **12**(6), 779–786 (2018)

17. Stephen, K., James, D., McCluggage, G., et al.: An automated machine vision system for the histological grading of cervical intraepithelial neoplasia (CIN). J. Pathol. **192**(3), 351–362 (2000)

# OCD Diagnosis via Smoothing Sparse Network and Stacked Sparse Auto-Encoder Learning

Peng Yang[1], Lili Jin[2], Chuangyong Xu[2], Tianfu Wang[1], Baiying Lei[1(✉)],
and Ziwen Peng[2,3(✉)]

[1] National-Regional Key Technology Engineering Laboratory for Medical Ultrasound,
Guangdong Key Laboratory for Biomedical Measurements and Ultrasound Imaging,
School of Biomedical Engineering, Health Science Center,
Shenzhen University, Shenzhen 518060, China
leiby@szu.edu.cn

[2] College of Psychology and Sociology, Shenzhen University, Shenzhen 518060, China
pengzw@email.szu.edu.cn

[3] Department of Child Psychiatry, Shenzhen Kangning Hospital, Shenzhen University School
of Medicine, Shenzhen, China

**Abstract.** Obsessive-compulsive disorder (OCD) is a serious mental illness that affects the overall quality of patients' daily life. Since sparse learning can remove redundant information in resting-state functional magnetic resonance imaging (rs-fMRI) data via the brain functional connectivity network (BFCN) and retain good biological characteristics, it is an important method for OCD analysis. However, most existing methods ignore the relationship among subjects. To solve this problem, we propose a smoothing sparse network (SSN) to construct BFCN. Specifically, we add a smoothing term in the model to constrain the relationship and increase the similarity among the subjects. As a kind of deep learning method, the stacked sparse auto-encoder (SSAE) can learn the high level internal features from data and reduce its dimension. For this reason, we design an improved SSAE to learn the high level features of BFCN and reduce the data dimension. We add a $\ell_2$-norm to prevent overfitting as well. We apply this framework on OCD dataset self-collected from local hospitals. The experimental results show that our method can achieve quite promising performance and outperform the state-of-the-art methods.

**Keywords:** Obsessive-compulsive disorder · Stacked sparse auto-encoder · Smoothing sparse network · Brain functional connectivity network

This work was supported partly by National Natural Science Foundation of China (Nos. 31871113, 61871274, 61801305 and 81571758), National Natural Science Foundation of Guangdong Province (No. 2017A030313377), Guangdong Pearl River Talents Plan (2016ZT06S220), Shenzhen Peacock Plan (Nos. KQTD2016053112051497 and KQTD2015033016 104926), and Shenzhen Key Basic Research Project (Nos. JCYJ2017 0413152804728, JCYJ20180507184647636, JCYJ20170818142347251 and JCYJ20170818094109846).

D. Zhang et al. (Eds.): GLMI 2019, LNCS 11849, pp. 155–163, 2019.
https://doi.org/10.1007/978-3-030-35817-4_19

# 1 Introduction

Obsessive-compulsive disorder (OCD) is a mental disease characterized by compulsive thoughts or behaviors, which often causes negative impacts on the daily life of patients [1]. According to clinical studies, OCD is hereditary and the siblings show similar symptoms. About 2% to 3% of people are affected by this disease in the world. However, there are still no accurate physiological and biochemical indicators for the diagnosis of patients with OCD in the clinic. Also, OCD often co-occurs with depression and anxiety, which may cause misdiagnosis [2].

For accurate and objective OCD diagnosis, it is known that resting functional magnetic resonance imaging (rs-fMRI) can show a steady-state pattern of brain co-activation. To achieve this, the brain functional connectivity network (BFCN) is first built from rs-fMRI to understand the functional interactions among the brain areas. Recently, many BFCN methods have been proposed. For example, Sen *et al.* [2] combined Pearson's correlation (PC) network and adjacent matrices features selected by minimum redundancy maximum relevance method for OCD diagnosis. However, this method only considers the relationship between the two brain regions, which ignores the relationship among the target brain region and other multiple brain regions. To enhance it, Xing *et al.* [3] proposed the Riemann kernel to build BFCN and used principal components analysis (PCA) to reduce feature dimensions. However, this BFCN is too dense to represent features well. To construct a BFCN with less density, Wee *et al.* [4] proposed a group-constrained sparse (GCS) model to construct BFCN for mild cognitive impairment identification. Although this method removes a lot of irrelevant information, the data dimension of the BFCN features is still very high. Also, this method ignores the similarity among subjects. There are some commonly used methods (e.g., Lasso, PCA) for reducing the data dimension, but these methods cannot learn the inside relation of BFCN features. First, we propose a smoothing sparse network (SSN) to construct the BFCN based on GCS method, which can control the BFCN density and add similarity constraints among subjects.

The deep learning method has witnessed great success by addressing the issue of dimensionality curse. For example, Chen *et al.* [5] used the sparse auto-encoder (SAE) in polarimetric synthetic aperture radar image for reducing the data dimension. The stacked sparse auto-encoder (SSAE) can stack multiple SAEs to learn high level features and reduce the data dimension. This method has achieved good results for nuclei detection [6]. Inspired by these methods, we propose a novel method which combines the techniques of traditional machine learning and deep learning for OCD diagnosis. Specifically, the features extracted from BFCN are fed to the $\ell_2$ regularized SSAE to learn high level features, which can express disease-related features and reduce the data dimension as well. Our method can learn the nonlinear relationship inside the feature to reduce feature dimension and the high level features are exploited for OCD diagnosis. Our method can not only consider the similarities of the subjects, but also learn the advanced features in BFCN to reduce the dimensions of the data. Experimental results on our self-collected data show that our method has achieved quite promising performance.

## 2  Methodology

### 2.1  Proposed Framework

Figure 1 shows our framework combining the traditional machine learning and deep learning techniques for OCD diagnosis. Firstly, we preprocess the original rs-fMRI data in a standard way. Secondly, we construct BFCN by the SSN method. Then, SSAE is applied to learn high level features, which can reduce the feature dimension effectively and enhance the feature representation ability for final classification.

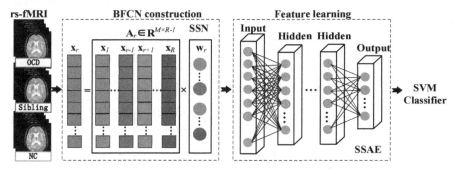

**Fig. 1.** The flow chart of our method.

### 2.2  Data Acquisition and Image Preprocessing

A Philips Medical Systems with 3.0-T MR was used for data acquisition. Subjects were instructed to relax with his eyes closed and remain awake without moving. The parameters are defined as follow: $TR = 2000$ ms; $TE = 60$ ms; flip angle $= 90°$, 33 slices, field of view $= 240$ mm $\times 240$ mm, matrix $= 64 \times 64$; slice thickness $= 4.0$ mm. The Statistical Parametric Mapping toolbox (SPM8), and Data Processing Assistant for Resting-State fMRI (DPARSFA, version 2.2) were used to preprocess the data. We discard the first 10 rs-fMRI volumes of each subject before any further processing to keep the magnetization equal. The remaining 170 volumes are corrected by the staggered sequence of slice collection, which takes advantage of the echo planar scan to ensure that the data on each slice corresponds to the unanimous point in time. The image preprocessing including: slice timing correction; head motion correction; realignment with the corresponding T1-volume; nuisance covariate regression (six head motion parameters, white matter signal and cerebrospinal fluid signal); spatial normalization into the stereotactic space of the Montreal Neurological Institute and resampling at $3 \times 3 \times 3$ mm$^3$; spatial smoothing with a 6-mm full-width half-maximum isotropic Gaussian kernel, and band-pass filtered (0.01–0.08 Hz).

The rs-fMRI is divided into 116 regions of interest (ROIs) using the automatic anatomical labeling (AAL) template. In addition, a high-pass filter is used to refine the average rs-fMRI time series of each brain region. Furthermore, we regress out head movement parameters, cerebrospinal fluid, and mean BOLD time series of the white matter. We extract the mean of the BOLD signal as the original rs-fMRI signal [7].

## 2.3  Smoothing Sparse Network

In this paper, matrices are represented in bold capital letters, the vectors are in bold lowercase letters, and the scalars are in normal italic letters. Assuming that there are $N$ subjects and $\mathbf{X} = [\mathbf{x}_1, \ldots, \mathbf{x}_r, \ldots, \mathbf{x}_R] \in \mathbb{R}^{R \times N}$ denotes our input data, the AAL template is utilized to divide the brain into $R$ ROIs and the $r$-th ROI with a BOLD regional mean time series ($M$ length) is represented $\mathbf{x}_r^n = \left[x_{1r}^n, x_{2r}^n, \ldots, x_{Mr}^n\right] \in \mathbb{R}^{M \times 1}$. $\mathbf{A}_r^n$ denotes all ROIs signal matrix except $\mathbf{x}_r^n$, $\mathbf{A}_r^n = \left[\mathbf{x}_1^n, \ldots \mathbf{x}_{r-1}^n, \ldots \mathbf{x}_{r+1}^n, \ldots \mathbf{x}_R^n\right]$, $\mathbf{w}_r^n \in \mathbb{R}^{R-1}$ is a weighting regression coefficient vector, and $\mathbf{W}_r = \left[\mathbf{w}_r^1, \ldots \mathbf{w}_r^n, \ldots, \mathbf{w}_r^N\right]$. The sparse networks used to represent brain functional connectivity can be constructed using GCS, which is defined as

$$J(\mathbf{W}_r) = \min_{\mathbf{W}_r} \frac{1}{2} \sum_{n=1}^{N} \left|\left|\mathbf{x}_r^n - \mathbf{A}_r^n \mathbf{w}_r^n\right|\right|_2^2 + R_g(\mathbf{W}_r), \tag{1}$$

where $R_g(\mathbf{W}_r)$ is a group regularization and defined as

$$R_g(\mathbf{W}_r) = \lambda_1 ||\mathbf{W}_r||_{2,1} = \lambda_1 \sum_{d=1}^{R-1} \left|\left|\mathbf{w}_r^d\right|\right|_2, \tag{2}$$

where $\lambda_1$ is the group regularization parameter, $||\mathbf{W}_r||_{2,1}$ is the summation of $l_2$-norm of $\mathbf{w}_r^n$. Specifically, we jointly select information by $R - 1$ ROIs' weights. $\mathbf{w}_r^d$ is the $d$-th row vector of $\mathbf{W}_r$. As a sparse regression network method, GCS ensures all models in the unequal group with identical connections. The $l_2$-norm is imposed on identical elements across the unequal matrix $\mathbf{W}_r$, which forces the weight corresponding to connections across different subjects to be grouped together. The constraint imposes a common connection topology among subjects, and leverages variation of connection weights among them. Therefore, the model is able to rebuild the target ROI using the remaining ROIs. Moreover, the reconstruction of each ROI is independent from others. However, the existing GCS model with penalty ignores the smoothing properties of different subjects within the model. To overcome this drawback, a novel model is devised to jointly learn shared functional brain networks of each subject by the group sparse regularization and the smoothness regularization. The objective function is defined as

$$J(\mathbf{W}_r) = \min_{\mathbf{W}_r} \frac{1}{2} \sum_{n=1}^{N} \left|\left|\mathbf{x}_r^n - \mathbf{A}_r^n \mathbf{w}_r^n\right|\right|_2^2 + R_g(\mathbf{W}_r) + R_s(\mathbf{W}_r), \tag{3}$$

where $R_g(\mathbf{W}_r)$ is the group regularization, and $R_s(\mathbf{W}_r)$ denotes the smoothness regularization, which is denoted as

$$R_s(\mathbf{W}_r) = \lambda_2 \sum_{n=1}^{N-1} \left|\left|\mathbf{w}_r^n - \mathbf{w}_r^{n+1}\right|\right|_1, \tag{4}$$

where $\lambda_2$ is the parameter of smoothness regularization. The second term $\left|\left|\mathbf{w}_r^n - \mathbf{w}_r^{n+1}\right|\right|_1$ constrains the diversity between two consecutive weighting vectors from the same groups to be as small as possible. When the smoothness regularization parameter $\lambda_2$ is zero, the proposed method reproduces the original GCS method. Due to the use of $l_1$-norm in the fused smoothness term that encourages the sparsity on difference of weight vectors, there will be a lot of zero components in the weight difference vectors. The informative features will be selected due to the non-zero weights in our task. We introduce the smoothness terms to smooth the connectivity coefficients of the subjects. In addition, we fuse the regularization terms to impose a high level of constraints. We call this sparse learning model as smoothing sparse network. The asymmetrical BFCN does not contribute to the final classification accuracy. Hence, $\mathbf{W}^* = \left(\mathbf{W}_n + \mathbf{W}_n^T\right)/2$ is defined to obtain symmetry. The local clustering coefficients of weighted graphs are used to extract features from each established BFCN [8, 9].

## 2.4 Stacked Sparse Auto-Encoder

Auto-encoder (AE) mainly consists of an encoding network and a decoding network, which is a symmetric neural network with only one hidden layer. The encoder network converts the input data from a high dimensional space to a feature space with a lower dimension, and the decoder network can reconstruct the input data from the feature space. Multiple auto-encoders can form a stacked AE, which can learn the high level features from the original features. SAE is one of the classic variants of learning relatively sparse features by penalizing hidden unit deviations. It improves the performance of traditional AEs and demonstrates more practical application. Our proposed SSAE not only learns high level features, but also controls the sparsity of features, which is more beneficial to the improvement of classification performance. The function of SSAE is denoted as:

$$J(W, b) = \frac{1}{n} \sum_{n=1}^{N} \sum_{f=1}^{F} \left(y_{nf} - x_{nf}\right)^2 + \beta_1 S_1\left(\mathbf{w}_{nf}\right) + \beta_2 S_2(\rho), \tag{5}$$

$$S_1\left(\mathbf{w}_{nf}\right) = \frac{1}{2}\left\|\mathbf{w}_{nf}\right\|_2, \tag{6}$$

$$S_2(\rho\|\rho_k') = \sum_{k=1}^{K} \rho \log \frac{\rho_k'}{\rho} + (1-\rho) \log \frac{1-\rho_k'}{1-\rho}. \tag{7}$$

The first item is the mean squared error. The second item is the $\ell_2$ regularization part on encoding weights, $\beta_1$ is the penalty coefficient of $\ell_2$ regularization term. The third item is the sparsity constraint term, where $\beta_2$ is the coefficient of the sparsity constraint term. $S_2(\rho)$ is the Kullback-Leibler (KL) divergence. $\mathbf{X} \in \mathbb{R}^{N \times F}$ denotes the input data, and $\mathbf{Y} \in \mathbb{R}^{N \times D}$ denotes the reconstructed data. For $N$ subjects, $F$ and $D$ represent the feature dimensions of the input data and the reconstructed data, respectively. $\mathbf{Z} \in \mathbb{R}^{N \times K}$ means the activation matrix of a hidden layer, which has $K$ nodes. The weights $\mathbf{w}_1$ and the bias $\mathbf{b}_1$ are used to encode the input data $\mathbf{X}$ as the activation matrix $\mathbf{Z}$, where $\mathbf{Z} = f(\mathbf{w}_1\mathbf{X} + \mathbf{b}_1)$. The weights $\mathbf{w}_2$ and bias $\mathbf{b}_2$ decode activation matrix $\mathbf{Z}$, $\mathbf{Y} = f(\mathbf{w}_2\mathbf{Z} + \mathbf{b}_2)$. $\rho_k' = \frac{1}{N} \sum_{n=1}^{N} [Z_k(\mathbf{x}_n)]$ is the average activation of the $k$-th hidden node, and $\rho$ is a constant. Then, the weights $\mathbf{w}$ and bias $\mathbf{b}$ are optimized by the scaled conjugate gradient descent algorithm. Therefore, the output $\mathbf{Z}$ of each layer in AE is regarded as the input data of the next layer. In this paper, the $\ell_2$ regularized SSAE contains two different AEs.

## 3 Experiments and Results

### 3.1 Experimental Setup

In this paper, we collect 180 subjects' rs-fMRI data from local hospital, which contains 62 OCD patients, 53 OCD patients' sibling and 65 normal control (NC) people. All data was collected from the Chinese Han population and was marked by two highly trained and experienced clinical psychiatrists and psychologists.

Since we have a small amount of data, the leave-one-out cross-validation (LOOCV) strategy is used to assess our proposed method. Specifically, given $N$ subjects, one of them is left out for testing, and the rest $N$-1subjects are utilized for training. The hyperparameters in each method are empirically set by the greedy search to identify the optimal parameters. The three quantitative measurements are utilized to evaluate the diagnosis performance: accuracy (ACC), area under receiver operating characteristic curve (AUC) and sensitivity (SEN). The experiments are conducted using MATLAB 2018a to verify our proposed method. The SLEP and LibSVM toolboxes are used to construct sparse representation and classification, respectively.

### 3.2 Classification Performance

The experimental results are shown in Table 1 (boldfaces represent the best performance). The receiver operating characteristic (ROC) curves is shown in Fig. 2. To demonstrate the effectiveness of our proposed SSN approach, our BFCN construction method is compared to typical BFCN such as PC and GCS. Also, our classification results are compared to typical dimensionality reduction (DR) methods such as PCA, Lasso and SAE.

**PCP**: PCP uses PC for BFCN construction and PCA to reduce the features.
**PCL**: PCL uses PC to construct BFCN and Lasso for feature selection.
**PCS**: PCS utilizes PC to generate the BFCN and SAE to reduce the data dimension.
**PCSS**: PCSS uses PC to generate the BFCN and SSAE to reduce the data dimension.
**GCSP**: GCSP uses GCS to get BFCN and PCA to reduce the features.
**GCSL**: GCSL uses GCS to get BFCN and Lasso for feature selection.
**GCSS**: GCSS uses GCS to get BFCN and SAE to reduce the features.
**GCSSS**: GCSSS uses GCS to get the BFCN and SSAE to reduce the data dimension.
**SSNP**: SSNP uses SSN to get BFCN and PCA to reduce the features.
**SSNL**: SSNL utilizes SSN to get BFCN and Lasso for feature selection.
**SSNS**: SSNS uses SSN to get BFCN and SAE to reduce the data dimension.
**SSNSS**: SSNSS uses SSN to get BFCN and SSAE for feature dimension reduction.

Obviously, the SSNSS method achieves the best performance. In the classification task of OCD vs. NC, the highest accuracy of our SSNSS method is 88.82%, which is 6.30% higher than other methods. Similarly, for Sibling vs. NC task, our SSNSS model achieves an accuracy of 79.15%, which is 2.03% higher than other methods. For OCD vs. Sibling task, our SSNSS model obtains an accuracy of 79.48%, which is 1.74% higher

**Table 1.** Classification performance of all methods used in this study (%).

| BFCN | DR | OCD vs. NC | | | Sibling vs. NC | | | OCD vs. Sibling | | |
|---|---|---|---|---|---|---|---|---|---|---|
| | | ACC | AUC | SEN | ACC | AUC | SEN | ACC | AUC | SEN |
| PC | PCA | 47.87 | 52.28 | 64.52 | 55.42 | 54.46 | 59.25 | 40.00 | 12.78 | 22.90 |
| | Lasso | 51.18 | 54.52 | 36.77 | 52.28 | 70.89 | 36.45 | 50.61 | 46.87 | 48.06 |
| | SAE | 55.28 | 58.26 | 50.97 | 50.34 | 60.23 | 47.92 | 54.09 | 32.59 | 58.71 |
| | SSAE | 56.38 | 53.25 | 59.68 | 55.42 | 54.08 | 47.92 | 58.26 | 54.81 | 64.52 |
| GCS | PCA | 63.46 | 69.08 | 57.10 | 59.66 | 62.00 | 55.47 | 56.70 | 55.30 | 52.90 |
| | Lasso | 67.72 | 58.98 | 49.68 | 60.34 | 47.02 | 12.45 | 56.17 | 53.74 | 58.71 |
| | SAE | 57.95 | 64.86 | 58.71 | 44.92 | 45.98 | 36.23 | 54.43 | 58.52 | 57.74 |
| | SSAE | 71.97 | 71.61 | 70.00 | 55.08 | 30.68 | 43.72 | 56.87 | 57.61 | 60.97 |
| SSN | PCA | 78.90 | 77.99 | 84.84 | 72.20 | 71.93 | 38.87 | 61.22 | 69.29 | 58.06 |
| | Lasso | 80.16 | 82.68 | 61.29 | 70.34 | **90.71** | **64.15** | 72.87 | 80.13 | 76.13 |
| | SAE | 82.52 | 88.29 | 80.65 | 77.12 | 75.91 | 51.32 | 77.74 | 84.05 | 83.55 |
| | SSAE | **88.82** | **97.62** | **92.90** | **79.15** | 80.93 | 53.58 | **79.48** | **86.18** | **80.00** |

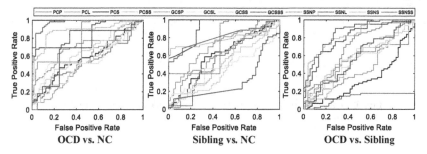

**Fig. 2.** The receiver operating characteristic curves of different tasks.

than other methods. The above results demonstrate that our SSNSS model is effective and outperforms other competing methods.

We use the proposed method to build functional connectivity network of OCD, Sibling and NC. The feature maps of our BFCN are shown in Fig. 3. The image below is the whole brain BFCN, while the image above is a partial area magnified image. It can be seen that the network constructed by SSN is sparse.

The brain functional connectivity networks are shown in Fig. 4. Our method can clearly express the activity of the brain, which has been verified in the classification results. It can be clearly seen from the BFCN that there are some differences between

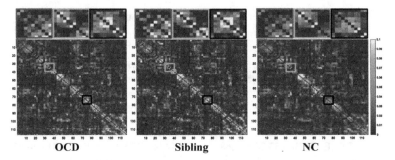

**Fig. 3.** The feature map of BFCN of different groups.

OCD and NC. The OCD patients have similar characteristics to Siblings. The differences between OCD and NC brain activity status include frontal_sup_orb, hippocampus, caudate, putamen. These ROIs are similar to OCD related areas found by previous researchers [1, 10].

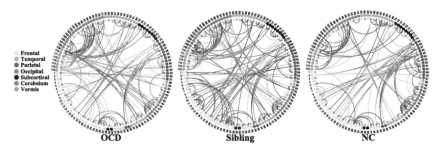

**Fig. 4.** The brain functional connectivity network of different groups.

## 4    Conclusions

In this paper, a novel method of diagnosing OCD and OCD's sibling has been proposed, which integrates the merits of both traditional machine learning and deep learning techniques. Specifically, the SSN model based on sparse learning has been proposed to construct the BFCN, which not only can control the density of BFCN, but also take into account the similarity among subjects. The SSAE is used to learn high-level features to obtain discriminative features for final classification. In our future work, we will consider more modalities and constraints to enhance the disease diagnosis accuracy. Also, the dynamic and high-order BFCN can be incorporated into our framework to enhance the performance of the entire framework as well.

# References

1. Zhou, C., Cheng, Y., Ping, L., et al.: Support vector machine classification of obsessive-compulsive disorder based on whole-brain volumetry and diffusion tensor imaging. Front. Psychiatry **9**, 1–9 (2018). https://doi.org/10.3389/fpsyt.2018.00524

2. Sen, B., Bernstein, G.A., Xu, T., et al.: Classification of obsessive-compulsive disorder from resting-state fMRI. In: 38th Annual International Conference of the IEEE Engineering in Medicine and Biology Society, pp. 3606–3609. IEEE Press, New York (2016). https://doi.org/10.1109/embc.2016.7591508

3. Xing, X., Jin, L., Shi, F., et al.: Diagnosis of OCD using functional connectome and Riemann kernel PCA. In: SPIE Medical Imaging. SPIE, Washington DC (2019). https://doi.org/10.1117/12.2512316

4. Wee, C.Y., Yap, P.T., Zhang, D., et al.: Group-constrained sparse fMRI connectivity modeling for mild cognitive impairment identification. Brain Struct. Funct. **219**, 641–656 (2014). https://doi.org/10.1007/s00429-013-0524-8

5. Chen, Y., Jiao, L., Li, Y., et al.: Multilayer projective dictionary pair learning and sparse autoencoder for PolSAR image classification. IEEE Trans. Geosci. Remote Sens. **55**, 6683–6694 (2017). https://doi.org/10.1109/TGRS.2017.2727067

6. Xu, J., Xiang, L., Liu, Q., et al.: Stacked sparse autoencoder (SSAE) for nuclei detection on breast cancer histopathology images. IEEE Trans. Med. Imaging **35**, 119–130 (2016). https://doi.org/10.1109/TMI.2015.2458702

7. Wee, C.Y., Yang, S., Yap, P.T., et al.: Sparse temporally dynamic resting-state functional connectivity networks for early MCI identification. Brain Imag. Behav. **10**, 342–356 (2016). https://doi.org/10.1007/s11682-015-9408-2

8. Chen, X., Zhang, H., Gao, Y., et al.: High-order resting-state functional connectivity network for MCI classification. Hum. Brain Mapp. **37**, 3282–3296 (2016). https://doi.org/10.1002/hbm.23240

9. Rubinov, M., Sporns, O.: Complex network measures of brain connectivity: uses and interpretations. NeuroImage **52**, 1059–1069 (2010). https://doi.org/10.1016/j.neuroimage.2009.10.003

10. Fan, J., Zhong, M., Zhu, X., et al.: Resting-state functional connectivity between right anterior insula and right orbital frontal cortex correlate with insight level in obsessive-compulsive disorder. NeuroImage Clin. **15**, 1–7 (2017). https://doi.org/10.1016/j.nicl.2017.04.002

# A Longitudinal MRI Study of Amygdala and Hippocampal Subfields for Infants with Risk of Autism

Guannan Li[1,2], Meng-Hsiang Chen[3], Gang Li[2], Di Wu[4], Chunfeng Lian[2], Quansen Sun[1], Dinggang Shen[2(✉)], and Li Wang[2(✉)]

[1] School of Computer Science and Engineering, Nanjing University of Science and Technology, Nanjing 210094, China
[2] Department of Radiology and Biomedical Research Imaging Center, University of North Carolina at Chapel Hill, Chapel Hill, NC 27599, USA
{dgshen,li_wang}@med.unc.edu
[3] Department of Diagnostic Radiology, Kaohsiung Chang Gung Memorial Hospital, Chang Gung University College of Medicine, Kaohsiung, Taiwan
[4] Department of Biostatistics, University of North Carolina at Chapel Hill, Chapel Hill, NC 27599, USA

**Abstract.** Currently, there are still no early biomarkers to detect infants with risk of autism spectrum disorder (ASD), which is mainly diagnosed based on behavioral observations at three or four years of age. Since intervention efforts may miss a critical developmental window after 2 years old, it is clinically significant to identify imaging-based biomarkers at an early stage for better intervention, before behavioral diagnostic signs of ASD typically arising. Previous studies on older children and young adults with ASD demonstrate altered developmental trajectories of the amygdala and hippocampus. However, our knowledge on their developmental trajectories in early postnatal stages remains very limited. In this paper, for the first time, we propose a volume-based analysis of the amygdala and hippocampal subfields of the infant subjects with risk of ASD at 6, 12, and 24 months of age. To address the challenge of low tissue contrast and small structural size of infant amygdala and hippocampal subfields, we propose a novel deep-learning approach, dilated-dense U-Net, to digitally segment the amygdala and hippocampal subfields in a longitudinal dataset, the National Database for Autism Research (NDAR). A volume-based analysis is then performed based on the segmentation results. Our study shows that the overgrowth of amygdala and cornu ammonis sectors (CA) 1–3 May start from 6 months of age, which may be related to the emergence of autistic spectrum disorder.

**Keywords:** Autism · Convolutional neural network · Trajectory · Amygdala · Hippocampus

---

G. Li and M.-H. Chen—Co-first authors.

© Springer Nature Switzerland AG 2019
D. Zhang et al. (Eds.): GLMI 2019, LNCS 11849, pp. 164–171, 2019.
https://doi.org/10.1007/978-3-030-35817-4_20

# 1 Introduction

Autism, or autism spectrum disorder (ASD), refers to a range of conditions characterized by challenges with social skills, repetitive behaviors, speech, and nonverbal communication, as well as by unique strengths and differences. Globally, autism is estimated to affect 70 million people as of 2017[1]. The diagnosis of ASD is mainly based on a thorough behavioral assessment. Studies demonstrate that behavioral signs can begin to emerge as early as 6 to 12 months [2]. However, most professionals who specialize in diagnosing the disorder won't attempt to make a definite diagnosis until 2 or 3 years of age [3]. As a result, the time window of opportunity for effective intervention may have passed when the disorder is detected. Thus, it is of great importance to detect ASD earlier in life for better intervention.

Magnetic resonance (MR) examination allows researchers and clinicians to noninvasively examine brain anatomy. Structural MR examination is widely used to investigate brain morphology and plays an increasingly pivotal role in early diagnosis and intervention of ASD because of its high contrast sensitivity and spatial resolution [4]. Many neuroscience studies on older children and young adults with ASD demonstrate abnormalities in the amygdala [5, 6] and hippocampus [7, 8]. For example, some studies have reported increased amygdala and hippocampal volumes [9–11]. However, most of previous studies are based on cross-sectional subjects larger than 2 years of age. Hence, our knowledge on the volumetric growth of autistics in early postnatal stages remains very limited. Moreover, the studies on hippocampal subfields, i.e., the subiculum, the cornu ammonis sectors (CA) 1–3, and the dentate gyrus (DG) [8], are rare at early stages. In fact, each subfield has different functions. For example, CA3 and DG are involved in memory encoding and early retrieval, while CA1 is involved in late retrieval, consolidation, and recognition [12].

Therefore, longitudinal studies of the amygdala and hippocampal subfields development could identify critical periods of abnormal trajectory as a first step towards establishing neurobiological factors responsible for the autism. To characterize trajectories of the amygdala and hippocampal subfields at early stages, i.e., 6-, 12-, and 24-months of age, it is critically important to accurately segment them from MR images. Manual segmentation is often treated as a gold standard, but it is time-consuming and tedious, along with large inter- and intra-observer variability. In recent years, deep neural networks have been widely applied in medical image segmentation. Fully convolutional networks (FCNs) [13], as a natural extension of convolutional neural networks (CNNs), were developed for semantic segmentation of natural images and have been rapidly applied to biomedical images due to their powerful end-to-end training. 3D U-Net [14] extends the FCNs for volumetric segmentation by using skip connections to capture both the local and contextual information. To date, many network architectures further incorporate the residual connections [15] or dense connections [16] to get efficient improved flow of information and gradients throughout the network [17, 18]. A new convolutional network module, which is specifically designed for dense prediction, was proposed in [19]. The module uses dilated convolutions to systematically aggregate multiscale contextual information without losing resolution. Inspired by [20], in this paper, we propose a

---

[1] https://www.autismspeaks.org/science-news/autism-and-health-special-report-autism-speaks.

Dilated-Dense U-Net for accurate segmentation of amygdala and hippocampal subfields from around 6-, 12-, and 24-month-old infant brain MRI. Based on the segmentation results, for the first time, our study reveals that the amygdala and CA1-3 start to overgrow from 6 months of age, which may be related to the emergence of ASD.

## 2    Materials and Methods

**Data Description.** Totally 276 subjects gathered from the National Database for Autism Research (NDAR) [21] were used in the study. More specifically, the dataset consists of 30 autistic subjects (25 males/5 females), 31 mild condition autism spectrum subjects (21 males/10 females), and 215 normal controls (133 males/82 females). In the experiment, we regard the first two types as one group. All images were acquired on a Siemens 3T scanner. T1-weighted MR images were acquired with 160 sagittal slices using parameters: TR/TE = 2400/3.16 ms and voxel resolution = $1 \times 1 \times 1$ mm$^3$. Then, in-house tools were used to perform skull stripping, intensity inhomogeneity correction, and histogram matching for MR images. There are 12, 13, and 15 MR images acquired at 6, 12, and 24 months, which were manually labeled by an experienced neuroscientist. These subjects were randomly selected, and, during manual annotations, diagnosis information is unknown to the neuroscientist. The longitudinal analyses were conducted on a subset of 29 ASD subjects and 113 normal control (NC) subjects, who have all the three longitudinal scans acquired at 6, 12 and 24 months of age. The age of participant did not differ significantly ($p$-value $> 0.05$) between ASD and NC group at each time point.

**Dilated-Dense U-Net:** In this study, a novel network architecture, Dilated-Dense U-Net (DDUNET), is proposed to segment the amygdala and hippocampal subfields. Inspired by [20], the proposed network is a fully convolutional neural network taking advantages of the U-Net skip connections, dense blocks, and dilated convolutions. The U-Net skip connections facilitate the joint capturing of both the local and contextual information, while the dilated dense blocks bring a better flow of the gradient information without losing resolution. As the structure size of the amygdala and hippocampal subfields is very small, some details may be missed in max-pooling layer. Thus, dilated convolutions are used to support exponential expansion of the receptive field without loss of resolution or coverage.

The proposed network architecture is shown in Fig. 1. It consists of a contracting path and an expansive path going through 7 dense blocks. Each path consists of one standard dense block and two dilated dense blocks. After the first standard dense block in the contracting path, a max-pooling layer of size $2 \times 2 \times 2$ is used to reduce the dimensionality and exploit the contextual information. Each dense block consists of three BN-ReLU-Conv-Dropout operations, in which each Conv includes 16 $3 \times 3 \times 3$ kernels and the dropout rate was 0.1during training. It should be noted that two dilated dense blocks with dilation rates d = 2 are used in the downsampling path to expand receptive fields. Then, a dense block with a dilation rate d = 2 is used to transfer the features from the contracting path to the expansive path. Skip connections are established between the contracting path and the expansive path to recover the spatial information lost during the downsampling.

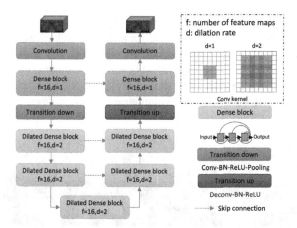

**Fig. 1.** DDUNET consists of two paths: a contracting path to capture contextual information and an expansive path to capture local information. There are seven dense blocks in total: two standard dense blocks (i.e., d = 1), and five dilated dense blocks (i.e., d = 2).

**Network Implementation.** Due to large appearance differences in MRI between 6, 12, and 24 months, we trained three individual models for each age period. During training, we randomly extracted 3D patches from training images. The patch size was optimized as $16 \times 64 \times 16$ based on cross-validation, by using cross-entropy as a loss function. We used SGD optimization strategy. The initial learning rate was 0.005, which was multiplied by 0.1 after each epoch. Training and test were performed on a NVIDIA Titan X GPU. Training a DDUNET takes around 72 h, and, in the application stage, segmenting a 3D image takes 60 s.

## 3   Experiments and Results

In this section, we present our segmentation results of the amygdala and hippocampal subfields using the proposed Dilated-Dense U-Net, by comparison with 3 state-of-the-art methods. Based on the segmentation results, we further measured the volumetric differences of the amygdala and hippocampal subfields between ASD group and NC group.

### 3.1   Segmentation Results and Performance

Leave-one-out cross-validation was used in the experiment, e.g., for 24 months, in each fold, we selected 12 subjects for training, 2 subjects for validation, and 1 subject for testing. Figure 2 shows the 2D and 3D views of segmented amygdala and hippocampal subfields for one randomly-selected subject acquired at 24 months old by different methods, including DRUNET [18], SegNet [22], U-Net [14], our proposed DDUNET, and manual segmentation. It can be seen that the comparison methods cannot accurately identify these ROIs, especially for CA1-3. By contrast, our method has achieved a consistent result with the manual result. Table 1 reports the Dice coefficients (mean ± std) of the segmentation results obtained by different networks. Our proposed method achieves the highest Dice coefficients for all age periods. We further calculate $p$-values between proposed results and any comparison results, and mark the significantly better performance in bold ($p$-value $< 0.05$). For most cases, our proposed method can achieve a significantly better result. We then apply our trained model to the remaining subjects and further perform ROI-based volumetric measurements.

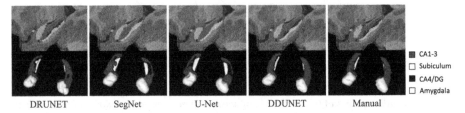

DRUNET          SegNet          U-Net          DDUNET          Manual

**Fig. 2.** Segmented amygdala and hippocampal subfields from one randomly-selected subject acquired at 24 months of age, by four different networks and manual segmentation.

**Table 1.** Comparison between different networks in term of Dice coefficients (mean ± std) for each segmented structure. The best accuracy is shown in **bold** with $p$-value $< 0.05$.

|        | Age       | Amygdala          | CA1-3             | Subiculum         | CA4/DG            |
|--------|-----------|-------------------|-------------------|-------------------|-------------------|
| DRUNET | 6 months  | 0.754 ± 0.013     | 0.728 ± 0.007     | 0.652 ± 0.020     | 0.685 ± 0.019     |
|        | 12 months | 0.804 ± 0.016     | 0.810 ± 0.009     | 0.825 ± 0.017     | 0.800 ± 0.015     |
|        | 24 months | 0.846 ± 0.008     | 0.827 ± 0.008     | 0.842 ± 0.012     | 0.801 ± 0.002     |
| SegNet | 6 months  | 0.695 ± 0.015     | 0.688 ± 0.014     | 0.646 ± 0.018     | 0.638 ± 0.007     |
|        | 12 months | 0.792 ± 0.012     | 0.762 ± 0.012     | 0.692 ± 0.016     | 0.690 ± 0.004     |
|        | 24 months | 0.834 ± 0.017     | 0.764 ± 0.021     | 0.705 ± 0.016     | 0.695 ± 0.006     |
| U-Net  | 6 months  | 0.687 ± 0.006     | 0.624 ± 0.003     | 0.621 ± 0.006     | 0.600 ± 0.010     |
|        | 12 months | 0.754 ± 0.008     | 0.707 ± 0.004     | 0.679 ± 0.009     | 0.637 ± 0.012     |
|        | 24 months | 0.795 ± 0.006     | 0.720 ± 0.010     | 0.695 ± 0.018     | 0.674 ± 0.008     |
| DDUNET | 6 months  | **0.882 ± 0.007** | **0.863 ± 0.009** | **0.832 ± 0.005** | **0.809 ± 0.010** |
|        | 12 months | **0.898 ± 0.010** | **0.878 ± 0.009** | **0.846 ± 0.009** | 0.820 ± 0.006     |
|        | 24 months | **0.909 ± 0.014** | **0.880 ± 0.016** | 0.854 ± 0.006     | 0.815 ± 0.010     |

## 3.2 Volumetric Measures and Discussion

**Cross-Sectional Studies:** The volumetric measurements for all 276 subjects are provided in Fig. 3. At 6 months of age, compared with NC group, ASD group has significant enlargements ($p < 0.05$) in amygdala in both left and right hemispheres (with 4.7% and 3.4% enlargement, respectively), and in CA1-3 in left and right hemispheres (with 5.8% and 3.3% enlargement, respectively). At 12 months of age, for male subjects, the CA1-3 in both left and right hemisphere show 4.4% and 3.3% enlargement, respectively. For female subjects, there is no significant difference between ASD group and NC group, which may be caused by limited female subjects in the ASD group. At 24 months of age, compared with the NC group, the ASD group shows significant enlargement in amygdala (both hemispheres, $p$-value $< 0.01$), CA1-3 (left hemisphere, $p$-value $< 0.01$), and subiculum (left hemisphere, $p$-value $< 0.05$).

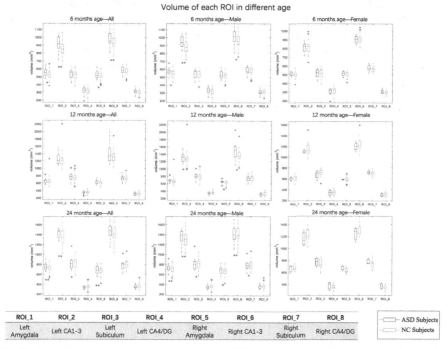

**Fig. 3.** The volumetric data for all participants at different age stages. Significance of the $p$-value of each ROI is shown at the corner of each plot figure, with * indicating $p$-value $< 0.05$ and ** indicating $p$-value $< 0.01$.

**Longitudinal Study:** Figure 4 shows the longitudinal trajectory of each ROI volume from a subset of 29 ASD subjects and 113 NC subjects with all three longitudinal MR images acquired at around 6, 12, and 24 months of age. At 6 months of age, compared with the NC group, the ASD group shows significant enlargement in amygdala (both left and right hemispheres, $p$-value $< 0.05$), and hippocampus in CA1-3 (both left and right hemispheres, $p$-value $< 0.01$). At 12 months of age, compared with the NC group, the ASD group shows significant enlargement in amygdala (left hemisphere, $p$-value $< 0.05$), and hippocampus in CA1-3 (both left and right hemispheres, $p$-value $< 0.05$). At 24 months of age, the difference between ASD and NC groups becomes larger, and it is significantly different in the amygdala (both left and right hemispheres, $p$-value $< 0.05$), and CA1-3 (both left and right hemispheres, $p$-value $< 0.01$).

We further investigate the growth rates from 6 to 12 months of age and find that the growth rates of the two groups are not significantly different. However, in the second year, the average ROI volumetric growth rates of ASD group become larger than the NC group in CA1-3 (left hemisphere, $p$-value $= 0.0101$), and hippocampus (left hemisphere, $p$-value $= 0.0365$). We further normalized the ROI volumes with total brain volumes (ROI volume/total brain volume) and still find that the ASD group shows significant increase of growth rate in CA1-3 (left hemisphere, $p$-value $= 0.0053$), and hippocampus (left hemisphere, $p$-value $= 0.0146$).

The degree of amygdala enlargement at the early age is associated with the severity of social and communication and emotional perception [5]. The enlargement of CA1-3 may represent up-regulation, strengthen emotion of fear to communicate with surrounding or others. These findings suggest that there are developmental abnormalities in amygdala and hippocampus (especially for CA1-3) in the early age of ASD, which is also confirmed by previous reports on older children and young adults [5, 6].

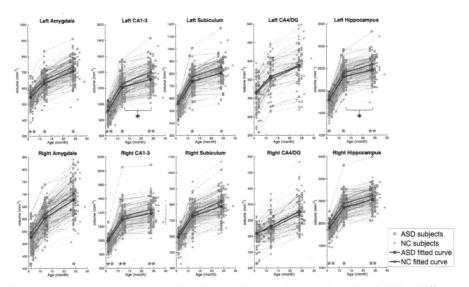

**Fig. 4.** The growth trajectory of each ROI. Significance of the $p$-value of each ROI at different ages is indicated by * with $p$-value $< 0.05$, and by ** with $p$-value $< 0.01$. While, significance of the $p$-value of growth rate is indicated by ✳ with $p$-value $< 0.05$.

In conclusion, for the first time, our study finds that the overgrowth of amygdala and CA1-3 in hippocampal subfields starts from 6 months of age, which may be linked to early emergence of ASD.

**Acknowledgements.** Part of this work was done when Guannan Li was in UNC (supported in part by NIH grants MH109773). Gang Li and Dinggang Shen were supported in part by NIH grants (MH117943). Li Wang was supported by NIH grants MH109773 and MH117943.

# References

1. Newschaffer, C.J., et al.: The epidemiology of autism spectrum disorders. Dev. Disabil. Res. Rev. **8**, 151–161 (2002)
2. Filipek, P.A., et al.: The screening and diagnosis of autistic spectrum disorders. J. Autism Dev. Disord. **29**, 439–484 (1999)
3. Baird, G., et al.: Diagnosis of autism. BMJ Br. Med. J. **327**, 488–493 (2003)
4. Chen, R., et al.: Structural MRI in autism spectrum disorder. Pediatr. Res. **69**, 63R (2011)
5. Avino, T.A., et al.: Neuron numbers increase in the human amygdala from birth to adulthood, but not in autism. Proc. Natl. Acad. Sci U. S. A. **115**, 3710–3715 (2018)
6. Aylward, E., et al.: MRI volumes of amygdala and hippocampus in non–mentally retarded autistic adolescents and adults. Neurology **53**, 2145 (1999)
7. Schumann, C.M., et al.: The amygdala is enlarged in children but not adolescents with autism; the hippocampus is enlarged at all ages. J. Neurosci. **24**, 6392 (2004)
8. Duvernoy, H.M.: The Human Hippocampus: Functional Anatomy, Vascularization and Serial Sections with MRI. Springer, Heidelberg (2005). https://doi.org/10.1007/b138576
9. Howard, M.A., et al.: Convergent neuroanatomical and behavioural evidence of an amygdala hypothesis of autism. NeuroReport **11**, 2931–2935 (2000)
10. Sparks, B., et al.: Brain structural abnormalities in young children with autism spectrum disorder. Neurology **59**, 184–192 (2002)
11. Avino, T.A., et al.: Neuron numbers increase in the human amygdala from birth to adulthood, but not in autism. Proc. Natl. Acad. Sci. **115**, 3710–3715 (2018)
12. Mueller, S.G., et al.: Evidence for functional specialization of hippocampal subfields detected by MR subfield volumetry on high resolution images at 4 T. Neuroimage **56**, 851–857 (2011)
13. Long, J., et al.: Fully convolutional networks for semantic segmentation. In: CVPR, pp. 3431–3440 (2016)
14. Ronneberger, O., Fischer, P., Brox, T.: U-Net: convolutional networks for biomedical image segmentation. In: Navab, N., Hornegger, J., Wells, William M., Frangi, Alejandro F. (eds.) MICCAI 2015, Part III. LNCS, vol. 9351, pp. 234–241. Springer, Cham (2015). https://doi.org/10.1007/978-3-319-24574-4_28
15. He, K., et al.: Deep residual learning for image recognition. In: CVPR, pp. 770–778 (2018)
16. Huang, G., et al.: Densely connected convolutional networks. In: CVPR, p. 3 (2017)
17. Jégou, S., et al.: The one hundred layers tiramisu: fully convolutional DenseNets for semantic segmentation. In: CVPRW, pp. 1175–1183 (2017)
18. Devalla, S.K., et al.: DRUNET: a dilated-residual U-Net deep learning network to digitally stain optic nerve head tissues in optical coherence tomography images. arXiv preprint: arXiv: 1803.00232 (2018)
19. Yu, F., Koltun, V.: Multi-scale context aggregation by dilated convolutions. arXiv preprint arXiv:1511.07122 (2015)
20. Wang, L., et al.: Volume-Based Analysis of 6-Month-Old Infant Brain MRI for Autism Biomarker Identification and Early Diagnosis. In: Frangi, Alejandro F., Schnabel, Julia A., Davatzikos, C., Alberola-López, C., Fichtinger, G. (eds.) MICCAI 2018, Part III. LNCS, vol. 11072, pp. 411–419. Springer, Cham (2018). https://doi.org/10.1007/978-3-030-00931-1_47
21. Payakachat, N., et al.: National Database for Autism Research (NDAR): big data opportunities for health services research and health technology assessment. PharmacoEconomics **34**, 127–138 (2016)
22. Badrinarayanan, V., et al.: SegNet: a deep convolutional encoder-decoder architecture for image segmentation. arXiv preprint: arXiv:1511.00561 (2015)

# CNS: CycleGAN-Assisted Neonatal Segmentation Model for Cross-Datasets

Jian Chen[1], Zhenghan Fang[2], Deqiang Xiao[2], Duc Toan Bui[2], Kim-Han Thung[2], Xianjun Li[3], Jian Yang[3], Weili Lin[2], Gang Li[2], Dinggang Shen[2(✉)], and Li Wang[2(✉)]

[1] School of Information Science and Engineering, Fujian University of Technology, Fuzhou, China
[2] Department of Radiology and BRIC, University of North Carolina at Chapel Hill, Chapel Hill, USA
`{dgshen,li_wang}@med.unc.edu`
[3] Department of Diagnostic Radiology, The First Affiliated Hospital of Xi'an Jiaotong University, Xi'an, China

**Abstract.** Accurate segmentation of neonatal brain MR images is critical for studying early brain development. Recently, supervised learning-based methods, i.e., using convolutional neural networks (CNNs), have been successfully applied to infant brain segmentation. Although these CNN-based methods have achieved reasonable segmentation results on the testing subjects acquired with similar imaging protocol as the training subjects, they are typically not able to produce reasonable results for the testing subjects acquired with different imaging protocols. To address this practical issue, in this paper, we propose leveraging a cycle-consistent generative adversarial network (CycleGAN) to transfer each testing image (of a new dataset/cross-dataset) into the domain of training data, thus obtaining the transferred testing image with similar intensity appearance as the training images. Then, a densely-connected U-Net based segmentation model, which has been trained on the training data, can be utilized to robustly segment each transferred testing image. Experimental results demonstrate the superior performance of our proposed method, over existing methods, on segmenting cross-dataset of neonatal brain MR images.

**Keywords:** Neonatal brain · Cross-dataset · Segmentation · CycleGAN

## 1 Introduction

The first year of life is the most dynamic phase of postnatal human brain development, characterized by rapid tissue growth and development of a wide range of cognitive and motor functions [1]. Accurate and automatic segmentation of neonatal brain MR images into different tissue types, e.g., gray matter (GM) and white matter (WM), is an important step to accurately characterize early brain development [2].

Recently, deep learning-based methods have been successfully applied to infant brain MR image segmentation, especially for neonatal [3] and 6-month-old infant brain

© Springer Nature Switzerland AG 2019
D. Zhang et al. (Eds.): GLMI 2019, LNCS 11849, pp. 172–179, 2019.
https://doi.org/10.1007/978-3-030-35817-4_21

images [4]. Although these methods have achieved reasonable results, there are still several unresolved challenges: (1) neonatal and infant brain images are often degraded in quality due to motions and uneven illuminations during image acquisition [5], as shown in Fig. 1(a) and (b); and (2) deep learning-based methods typically trained on one dataset with a specific imaging protocol are not able to generalize well on other datasets with different imaging acquisition protocols. This is because, with different imaging parameters, field strengths, or receiving coils during scanning, the acquired images would have different intensity contrast and distribution. For example, two neonatal brain MR images with different imaging protocols are shown in Fig. 2, in which we can see tissue intensities in Fig. 2(a) are more inhomogeneous than those in Fig. 2(b). These differences hamper the generalization capabilities of the trained deep learning-based methods in tissue segmentation.

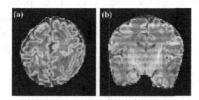

**Fig. 1.** Motion artifacts (a) and uneven illumination (b) during neonatal MR image acquisition.

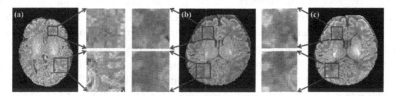

**Fig. 2.** Comparison between two T1-weighted MR images from the source domain (a) and the target domain (b). (c) shows the transferred image of (b) with trained CycleGAN, and has more consistent appearance with (a), compared to (b).

To alleviate the imaging appearance gaps between different datasets, inspired by the cycle-consistent generative adversarial networks (CycleGAN) [6], which can successfully transfer images from different domains without requiring any paired images for training, we propose a CycleGAN-assisted Neonatal Segmentation (CNS) model for cross-datasets of brain MR images. Specifically, we first train a densely-connected U-Net (DU-Net) for neonatal image segmentation in the source domain. Then, given any new images in the target domain, we employ our trained CycleGAN to transfer each target image to the source domain, and then apply the trained segmentation model onto the transferred target image for deriving the segmentation result. In this way, we only need to train the segmentation model in the source domain for one time, and then directly apply the trained model to any new dataset after being transferred to the source domain.

## 2 Method

**Dataset and Image Preprocessing.** The source dataset consists of 30 neonatal T1-weighted MR images acquired on a Siemens head-only 3T scanners, with 144 sagittal slices, TR/TE = 1900/4.38 ms, and resolution = $1 \times 1 \times 1$ mm$^3$. The target dataset contains 20 T1-weighted neonatal MR images acquired on a GE 3T scanner, with 120 slices, TR/TE = 10.47/4.76 ms, and resolution = $0.9375 \times 0.9375 \times 1$ mm$^3$. Standard preprocessing steps are performed prior to tissue segmentation, including resampling to the resolution of $1 \times 1 \times 1$ mm$^3$, skull stripping, intensity inhomogeneity correction [7], and cerebellum and brain stem removal. Five images from the source dataset were manually labeled by experts, thus providing ground-truth labels for training the segmentation network.

**Framework.** Figure 3 illustrates the framework of our proposed method, consisting of two training stages and one testing stage. The target domain ($T$ for short) contains images without labels for testing, while the source domain ($S$ for short) contains images with labels for training our tissue segmentation network. We first introduce a densely-connected U-Net as the segmentation network and train it in the source domain, and then leverage CycleGAN to train the generator networks for intensity transferring between the target domain and the source domain. Finally, the testing stage is implemented for new subjects from the target domain.

**Training of Segmentation Network.** Training of the tissue segmentation module is indicated by black arrows in the top-left part of Fig. 3. We use a densely-connected U-Net architecture (DU-Net) derived from [8], as shown in Fig. 4. It consists of an encoder path and a decoder path. The encoder (decoder) path consists of one convolutional layer, three dense blocks, and three transition down (up) blocks. Each dense block consists of three BN-ReLU-Conv-Dropout operations, in which each Conv includes 16 kernels and the dropout rate is 0.1. The transition down block (i.e., Conv-BN-ReLU followed by a max pooling layer) is to reduce the feature map resolution and increase the receptive field. While, in the decoder path, the transition up block (i.e., Deconv-BN-ReLU) is to recover the feature map resolution. Feature maps in the same level of encoder and decoder paths are concatenated through a skip connection. The final layer in the network is a convolution layer, followed by a softmax non-linearity to provide the per-class probability at each voxel. For all the convolutional layers, the kernel size is $3 \times 3 \times 3$ with stride size 1 and 0-padding. The loss function is cross-entropy in the network, which is represented as $L_{Seg}$ in Fig. 3. In network implementation, we randomly extracted 3D patches with a size of $32 \times 32 \times 32$ from source images for training. During training, learning rate was set as 0.01 with step decreasing, gamma was set as 0.1, momentum was set as 0.9, and weight decay was set as 0.0005.

**Training of CycleGAN.** Image synthesis training is performed using the 3D Cycle-GAN illustrated by green arrows in the top-right part of Fig. 3. Let two generators be $G_1$ and $G_2$ for, respectively, learning the mapping from $T$ to $S$ and the mapping from $S$ to $T$. While two discriminators, $D_1$ and $D_2$, determine whether the input image is real

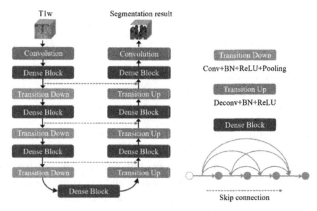

**Fig. 4.** Diagram of the architecture of the densely-connected U-Net (DU-Net).

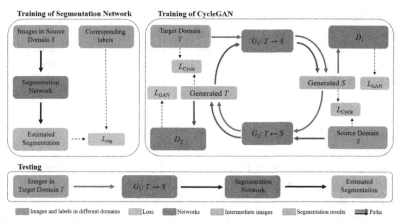

**Fig. 3.** Illustration of our proposed CycleGAN-assisted neonatal segmentation method. The top-left part is the 3D tissue segmentation network (i.e., densely-connected U-Net) in the training stage, and the top-right part is the 3D CycleGAN in the training stage. The lower part shows the testing stage for images in the target domain, which needs a trained generator $G_1$ $(T \rightarrow S)$ for transferring each testing image to the source domain and also a trained segmentation network for tissue segmentation. (Color figure online)

or not for $S$ and $T$, respectively. CycleGAN applies adversarial losses for both mapping functions, and the discrimination loss can be written as [6]:

$$L_{GAN} = E_{y \sim S}[\log D_1(y)] + E_{x \sim T}[\log(1 - D_1(G_1(x)))] \\ + E_{x \sim T}[\log D_2(x)] + E_{y \sim S}[\log(1 - D_2(G_2(y)))] \quad (1)$$

Meanwhile, CycleGAN also introduces the cycle-consistent loss to avoid a network that maps the same set of input images to any random permutation of images in the target domain with large enough capacity, where any of the learned mappings can induce an output distribution that matches the target domain. The cycle consistency loss can be described as [6]:

$$L_{\text{Cycle}} = E_{y \sim S}[||G_1(G_2(y)) - y||_1] + E_{x \sim T}[||G_2(G_1(x)) - x||_1] \qquad (2)$$

The overall objective for the CycleGAN is:

$$L = L_{\text{GAN}} + \lambda L_{\text{Cycle}} \qquad (3)$$

We use 3D convolution kernels, instead of 2D kernels, in the convolution layers of generators and discriminators to fully exploit spatial information of 3D images. ResNet [9] with three residual blocks and the fully convolutional network with five convolutional layers are applied, respectively, for the generators and discriminators. To increase the number of training samples and also avoid overload of GPU memory usage, we extracted 3D patches with a size of $32 \times 32 \times 32$ as inputs to the generators and discriminators. Learning rate was set as 0.0002, $\lambda$ was set as 10, and momentum was set as 0.5.

**Testing of CycleGAN and Segmentation.** In the testing stage, the original images in the target domain are translated by the trained CycleGAN to yield synthetic images, which have similar intensity distribution with the images in the source domain. Then, the transferred images are segmented by the trained DU-Net in the source domain to obtain the segmentation results.

## 3   Experimental Results

To train the segmentation network DU-Net, we used 5 images with manual labels from the source domain. To train the 3D CycleGAN, we used 20 images from the source domain and 20 images from the target domain. Regarding the number of subjects with artifacts, among 20 images from target domain for CycleGAN training, 4 images of them have motion artifact and 8 of them have uneven illumination problem. For comparison, we first directly applied the DU-Net on the target images without using CycleGAN. Two representative results by U-Net [10] and DU-Net are shown in the first two rows of Fig. 5(a). Due to the intensity distribution difference between datasets, the model trained on the source images cannot generalize well to the target images, with WM incorrectly identified as GM within the dashed contour. In contrast, with the proposed CycleGAN-assisted strategy, both segmentation results of U-Net and DU-Net are greatly improved, especially in the region indicated by the dashed contour, demonstrating effectiveness of CycleGAN in assisting neonatal image segmentation. Examples of the transferred target images and their corresponding results are shown in the third row and fourth row of Fig. 5. For better evaluating WM segmentation results, 3D renderings of segmented WM are also in Fig. 5. Figure 5(b) shows comparison results for the case with uneven illumination shown in Fig. 1. It can be observed that the artifact as uneven illumination were corrected by CycleGAN, and thus those segmentation errors as holes and handles are eliminated by using CycleGAN-assisted methods.

For a quantitative comparison, we evaluated 8 images from the target domain. Among these 8 images, 2 of them have motion artifact and 2 of them have uneven illumination.

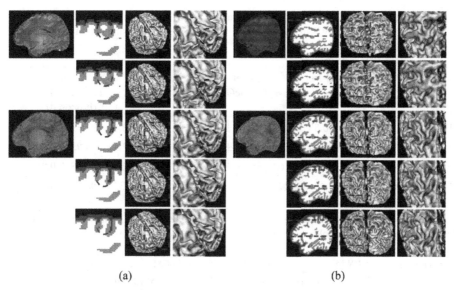

(a)                                                    (b)

**Fig. 5.** Comparisons of results without/with CycleGAN for two subjects (left and right panels). The first row shows the images in the target domain and segmentation results obtained by the U-Net, and the second row shows segmentation results obtained by the DU-Net. The third row shows the transferred target images and their corresponding segmentation results by U-Net + CycleGAN, and the fourth row shows segmentation results by DU-Net + CycleGAN. The fifth row shows the manual segmentation.

Manual labels generated by experts on these 8 subjects are provided as the ground truth. Due to artifacts, it took longer time for manual labeling voxel by voxel using ITK-SNAP software. The average Dice coefficient [11] and the modified Hausdorff distance (MHD) for the results without/with CycleGAN are presented in Table 1. It can be seen the proposed strategy achieves higher Dice coefficient, with a significantly improved performance in WM ($p$-value $< 0.05$). It is worth noting that the input images for U-Net and DU-Net without CycleGAN were preprocessed by histogram matching before using segmentation model. Training and testing were performed on a NVIDIA Titan X GPU. Basically, training a DU-Net and CycleGAN took around 48 h and 60 h respectively and in testing stage, segmenting a 3D image by the proposed strategy requires 180–200 s totally.

In the MICCAI Grand Challenge of Neonatal Brain Segmentation (NeoBrainS12), two preterm born infants acquired at 30.86 and 30.00 gestation corrected age (GCA) weeks were provided for training, while five preterm born infants acquired at 30.00, 25.57, 26.14, 30.86 and 28.71 GCA weeks were provided for testing. A detailed description of the data and the protocol is available at http://neobrains12.isi.uu.nl. Due to fast growth rate and 0–5 weeks gap between training subjects and testing subjects, there are large differences in terms of tissue contrast and intensity distribution. To deal with these differences, we use our proposed model by considering those 2 training images as in the source domain and those 5 testing images as in the target domain. The performance was evaluated by DC, mean surface distance (MSD), and Hausdorff distance (HD), as

**Table 1.** Averaged Dice coefficient (in percentage) and MHD (in mm) for different methods. Bold indicates a significantly better performance with p-value < 0.05 using paired t-test for Dice coefficient

| Method | Tissue | U-Net | U-Net + CycleGAN | DU-Net | DU-Net + CycleGAN (Proposed) |
|---|---|---|---|---|---|
| DC | WM | 90.89 ± 2.12 | 93.23 ± 0.68 | 91.93 ± 2.40 | **93.79 ± 0.67** |
| | GM | 83.94 ± 1.76 | 85.50 ± 0.84 | 85.22 ± 2.30 | **86.95 ± 0.60** |
| | CSF | 83.38 ± 1.62 | 84.38 ± 1.24 | 86.54 ± 2.30 | **87.35 ± 0.96** |
| MHD (in mm) | WM | 1.43 ± 0.29 | 0.99 ± 0.14 | 1.19 ± 0.33 | **0.95 ± 0.02** |

**Table 2.** Results of different methods on NeoBrainS12 challenge data. The highest DC and lowest MSD/HD are indicated in bold.

| Team name | UWM | | | MWM | | | CoGM | | | CSF | | |
|---|---|---|---|---|---|---|---|---|---|---|---|---|
| | DC | MSD | HD | DC | MSD | HD | DC | MSD | HD | DC | MSD | HD |
| UNC-IDEA-II | **0.94** | **0.09** | 10.57 | 0.53 | 0.60 | **9.19** | **0.89** | **0.10** | 18.79 | **0.85** | **0.16** | **8.66** |
| INFANT-INSIGHT | 0.93 | 0.11 | 12.40 | 0.51 | 0.73 | 11.42 | 0.88 | 0.14 | 22.56 | 0.83 | 0.19 | 9.42 |
| LRDE_LTCI | 0.93 | 0.11 | 20.63 | 0.06 | 5.84 | 20.74 | 0.87 | 0.11 | 26.02 | 0.83 | 0.20 | 10.15 |
| Anonymous2 | 0.92 | 0.14 | 6.38 | – | – | – | 0.87 | 0.13 | 7.29 | 0.68 | 0.61 | 14.60 |
| UPF_SIMBioSys | 0.91 | 0.17 | **5.90** | 0.54 | 0.62 | 20.62 | 0.85 | 0.15 | **6.56** | 0.79 | 0.29 | 9.71 |
| The proposed method without CycleGAN | 0.93 | 0.11 | 15.32 | 0.53 | 0.62 | 9.29 | 0.88 | 0.10 | 20.46 | 0.84 | 0.19 | 9.21 |
| **The proposed** | 0.93 | **0.09** | 10.16 | **0.54** | **0.58** | 9.27 | **0.89** | **0.10** | 18.90 | **0.85** | 0.17 | **8.66** |
| Team Name | Vent | | | CB | | | BS | | | BGT | | |
| | DC | MSD | HD | DC | MSD | HD | DC | MSD | HD | DC | MSD | HD |
| UNC-IDEA-II | **0.90** | **0.14** | 13.76 | **0.95** | 0.26 | 16.40 | **0.86** | 0.24 | 7.13 | **0.94** | 0.30 | 19.84 |
| INFANT-INSIGHT | 0.89 | 0.15 | 14.91 | 0.92 | 0.51 | 27.61 | 0.82 | 0.32 | 14.10 | 0.91 | 0.56 | 24.53 |
| LRDE_LTCI | 0.87 | 0.24 | 12.76 | 0.94 | 0.33 | 14.74 | 0.85 | 0.49 | 13.63 | 0.91 | 0.51 | 16.85 |
| Anonymous2 | 0.83 | 0.24 | **7.65** | – | – | – | – | – | – | 0.91 | 0.62 | 7.84 |
| UPF_SIMBioSys | 0.83 | 0.44 | 10.72 | 0.94 | 0.28 | **5.40** | 0.85 | **0.15** | 6.56 | 0.93 | 0.29 | **5.29** |
| The proposed method without CycleGAN | 0.87 | 0.32 | 23.94 | 0.95 | 0.28 | 20.28 | 0.85 | 0.25 | 3.64 | 0.93 | 0.32 | 17.38 |
| **The proposed** | 0.89 | **0.14** | 14.51 | **0.95** | **0.25** | 16.08 | **0.86** | 0.23 | 7.13 | **0.94** | **0.28** | 19.50 |

shown in Table 2. In most classes, our method achieves competitive results, compared to the top method, where the highest DC and lowest MSD/HD are indicated in bold. Compared with the results by the proposed method without CycleGAN, the results by the proposed method are outperforming. More detailed results can be found at https://neobrains12.isi.uu.nl/?page_id=143.

# 4 Conclusion

This paper presented a novel CycleGAN-assisted neonatal brain segmentation method for cross-dataset scenarios. We first introduced a densely-connected U-Net to train a segmentation network in the source domain. To alleviate intensity distribution difference between the source domain and the target domain, we employed CycleGAN to transfer the target images into the source domain. Experimental results demonstrate the effectiveness of our proposed method, which also achieved competitive results compared to the top method in a MICCAI challenge. In the future, we will extensively validate our method on more datasets.

# References

1. Shen, D., et al.: Deep learning in medical image analysis. Annu. Rev. Biomed. Eng. **19**(3), 221–248 (2017)
2. Wang, L., et al.: LINKS: Learning-based multi-source IntegratioN frameworK for Segmentation of infant brain images. NeuroImage **108**(3), 160–172 (2015)
3. Moeskops, P., et al.: Automatic segmentation of MR brain images with a convolutional neural network. IEEE Trans. Med. Imaging **35**(5), 1252–1261 (2016)
4. Nie, D., et al.: 3-D fully convolutional networks for multimodal isointense infant brain image segmentation. IEEE Trans. Cybern. **99**(2), 1–14 (2018)
5. Li, G., et al.: Computational neuroanatomy of baby brains: a review. NeuroImage **185**(1), 906–925 (2018)
6. Zhu, J., et al.: Unpaired image-to-image translation using cycle-consistent adversarial networks. In: CVPR (2017)
7. Sled, J.G., et al.: A nonparametric method for automatic correction of intensity nonuniformity in MRI data. IEEE Trans. Med. Imaging **17**(1), 87–97 (1998)
8. Wang, L., et al.: Volume-based analysis of 6-month-old infant brain MRI for autism biomarker identification and early diagnosis. In: Frangi, A.F., Schnabel, J.A., Davatzikos, C., Alberola-López, C., Fichtinger, G. (eds.) MICCAI 2018. LNCS, vol. 11072, pp. 411–419. Springer, Cham (2018). https://doi.org/10.1007/978-3-030-00931-1_47
9. He, K., et al.: Deep residual learning for image recognition. In: CVPR (2016)
10. Milletari, F., et al.: V-Net: fully convolutional neural networks for volumetric medical image segmentation. In: Fourth International Conference on 3D Vision (2016)
11. Litjens, G., et al.: Evaluation of prostate segmentation algorithms for MRI: the PROMISE12 challenge. Med. Image Anal. **18**(2), 359–373 (2014)

# Author Index

Printed in the United States
By Bookmasters